THE DEFENCE INDUSTRIAL BASE
AND THE WEST

THE
DEFENCE
INDUSTRIAL
BASE
AND THE WEST

EDITED BY DAVID G. HAGLUND
CENTRE FOR INTERNATIONAL RELATIONS
QUEEN'S UNIVERSITY

ROUTLEDGE
London and New York

First published 1989 by Routledge
11 New Fetter Lane, London EC4P 4EE
29 West 35th Street, New York, NY 10001

Printed and bound in Great Britain by
Mackays of Chatham PLC, Chatham, Kent
Page layout and typesetting by
Academic Horizons, Kingston, Ontario, Canada

British Library Cataloguing in Publication Data

Defence industrial base and the west.
    1. Western world. Military equipment industries
    I. Haglund, David G.
    338.4′7623′0911821
    ISBN 0-415-00923-5

Library of Congress Cataloging in Publication Data

Defence industrial base and the West / edited by David G. Haglund.
    p. cm.
    Includes index.
    ISBN 0-415-00923-5
    1. Industrial mobilization — Europe. 2. Industrial mobilization —
Israel. 3. Industrial mobilization — United States. 4. Munitions —
Europe. 5. Munitions — Israel. 6. Munitions — United States.
7. North Atlantic Treaty Organization — Armed Forces — Weapons
systems. I. Haglund, David G.
UA18.E8D44   1989
355.2′6′091812–dc19   89-3514
                                     CIP

Contents

Tables and Figures

Tables:

Figures:

Appendices:

Acknowledgements

The concept of the "defence industrial base" increasingly figures in the discussion of the security postures of NATO members and other Western countries. The concept itself, like so many political concepts, is not without ambiguity; much less is it without policy significance. Especially is this the case for the United States, where analysis of the recent challenge to that country's defence industrial base has impelled policy initiatives in a variety of defence-related domains. Prominent among the policy concerns, and potential contradictions, inherent in defence-industrial-base considerations is the trade-off between the security gains thought to attach to enhanced self-sufficiency and the security losses invariably linked to the fostering of an inefficient, and protected, manufacturing sector in weapons and other defence equipment.

This book examines the current debate within Western countries over the defence industrial base, and pays close attention to the above-noted tensions, particularly as they manifest themselves in the most advanced technological domains of defence production. Although purists might question the utility of the oxymoron, we do argue in this volume that the "apex" of the defence industrial base — above all in such high-technology defence-production efforts-as the manufacture of sophisticated fighter aircraft — illustrates in perhaps the most dramatic form the contemporary dilemma posed for the Atlantic Alliance, its various members, and such non-allies as Sweden and Israel, in so far as defence procurement and production are concerned.

This volume's origins date back to a grant application made in 1985 by the Queen's Centre for International Relations to the Military and Strategic Studies Program (MSSP) sponsored by the Canadian Department of National Defence. Needless to say, the generous financial assistance provided by that grant has made possible the Centre's research into the defence industrial base. For that assistance, the Centre is deeply appreciative. Also very welcome has been the support for and interest in this project shown by the Canadian Defence Industrial Preparedness Task Force, headed at the time by Col. Cal Hegge.

Numerous individuals from the scholarly, governmental, and business communities have assisted this initiative in countless ways. In particular we wish to highlight the contributions made by the following Canadian academics, who commented on three of this volume's chapters, which were originally prepared for a June 1987 Centre conference on the defence industrial base: David Dewitt, Barbara Haskel, and Stephen Page.

In the no-less-important category of manuscript production, we remain, as always, greatly indebted to the excellent technical skills of Kay Ladouceur and Mary Kerr. Marilyn Banting's editorial prowess and constant good cheer have enabled us to complete and improve this book in so many ways, and to her we extend our heartfelt appreciation. Darrel Reid, of Academic Horizons, was of invaluable assistance in the laser typesetting of the copy. Finally, Ed Black, overburdened as usual with his own scholarly and administrative obligations, always seems to find the time to bail the Centre out of difficulties associated with its own high-tech dilemma, one no doubt attributable to the Luddite proclivities of its director. To him go our warm thanks.

Introduction

David G. Haglund

I

The U.S. Navy's downing of Iran Air Flight 655 in early July 1988 is yet another reminder that in the fog of combat, decisions get made and actions taken that can have tragically unintended consequences. In this instance, the death of 290 innocent civilians bespeaks human error of major proportions, and though the cruiser *Vincennes* was equipped with the most modern air-defence technology available, its crew was evidently unable properly to interpret the data it received from its Aegis combat system.[1] However, if the Iran air catastrophe brings to full view yet again the tragic human dimension of the Persian Gulf fighting, it also does something else. It highlights a central feature of modern warfare: the degree to which high-technology has permeated its very fabric. As well, the technology-intensity of armed conflict has, in turn, had an effect both on the manner in which adversaries confront each other *and* on the way in which allies cooperate with one another. Although it is not the only theme addressed by the several contributors to this volume, a central focus of their individual chapters is the dynamics of defence collaboration among friends and allies in an era of high-technology warfare. Each of the authors examines a set of strategic, political, and economic factors that are embedded in the contemporary debate over the West's defence industrial base.

For the purpose of this book, the term defence industrial base is taken to refer to those sectors of a country's economy that can be called upon to generate goods, services, and technology for ultimate consumption by the state's armed forces. Whatever else it may be expected to accomplish, a state's defence industrial base ideally must fulfill two principal requirements: it must be able to provide for the normal peacetime material requirements of the

1

country's military; and it must be rapidly expansible to meet the increased demand of wartime or emergency situations.[2]

Significantly, it is in the upper regions of the defence industrial base — at what might be termed the apex of the triangle of modern defence production — that the issues we explore take on their greatest intensity, for it is quickly apparent that no state's defence industrial base can, in fact, come close to fulfilling these ideal requirements. It is in the realm of high-technology that the dynamics of weapons procurement, production, and trade lay bare some of the fundamental dilemmas now confronting defence planners in a series of Western countries. Among these policy dilemmas, none is more important and vexing than resolving the contradiction between optimising, in the interests of security, armaments self-sufficiency, and minimising, also ironically in the interests of security, the costs of weapons production. This self-sufficiency/cost-minimisation trade-off is, to be sure, evident at some of the stages of the defence industrial base that might be considered foundational, or basal, ones (such as raw-material acquisition), but it is really at the higher reaches of the defence industrial base that one encounters this contradiction in its most developed form.

For a variety of reasons, modern Western industrialised states — whether members of NATO or not — will face an ongoing choice over the degree to which they should subject their defence industrial bases to the forces of economic interdependence. States desirous of insulating their defence–production sectors from the full effects of global competition are motivated by several considerations, the most compelling of which inheres in the desire to minimise the strategic vulnerability that might result from a forced cessation of trade in defence goods during wartime conditions. This worry over strategic vulnerability has been most pronounced in the case of the United States; nevertheless, it is of great importance to other states, especially to countries such as Sweden and Israel, as well as to the major European members of NATO.

However, the goal of self-sufficiency, if pursued with total disregard to the costs of autarky, can itself be counter-productive to the pursuit of security. Thus most Western states, lately the U.S. among them, have been showing great interest in arms collaboration, and while this objective too might be said to have a mixture of motives, again the most compelling one (at least for the U.S.) is the security-impelled desire to maximise the amount of weaponry available for defence. This goal becomes especially important as the technological sophistication of weapons grows. Some writers have observed that one of the West's principal security challenges in the next decade will stem from the problem of "structural disarmament," taken to be the process whereby the costs of modern weapons systems escalate at a much faster rate than the budget for weapons procurement. One analyst describes it succinctly as "more and more money deliver[ing] less and less capability."[3]

This is a situation with particular poignancy for NATO, given that the Alliance has for some time predicated its military capability on the assumption that its quantitative inferiority *vis à vis* the Warsaw Pact will continue to be offset by its qualitative (above all, technological) superiority. The Western allies, and to a remarkable degree both Sweden and Israel, continue to view technological prowess as the *deus ex machina* of their long-term security predicament. Thus their strategic attention is focused with increasing intensity on the upper reaches of the defence industrial base, where they often come into economic and political collision with each other in the effort to stay or become technologically relevant. In a very meaningful sense, the West's defence industrial base is "crowded at the top" — and becoming more so, as allies and trading partners, all ultimately consumed by a desire to become more secure against their great adversaries, engage in both economic collaboration and conflict in their respective bids to maximise security and, at the same time, pursue such other goals as economic development and technology enhancement. Although the level and risks of economic conflict between allies can be overstated, the current climate of competition in high-tech defence production and procurement can and does breed tension, and in some ways is reminiscent of what one of the characters of the American cartoon strip, *Pogo*, said in the 1950s: "We have seen the enemy, and they is us."

Before one jumps to the pessimistic conclusion that high-technology commercial rivalry must ineluctably prove to be yet another wedge separating allies, it would be well to consider evidence to the effect that arms collaboration is becoming a more pronounced tendency of the Western allies.[4] It is this topic that Michael Moodie and Brenton Fischmann address in their chapter 1, "Alliance Armaments Cooperation: Toward a NATO Industrial Base." Recent trends in the realm of nuclear-arms reduction, they argue, will have the effect of enhancing the relevance of conventional arms improvements, as well as the overall health of the West's defence industrial base. This will be so because contemplation of the conventional deterrent will inevitably attend any initiatives to alter the nuclear status quo between East and West. Indeed, one outcome of substantive arms reduction in the nuclear domain could well be an emphasis upon the capability of the Western alliance to demonstrate its ability to sustain its forces in a protracted conventional struggle — not because anyone wants to fight such a war, but because in the altered nuclear environment perceptions of conventional war-fighting capability may take on new significance for *deterrence*. Thus the contemporary mood of nuclear optimism may mean that more, rather than less, attention will get directed toward the goal of stimulating arms collaboration within the Alliance.

Moodie and Fischmann seek to determine the strategic, political, and economic conditions necessary for the fostering of a NATO defence industrial base. They note that one major condition seems to be already well on the road to fulfilment: the new-found disposition of the United States to encourage arms cooperation on an Alliance-wide basis — cooperation extending from the early stages of research through the processes of procurement. This commitment to collaboration in arms production derives from an analysis of the new funding reality facing American defence planners. With Pentagon budgets being reduced and weapons costs continuing to rise, each in real terms, arms collaboration is being seen as a way to utilise efficiency as a means of arresting the Alliance's drift toward structural disarmament. Moodie and Fischmann trace the emergence and current popularity of the arms-collaboration ideal in the context of both U.S. and NATO bureaucratic politics. It is their view that arms collaboration is now an objective upon which alliance consensus has been achieved; indeed, they argue that "armaments cooperation within NATO is profoundly affecting the way allied governments and industry do business, forging what might be called the beginnings of an Alliance defence industrial base."

Citing such recent developments in arms collaboration as the 1985 Nunn-Roth-Warner amendment (which has resulted in the so-called "Nunn programs") and NATO's establishment of a Conventional Arms Planning System (CAPS), Moodie and Fischmann foresee the potential for much greater transatlantic arms cooperation, with the ultimate result being a rationalisation and enhancement of NATO's conventional military capability. However, they note the existence of several potential impediments to further collaboration, and observe that, recent successes notwithstanding, "transatlantic armaments cooperation efforts are at a watershed." Among the challenges to further collaboration are: 1) conflict among allies over technology transfers within and without the

Alliance; 2) the growing commitment of the European allies to intra-European arms cooperation; and 3) advocacies on either side of the Atlantic for more protection from the forces of international competition.

NATO lacks a coherent policy on technology transfer and technology security, in large measure, say the authors, because of the failure of the Reagan administration to coordinate its own internal policy in this regard. Although there has been some recent progress in the reduction of bureaucratic rivalry within the Washington policy community (a topic that my research assistant Marc Busch and I address in chapter 6), Moodie and Fischmann find that "the flow of information on emerging defence technology research programs between NATO allies is inadequate." Without greater Alliance coordination in this sphere, it will be difficult for the allies to advance beyond current levels of technology sharing.

A second challenge, and one that is explored in some detail in the other two chapters of Part One, is the momentum for greater intra-European defence collaboration. On the one hand, the promise of such collaboration, as outlined in a 1987 report of the Independent European Program Group (IEPG), is that it will enable the European allies to harvest savings in research and development of weapons that are currently not being achieved, primarily because of excessive and costly duplications of effort in the design and other stages of weapons production. Although European collaboration has been far from problem-free even for European partners or potential partners, it is really in the transatlantic context that the dangers of a Europeans-only approach to arms collaboration become most evident. (This is a topic Andrew Latham covers in chapter 3, "Conflict and Competition over the NATO Defence Industrial Base: The Case of the European Fighter Aircraft.") Should European efforts to achieve further economic integration after 1992 embrace the realm of defence production, as seems probable, and should liberalisation internally be accompanied by the erection of external barriers, this will likely have an adverse effect upon NATO arms-collaboration efforts.[5]

The third major challenge Moodie and Fischmann identify is the potential of weapons procurement being undertaken not for military but for economic and social considerations. Students of Canadian weapons procurement have for some time noted that arms acquisition often seems to be motivated by few, if any, apparent military considerations. Though doubtless this is a caricature view, it does remain the case that in Canada major procurements must be accompanied by the closest attentiveness to economic and social benefits associated with the fabrication or importation of weapons.[6] Nor is Canada an exception; even the U.S., as the experience with the Orion so beautifully illustrates, undertakes a significant amount of weapons procurement without military operational requirements appearing as decisive factors.[7] The European allies can hardly be said to exempt themselves from the temptation to use defence spending for economic and social purposes. This in turn prompts some officials, such as U.S. Deputy Under Secretary of Defense for Planning and Resources, Dennis Kloske, to express the fear that current collaborative efforts may be turning into "industrial entitlements," by which Kloske means that goals other than the enhancement of military capability are intruding into and distorting the procurement process. In light of this and the other two challenges to joint weapons planning on an Alliance-wide basis, Moodie and Fischmann conclude by recommending that NATO members "take the necessary further steps toward an Alliance industrial base by rationalising industrial effort at the research and development level."

The promise and reality of intra-European collaboration in the aerospace sector is the subject of Alistair Edgar's chapter 2, "The MRCA/Tornado: The Politics and Economics of Collaborative Procurement." This major collaborative venture, which ultimately involved the United Kingdom, the Federal Republic of Germany, and Italy, offers the best case study to date of the processes of intra-European arms cooperation, one that touches upon some of the challenges discussed by Moodie and Fischmann. Above all, the Tornado case illustrates the political reality that underlies the process of arms collaboration in the European (and, one might generalise, Western) context; for collaboration is simply another way of expressing the time-consuming and often costly processes of negotiating and bargaining. Collaboration, then, is first and foremost a political process, and like any political process it is liable to do some violence to objectives such as efficiency. If the Tornado development is any guide to further arms cooperation between the Western allies, it is clear that not only will "industrial entitlements" continue to be a prominent feature of collaborative projects, but so too will a host of other considerations that are only marginally related, if that, to the presumed purpose of weapons purchasing, namely to safeguard the security interests of the allies.

Edgar's chapter shows that the various members of the Panavia consortium each had a different agenda to pursue when they got together 20 years ago to contemplate building in common a Multi-Role Aircraft intended to become operational by 1975. Three of the original six countries would withdraw from the project by the summer of 1969, for reasons related to their concern about costs, work sharing, and operational characteristics of the aircraft. The three countries that stayed with the venture each did so for different reasons — and operational requirements did not rank high on the list of reasons. For example, the Germans (and the Italians) saw British participation in the MRCA project as being instrumental to Britain's becoming a member of the European Economic Community; in an important sense, Bonn (and Rome) sought the collaborative venture as a way of ensuring that Britain would become more involved with the EEC. For their part, the British viewed collaboration on this project not only as a way of averting a lapse into weapons dependence upon the United States, but also as a means of maintaining employment levels in the country's aerospace industry. The Germans shared these other two interests, and the Italians similarly regarded the project as containing socioeconomic benefit. Indeed, in the Italian instance, military requirements took a distinct back seat to such concerns as the alleviation of regional unemployment and the acquisition of technology from the more advanced German and British aerospace sectors.

In addition to bargaining between states in the international context, there was bargaining within states in a national setting; and this too frames Edgar's analysis. The role of industry and of political parties in the respective member-countries is examined, and with the exception of the privately owned British aerospace sector, Edgar finds little opposition to the venture from these precincts. That there was so little opposition is an indication of the kinds of expensive compromises that were necessary to be made for the project to continue; and one of the most costly such compromises was that involving the trade-off between equity and efficiency in worksharing. Edgar argues that in the early stages of the project, the "broad shape of the collaborative effort, and the design configuration of the aircraft itself, were both influenced much more by political pressures than by military requirements."

Notwithstanding the problems associated with the collaborative task, Edgar believes that the Tornado project should be regarded as a "mixed success." Operationally, the aircraft reflected the objectives of the Royal Air Force much more than it did those of either the German or Italian air forces, in that its optimal role seems to be that of long-range strike/interdiction, which coincides with RAF requirements. The GAF probably found the Tornado a fairly expensive craft for its roles in such a high-attrition environment, but it has, Edgar notes, been able to take advantage of some additional operational capabilities associated with newer versions of the Tornado. Arguably, it was the Italian Air Force that benefited least from the plane; but then, in Italy's case, military operational characteristics never did rank particularly high as a basis for Rome's decision to participate. In terms of another desired objective of collaboration, cost-savings, the Tornado again gets mixed reviews. Compared with the expense of separate national aircraft-development programs, it is obvious that the Tornado project had some built-in advantages — ones that in Britain's case alone are estimated to have resulted in the saving of some £360 million.

Nevertheless, one major cost of collaboration must be taken into consideration: the extended development time necessitated by the exigencies of bargaining among the partners. It took nearly twice as long — or 12 years — for the Tornado to reach deployment than it did for either the F-111 or the F-15 to proceed from the project-definition phase to operational readiness. This drawn-out development schedule in turn meant that avionics systems required major updating even before the first craft ever flew. Illustratively, this resulted in the frustration of one of the goals of the project, namely the avoidance of substantial American participation; for in the critical area of avionics, American aerospace companies figured as prominent sources of technology for the Tornado, despite one of the avowed intentions of the venture, which was to assist in the construction and sustaining of a European defence industrial base in high-technology production.

Edgar concludes by stressing that if subsequent collaborative projects are to achieve their postulated ends, more care must be given to avoid two of the major problems associated with the Tornado: the relative neglect of military-operational requirements, and the propensity of the partners to insist upon the sacrifice of efficiency for the cause of industrial equity. With the current European Fighter Aircraft program in mind, he observes, "that the Tornado emerged as a capable aircraft is no guarantee that political imperatives will not in the future force similar but ever-more-costly projects against insurmountable technological requirements." It is with this prospect of on-going collaboration among European countries in high-technology aviation projects that Andrew Latham's chapter 3 on the European Fighter Aircraft is concerned. In contrast to the qualified optimism expressed in the

Moodie/Fischmann chapter, Latham's analysis of the impact that the EFA program might have upon long-term transatlantic cooperation can only be termed pessimistic, for he sees an inevitable contradiction underlying current efforts, through the EFA, to construct a solid European "pillar" of the NATO defence industrial base.

Why should this be so? As Latham views it, arms collaboration among the NATO countries cannot for a variety of reasons take the form of Alliance-wide free trade in defence products. As a result, "managed specialisation" perforce becomes the avenue of whatever collaboration there might be. However, this mode of cooperation has an inherent defect, one that is potentially highly divisive. It inheres in the reality of the Europeans having to undertake a series of measures that will, in the attempt to render their defence industrial base more competitive with that of the U.S., necessarily require European consortia to seek the exclusion of American participants. Latham sees transatlantic harmony to be an ultimate casualty of Western Europe's aspiration to re-organise its development and production of such high-tech defence systems as the next-generation fighter aircraft; because "as the active presence of U.S. defence firms in the European market is one of the chief impediments to this type of reorganisation, this transformation of the European defence industrial base from a collection of relatively small-scale competing firms to a truly competitive continental effort is likely to involve exactly the type of state-led industrial policy that the U.S. finds so distasteful, namely, tariff and non-tariff barriers to American participation in European defence projects."

To compete with American aerospace producers, European firms have to surmount two obstacles: they must avoid unnecessary duplication of research and development; and they must rearrange production to take advantage of gains associated with servicing a large and consolidated market. Many Europeans have regarded, and continue to regard, the presence of American aerospace firms in Europe as the major impediment to their own flourishing. As Alistair Edgar has discussed, for some Europeans the problem is "more" than a security matter; it is a matter of critical economic moment, given the extent to which the high-technology aerospace sector is seen to constitute a "commanding height" of the economy. Thus, some hold U.S. aerospace competition as a double challenge. In the first instance, American companies "steal" market share, as they currently account for some 35 percent of the combined value of NATO Europe military aircraft. Second, because of their dominance in export markets, U.S. aircraft producers pose a hindrance to European efforts to realise scale economies through increased foreign sales. These postulated problems have been brought into crisp focus in the current debate over the EFA program, for the European consortium members have articulated, as they did with the Tornado, the goal of limiting, if not altogether prohibiting, American participation in the project.

Latham considers that there is really little chance that U.S. firms will make any significant contribution to the EFA, unlike the case with the Tornado. Indeed, to many of the EFA consortium personnel, one of the "lessons" of the Tornado experience is that U.S. participation has to be rejected, else the mooted gains of intra-European collaboration become minimised. Moreover, not only is the logic of the EFA program such as to exclude U.S. producers, it is to go further and compete with them for a share of the global market; this logic reinforces and justifies the exclusion of the Americans in the first place, for U.S. export-licencing procedures and laws are invoked as exclusion's principal rationale (though it clearly cannot be this). Not surprisingly, this puts the Europeans who are participating in the EFA program on a potential collision course with the United States. As Latham explains, "in the context of an American defence budget that is unlikely to grow substantially in the next few years, the possibility that armaments cooperation among the European allies could significantly reduce U.S. exports to Europe and elsewhere naturally bodes ill for American interests."

To counter this, Washington has responded to the EFA challenge with a three-pronged effort. First, it has sought to encourage the European NATO allies to participate in the kinds of transatlantic collaborative-arms projects detailed by Moodie and Fischmann. Second, it has raised the prospect of reciprocating in kind to what it regards as unfair trading on the part of the European members of the consortium.[8] Third, it has sought to reduce the desirability of the EFA by offering Europeans a chance to participate along with the U.S. in the co-development of upgraded versions of contemporary U.S. fighter aircraft, either an enhanced F-18 (the Hornet 2000) or an F-16 (the Agile Falcon). Although the attempt to preempt the EFA by offering co-production of the Hornet 2000 seems not to have succeeded, the possibility remains that such European non-participants in the EFA as Belgium, Denmark, the Netherlands, and Norway might respond to the offer of co-development of the Agile Falcon.[9]

Latham is in agreement with Moodie and Fischmann that transatlantic arms-collaboration efforts are at a "watershed." However, he sees little prospect of the U.S. and Europe succeeding, through collaboration, in achieving the kinds of solutions to the problem of structural disarmament that collaboration is intended to produce. Managed specialisation, in his view, is fraught with too many political difficulties for it to result in the cost-savings for the Alliance that some envision. Ironically, he concludes, "there is every possibility that ... European efforts to rationalise their pillar of the NATO defence industrial base will increase rather than reduce the Alliance's military preparedness burden."

II

The opportunities and challenges of arms collaboration constitute, together, the conceptual focus of the first part of this book. Part II takes as its animating concern the discussion of a further problematique introduced by the contemporary debate over the defence industrial base in Western countries, namely the degree to which the goal of maintenance of the defence industrial base conditions and sometimes conflicts with other objectives of states. In this section, contributors concentrate on some of the major current dilemmas faced by Germany, Sweden, Israel, and the United States in their pursuit of strategies aimed at strengthening their respective defence industrial bases. Among the diverse policy issues addressed by the four chapters, one finds the following theme common to them all: the manner in which maintenance of a defence-production capability in high-technology sectors has had, and continues to have, an important bearing on the formulation of trade policies in arms and other strategic goods.

For instance, the first two chapters in this part of the book pay careful attention to the contemporary policy dilemma facing Germany and Sweden: both countries have adopted fairly restrictive arms-export stances, which each sometimes feels itself obliged to attempt to subvert. There is a small but growing body of literature directed at the general problem of international weapons flows; to many of the analysts who have explored this problem, it has been the motives of supplier countries that have been deemed most worthy of attention. Although among these motives one occasionally finds adduced the desire to preserve or enhance a defence industrial base, it is usually other considerations that are held to be more germane for arms suppliers — considerations such as the bid to achieve influence and leverage over other (recipient) states, to support allies and friends, or to secure general economic gain for one's own industries.[10] Bernd Huebner seeks to make explicit the connection between German arms exports and the security-conditioned quest for a strengthening of the country's defence industrial base in his chapter 4, "The Importance of Arms Exports and Armament Cooperation for the West German Defence Industrial Base." He observes a seeming paradox associated with Bonn's arms-export policy: on the one hand, the Federal Republic has adopted a set of self-imposed constraints on weapons export; on the other, it ranks as among the five most important arms exporters in the world. To Huebner, the paradox is explained by reference both to the nature of the export constraints and to the requirements of the German defence industry for access to foreign markets.

The German constitution imposes a burden on the defence industry that, on first glance, would seem nearly to rule out the possibility of armaments exports, save perhaps to close German allies within NATO. Moreover, some subsequent legislation and policy statements have been intended to further tighten the restrictive regime that regulates arms export. Two legislative measures dating to 1961, the War Weapons Control Act (KWKG) and the Foreign Trade Act (AWG), coupled with a 1982 statement on export principles, set the regulatory context within which consideration of arms exports is situated. Officially, Bonn's position is to accord high priority to arms cooperation within NATO, while at the same time discouraging the export of weapons outside the Alliance. In reality, Germany sells far more weaponry outside the Alliance than it does inside, by more than a ratio of 3:1 during the first half of the 1980s. How does one account for this apparent discrepancy? In part, says Huebner, by legerdemain. Bonn maintains a semantic distinction between war weapons and less "deadly" categories of goods that, to some, borders on the specious; as Huebner argues, the distinction between war weapons and defence products is, at best, artificial. Nevertheless, the German public and politicians continue by and large to take comfort in the rhetorical restrictiveness of the country's arms-export policies. Understandably, for reasons related to recent German history, weapons exporting does have a certain stigma attached to it.

Nevertheless, the moral reservations of public opinion and political leaders aside, the reality is that Germany is anything *but* a minor player in international weapons transfers. Huebner shows why arms exports are considered to be essential for German security interests, as well as important for political and economic interests. He has surveyed a set of annual defence white papers, issued during the 1970s and 1980s, and has identified therein five core premises associated with weapons manufacturing: 1) that autarky will be deliberately avoided by the Federal Republic; 2) that defence industry should be as integrated as possible within the civilian, market economy; 3) that by maintaining a healthy defence industrial base Germany can enhance its influence within NATO; 4) that high-technology weapons manufacture can and does have a beneficial effect upon civilian industry, through the generation of spin-offs; and 5) that the need of the Bundeswehr for materiel, within the context of NATO preparedness efforts, justifies the existence of an autonomous defence industry. Unstated in these core assumptions is yet another fundamental truth about German defence-industrial production: its need for export markets.

The overall economic significance of the German defence industrial base cannot be adjudged to be particularly high: defence production accounts for perhaps three to four percent of the value of all goods produced by German industry. Even those firms that are clearly within the country's defence industrial base rely on the military market for only seven percent of their total output, although such sectors as aerospace are obviously much more dependent upon the military market. Nor do arms exports rank as critical components of German trade, constituting only one percent of total exports (and a quarter-percent of total GNP) in 1984. Nevertheless, some sectors of the defence industrial base are in an important way dependent upon the export market, and it is this market that, in turn, contributes to reducing the unit costs of crucial weapons systems deployed by Germany and other NATO countries. One such sector is tank-manufacturing: Germany produces more than 60 percent of the main battle tanks intended for the defence of Central Europe, and exports contribute significantly to holding the forces of structural disarmament at bay in this weapon category. Even more dependent upon export orders is the German submarine industry, which since 1950 has produced more conventionally powered submarines than any other country with the exception of the Soviet Union.

It is Huebner's thesis that German arms-export policy is "currently in crisis," in large measure because of the conflict between the declaratory policy of restriction and the needs of the German defence industrial base for access to export markets. While the

German economy could get along without the manufacture of weapons, the country's security and political interests require the maintenance of a healthy defence industrial base. The military market, with the introduction of ever-more technologically sophisticated weapons, is becoming increasingly characterised by high development costs, small orders, and "lumpy" demand. The effect must be either the acquisition of additional markets outside of Germany and NATO, or a reduction in the production of defence goods. Huebner advocates that Bonn adopt a qualified liberalisation of its export policy; "above all," he states, "there is a compelling need to adapt the 'Export Principles 82' to the real world."

If the Federal Republic of Germany can be said to face a growing dilemma in balancing its arms-export policy against its defence-industrial-base interests, the same applies *a fortiori* to Sweden. In chapter 5, "The Swedish Defence Industrial Base: Implications for the Economy," Michael Hawes explores two major themes. The first is the difficult situation into which Swedish policy makers have been plunged as a result of the Bofors and FFV arms-export scandals, and relates to the challenge of finding some way to placate the country's conscience while at the same time not doing damage to Swedish national security. The second is a question that has been analysed by defence economists and others for some time, and concerns the contribution (or lack thereof) made by defence spending to a country's overall economic well-being.

Hawes argues that the conceptual glue holding these two themes together is Sweden's long-standing policy of being alliance-free in peacetime, and an armed neutral in wartime. It has been this commitment to a reasonably comprehensive, and self-sufficient, defence policy that has stimulated a degree of defence-industrial autarky greater than that found in Germany and other Western European states. Also it has, in turn, been the security-induced bid to remain a viable producer of sophisticated defence goods that has, Hawes says, enabled Swedish industry to become more competitive internationally than it otherwise would have been. For Sweden, however, armed neutrality has imposed a severe constraint upon defence-industrial planners. Although Germany and other members of NATO might have to sacrifice certain political and economic interests were they to reduce the size of their indigenous defence-industrial establishments, they could at least maintain their armaments levels through heightened reliance upon other members of the Alliance, either through more collaboration with European states, or through greater "off-the-shelf" procurement from, or co-production with, the United States. In the case of Sweden, however, such a policy course would be construed — and in the context, rightly so — as a weakening of the commitment of neutrality; indeed, collaboration with "allies" is logically excluded even from being considered. Hence the current controversy over the proper role of weapons exports for Sweden, a country that is sometimes seen to be riding two horses heading in different directions. One horse gallops along the path of disarmament, which is a policy goal frequently promoted by Sweden at international fora; the other bounds forward in quest of the security that armed neutrality is thought to provide. Occasionally, as at present, the contradiction becomes too apparent either for logic or conscience (or both) to bear, and Swedes turn to agonising over the proper arms-export policy. Officially, there should be little difficulty in reconciling foreign-policy and security-policy objectives, for the country's weapons-export law makes that of Germany seem positively flaccid by comparison. As Hawes relates, Swedish defence materials can be exported without difficulty only to other Nordic countries or to neutral countries in Europe, a legal situation that has prompted one Swedish defence-industry official to note acerbically that "the Swedish defence industry can only export to those customers who can clearly demonstrate that they do not need the weapons and that they will not use them."

Making Sweden's situation more problematical is the fact that its armed forces, like those of other Western countries, confront the prospect of structural disarmament. Unless the country is prepared to adopt what Steven Canby calls an "introverted" (and less ambitious) defence policy, which it appears not to want to do, then it must face the urgent task of having to somehow ensure that its defence industrial base retains its vigour in a competitive international marketplace for defence goods. One guaranteed way of handicapping that base is to make export-policy more restrictive, for the simple reality is that the absorptive capacity of the Swedish military is not large enough to keep the defence producers in business. "For neutrality to work," writes Hawes, "critical weapons systems must be developed (or adapted) and supplied by domestic producers. This would account for the recent decision to proceed with the next generation of Swedish fighter aircraft (the JAS 39 Gripen), as opposed to buying a foreign plane off the shelf."

The second substantive issue raised by Hawes is the economic effect of Swedish defence-industrial production. Although he is far from arguing that the country's defence industrial base had been largely shaped by economic motivations, he does suggest that there may well be economic benefit for the civilian industrial sector derivable from the defence-industrial one. There is a lively dispute among scholars over the question of the relationship between defence production and overall economic well-being — a dispute in which Seymour Melman has figured as perhaps the major, if provocative, participant.[11] Suffice it to note that not all analysts are as convinced as Melman about the iniquitous consequences for civilian productivity of investment in the defence sector.[12] Although not pronouncing judgement upon the generalisable relationship (if any exists) between defence production and economic health, Hawes does conclude that in the specific instance of Sweden, "there appear to be significant civil sector benefits accruing from a healthy and technologically sophisticated defence industry."

Economic development, particularly in high-technology industrial sectors, was certainly one of the goals of the Israeli government when it developed plans to construct a state-of-the-art fighter aircraft, the Lavi, in early 1980. However, as Galen Perras argues in his chapter 6, "Israel and the Lavi Fighter-Aircraft: The Lion Falls to Earth," it is apparent that a small economy such as Israel's cannot easily afford the development costs associated with top-notch aircraft manufacturing today. This is so even should export sales be realised for the plane. Israel's problem has been compounded by the high level of dependence — in economic, political, and military terms — that it has upon the U.S., for once it became obvious that Washington would construe the production of the Lavi as contrary to its interests, the death warrant for the craft was as good as signed. This case provides an excellent illustration of the economic difficulties associated with maintaining a defence-industrial capability in the harshly competitive business of military aircraft production; perhaps even more to the point, it shows how at the high-tech apex of the defence-industrial-base one state's interests and actions cannot but have an effect upon those of other states. Competition, fairly severe at the best of times, has become especially pronounced in fighter-aircraft manufacturing in the West, due to the combination of overcapacity in the industry and stagnating or declining defence budgets of major consuming countries.

At its inception, the Lavi project was being hailed by some in Israel as the country's own version of the U.S. moon effort, a program that would raise Israeli technological sights for the challenges not only of the present, but of the coming century, one that would be economically invigorating while at the same time it made a crucial contribution to national security. Although a small country, Israel has boasted an extraordinary capability for defence production, even in the most sophisticated technologies. Indeed, the president of the state-owned Israel Aircraft Industry (IAI), Gabriel Gidor, could make the assertion in 1979 that in the field of avionics, Israel was "one class ahead" of such American craft as the F-16. It has been said that Israel does not *have* a military in-dustrial complex; it *is* one. One measure of this is the proportion of the workforce — nearly 20 percent of the non-Arab industrial workers — involved in defence production. In the U.S., by com-parison, perhaps five percent of employment is in the defence sec-tor, while in Canada the figure would be closer to one percent.

Not only, it was thought, would economic benefit be achieved by the Lavi, so would security be enhanced. Israel, more than the Western European members of NATO, entertains the aspiration that defence-industrial autarky can and should be approximated, even though complete independence is obviously out of the ques-tion. In major weapons systems, however, self-sufficiency seemed to make economic, political, and strategic sense; for the Israelis had been taught, as a result of a series of arms embargoes applied to them in the 1950s and 1960s, the virtue of military self-reliance. Another important stimulus to the Lavi project was the 1973 war — a war in which the Israeli air force suffered heavy losses to Arab anti-air defences. The clear lesson of that conflict was that the country would need a very capable multi-mission aircraft that could demonstrate considerable effectiveness in air-ground attack. On paper, the Lavi looked to be that plane, and even some hostile Pentagon critics judged the plane to be potentially superior to the F-16 in the air-to-ground role.

The plane would never get a chance to be tested in combat con-ditions, for it fell victim to domestic and foreign (American) opposition that concentrated on the central question of cost. Originally costed in a way that made it price-competitive with U.S. fighters, by 1987 the project had experienced cost escalation suffi-cient to render the Lavi half again as expensive as the F-16. Remarked one prominent Israeli political figure, Ezer Weizman, "We set out to build an Austin Mini, and we have ended up with a Cadillac." As Perras details, much opposition within Israel came from the Israeli military, who were fearful of the effect upon other weapons systems of a Lavi program that was spinning out of

17

financial control; this was a particularly troublesome prospect for the Navy. Outside Israel, it would be the Pentagon that figured among the project's chief opponents, for reasons related both to a concern over the opportunity cost of the plane (interpreted in terms of the weapons the country could not afford to build as a result of the Lavi's existence) and to a fear that the Lavi, if ever built, would prove a competitor for American aircraft on world export markets. Since a large proportion (some 40 percent) of the Lavi would consist of American parts, the U.S. would have veto authority over export sales, and American officials made no secret of their desire to block the transfer of any American technology to third parties, if they ever got the opportunity.

Ultimately, the Lavi case is testimony to the incredibly rapid pace of technological change in weapons production; and even though Israel was one of only a handful of countries during the 1960s and 1970s with the ability to produce supersonic fighter aircraft, it found itself left with no alternative but to enter into a co-production arrangement to build the F-16C. In its outcome, though in few other ways, the Lavi episode would demonstrate some uncanny parallels with a modern independent fighter aircraft project envisioned by the Japanese, the FSX. This is one of the issues covered in our last chapter, "Techno-Nationalism and the Contemporary Debate over the American Defence Industrial Base," which I wrote with the assistance of Marc Busch. The connection between the "Japanese Lavi" and the phenomenon of techno-nationalism, while important, is only one of a set of matters we address in that chapter.

For the most part, our chapter is concerned with assessing the security implications associated with the process of high-technology interdependence. We argue that, in general, the U.S. is finding that the increased degree of economic interdependence it is experiencing — as measured by the extent to which imports and exports contribute to the gross national product — is having potentially adverse consequences for security in a number of industrial sectors. Perhaps the most evident and traumatic of these security-generated tensions have been those associated with such high-technology sectors as semiconductors, the silicon chips that are the brain cells of electronic products, including modern weapons systems. What has been happening in the global production of semiconductors represents to some in the U.S. the most sinister specific aspect of growing reliance upon foreign trade in general. A decade ago American chip manufacturers dominated world markets; today, they barely have 10 percent of global sales. Most importantly, U.S. civilian and military electronic production relies more and more on components produced by Japan. Currently, some 40 percent of the electronics in American weapons systems is made in Japan, prompting some in the Pentagon to quip that were the U.S. to become embroiled in a future conventional war, it would have to be sub-contracted to Japan.

Reliance on imports for a substantial share of consumption is nothing new internationally; states for some time seem to have forsaken whatever aspirations to total self-sufficiency they may once have had. In the case of the U.S., however, the reliance is a relatively recent development, and because of the obvious implications for security in the event lines of communication were cut in wartime, one can understand the anxiety of some defence analysts in Washington. While a future conventional war — one that might make the same call on the "arsenal of democracy" as was made in World Wars I and II — does not appear likely, one cannot obviously be ruled out. Indeed, as Moodie and Fischmann, among others, have noted, there is likely to be a stress on conventional defence and deterrence in the presence of nuclear-arms reduction measures.[13] Given its expansive defence commitments, and in view of the relative newness of its reliance on world trade, it is hardly surprising that in the U.S., perhaps more than anywhere else, attention should be rivetted upon the health of the defence industrial base.

We label "techno-nationalism" those policies that seek to isolate from the forces of international competition a portion of the U.S. high-technology sector. In the case of imports, we single out the semiconductor industry and note that one innovative strategy that has recently been adopted, with government subsidisation and industry collaboration, has been the formation of a consortium, Sematech, from which foreign enterprises will be excluded, and whose primary purpose will be to enable the U.S. to regain the competitive advantage in this industry that has been lost to Japan. However, imports are only one side of the coin of techno-nationalism. One of the realities to which Washington has been adjusting of late is the loss of U.S. control over sensitive technology that leaks to the Soviet Union, and this because the U.S. in many instances no longer is a major supplier of much of the high-technology that it deems necessary to be kept out of the East bloc.

Few disputes about allies' differing conceptions of "technology security" have caused such outrage in Washington as has the

Toshiba/Kongsberg affair, which we argue dramatised the dilemma in which U.S. defence officials found themselves as a result of the country's declining technological capability. In an earlier era, when it was a more dominant supplier of high-technology than it is today, the U.S. had less difficulty in stanching the flow of sensitive technology and equipment to the Soviet bloc; if the recent Japanese and Norwegian technology diversion showed anything, it has been the extent to which U.S. capability in this regard has been diminished over time. There has recently been an attempt by Washington, in the wake of the transfer of milling machines and computers that enabled the Soviets to make their submarines quieter, to rationalise the procedures by which the members of the Coordinating Committee for Multilateral Export Controls (COCOM) attempt to prevent the loss of technology with potential military applications to the Soviet Union and its allies. Although it is still too soon to determine the effect of these reforms, made in early 1988, it seems to us that unless the Western countries can resolve their difficulties over technology security and their conflicting interpretations over the propriety of export control, then the future of armaments collaboration within the Atlantic Alliance will be problematical.

As some of our authors have remarked, transatlantic arms collaboration is at an important juncture. Although the U.S. is hardly the most protectionist of the Western trading partners (indeed, it may be the least protectionist) one issue that is likely to have increasing relevance, both for relations within NATO and between the U.S. and Japan, is the contemporary mood of "technonationalism," coupled as it has been with the more diffuse concern for the state of the American defence industrial base. At the very least, one can expect that the defence industrial base concept will continue to generate debate among Western countries, and that unless some way can be found of resolving the contradictions that seem to inhibit the development of an alliance-wide industrial-base, this issue will loom as yet one more element of discord and tension between trading partners and allies.

Notes

[1]Bernard E. Trainor, "Errors by a Tense U.S. Crew Led to Downing of Iran Jet, Inquiry is Reported to Find," *New York Times*, 3 August 1988, p. 1.

[2]This introductory discussion is informed by the analysis of the defence industrial base given in John M. Treddenick, "The Economic Significance

of the Canadian Defence Industrial Base," in *Canada's Defence Industrial Base: The Political Economy of Preparedness and Procurement*, ed. David G. Haglund (Kingston, Ont.: Ronald P. Frye, 1988), pp. 15-48.

[3]Ibid., p. 26. The phenomenon of structural disarmament is analysed in Mary Kaldor, *The Baroque Arsenal* (New York: Hill and Wang, 1981); idem, "The Weapons Succession Process," *World Politics* 38 (July 1986):557-95; Jacques Gansler, *The Defense Industry* (Cambridge, Mass.: MIT Press, 1980); and James Fallows, *The National Defense* (New York: Random House, 1981).

[4]The current vogue of international arms collaboration is discussed in Stephen Aubin, "The Defense Marketplace and International Collaboration," *Defense Media Review* 2 (May 1988):1-6.

[5]See Steven Greenhouse, "On to 1992," *New York Times*, 31 July 1988, p. 4:1.

[6]A good study of the various factors associated with a major weapons procurement is Frank L. Boyd, Jr., "The Politics of Canadian Defence Procurement: The New Fighter Aircraft Decision," in *Canada's Defence Industrial Base*, pp. 137-58.

[7]The P3 Orion patrol plane continues to get purchased for the U.S. Navy, even though the Navy neither recommends nor wants this plane. Its procurement is primarily a function of the Pentagon's desire to keep Lockheed's assembly line in business. See Molly Moore, "For the Navy, the Lockheed Orion Turns Out to Be Lazarus," *Washington Post*, 30 September 1987, p. 17. On a more general level, the problems of weapons procurement have been approaching monumental proportions in the U.S., as the recent two-year FBI investigation into defence procurement reveals. See, for the allegations of widespread fraud in defence procurement, Cheryl Pellerin, "FBI Sweep Likely to Yield 'Profound Restructuring'," *Defense News*, 20 June 1988, p. 1; and "Pop Goes the Weasel," *Economist*, 25 June - 1 July 1988, pp. 26-29. The best recent study of the procurement process, one that well illustrates current deficiencies, is Thomas L. McNaugher, "Weapons Procurement: The Futility of Reform," *International Security* 12 (Fall 1987):63-104.

[8]In this regard, the 1988 American trade legislation can be expected to have some far-reaching implications. See Clyde H. Farnsworth, "U.S. Push On Exports Sets Up a New Battle of the Barriers," *New York Times*, 7 August 1988, p. 4:1.

[9]"Carlucci to Sign Off on Agile Falcon Alternative for Co-development with Allies," *Inside the Pentagon*, 1 April 1988, p. 1.

[10]Motives of supplier states are analysed in Andrew J. Pierre, *The Global Politics of Arms Sales* (Princeton: Princeton University Press, 1982). Also see, for the same question, the conference summary prepared by Keith Krause, *The International Trade in Arms: Problems and Prospects* (Ottawa: Canadian Institute for International Peace and Security, March 1988). One analysis that stresses the salience of perceived economic benefit is Lloyd J. Dumas, ed., *The Political Economy of Arms Reduction: Reversing Economic Decay*, AAAS Selected Symposium 80 (Boulder, Colo.: Westview Press, 1982).

[11]See Seymour Melman, *The Permanent War Economy* (New York: Simon and Schuster, 1974); and Idem, "Limits of Military Power: Economic and Other," *International Security* 11 (Summer 1986):72-87.

[12]For a flavour of this debate, see Ann Markusen, "The Militarized Economy," *World Policy Journal* 3 (Summer 1986):495-516; and Steve Chan, "The Impact of Defense Spending on Economic Performance: A Survey of Evidence and Problems," *Orbis* 29 (Summer 1985):403-34.

[13]For discussions of the likelihood of protracted conventional warfare, see Carl H. Builder, "The Prospects and Implications of Non-Nuclear Means for Strategic Conflict," *Adelphi Papers*, no. 200 (London: International Institute for Strategic Studies, 1985); and Jeffrey Record, *Revising U.S. Military Strategy: Tailoring Means to Ends* (Washington: Pergamon-Brassey's, 1984). Soviet thinking on the topic is treated in Joseph L. Nogee and John Spanier, *Peace Impossible — War Unlikely: The Cold War Between the United States and the Soviet Union* (Glenview, Ill.: Scott, Foresman, 1988), pp. 161-62.

PART ONE

Intra-Alliance Collaboration and Discord over Weapons Procurement

1
Alliance Armaments Cooperation: Toward a NATO Industrial Base

Michael L. Moodie and Brenton C. Fischmann

INTRODUCTION

The recent agreement eliminating intermediate nuclear weapons from the arsenals of the superpowers has thrown into high relief the imbalances in conventional forces deployed in Europe, and spurred NATO to re-examine its conventional deterrent. Yet, as the Alliance looks for options to redress the conventional imbalance, all NATO members face a growing gap between their Alliance commitments and the resources they are willing to commit to defence. This concentrated, post-INF focus on conventional forces and Alliance-wide pressure on defence resources has made a fundamental change in the way NATO organises its collective-defence industrial effort the order of the day.

As defence costs continue to soar, every Alliance member will be forced to undertake a fundamental review of its NATO responsibilities in the 1990s and beyond. Re-examination in some countries is already underway. Canada's 1987 White Paper on defence outlined a major change in the nature of that country's contribution to and role in the Alliance. In Germany, an examination of the future structure of the country's entire armed forces has been completed, and Bonn's responses to the demographic, economic, and military challenges facing NATO's largest army in the 1990s will have enormous implications for NATO strategy. In the United Kingdom, the Thatcher government has avoided a fundamental defence review to date, but analysis of an emerging "funding gap" in U.K. defence planning suggests that a major reassessment is in the offing.[1]

On Capitol Hill and in the Pentagon, reductions in defence expenditures forced by efforts to reduce the nation's massive trade deficit have accelerated the re-examination of U.S. defence commitments. The Pentagon's budget authority has declined, in real terms, every year since 1985, with much of the reduction coming in the procurement account, down $16 billion from the 1985 level.[2]

The critical challenge facing the Alliance today is the development of what former U.S. Ambassador to NATO David Abshire has termed an effective "defence investment strategy" to manage its resources.[3] The cost of the West's increasingly sophisticated arsenal is rising 5 to 6 percent with each generation of weapons system. These soaring costs, driven by rapid technological progress, have dramatically reduced the return on the West's collective-defence investment. Recent U.S. Defense Department estimates, for example, suggest that NATO's current inventory of first-line aircraft will be replaced by the next generation on no better than a 3:4 ratio.

NATO's preferred response to its advancing "structural disarmament" — fewer and fewer weapons at higher and higher costs — has been a revitalisation of armaments-cooperation efforts, the cornerstone of an effective defence-investment strategy. In his first *Report on the Allied Contributions to the Common Defense*, Secretary of Defense Frank Carlucci described the ambitious goals of Alliance arms cooperation thusly:

> Armaments cooperation continues to receive emphasis as a means of improving the distribution of the common defense burden. These programs help to increase efficiency in the allocation and use of Alliance-wide resources, minimize wasteful duplication of effort and promote economies of scale in production. They also improve U.S. and allied defense capabilities and operational effectiveness by access to, use of, and protection of the best technology to meet military requirements with compatible, interoperable, or standardized equipment. Finally, armaments cooperation promotes the military, industrial, and economic viability of allied defense industry upon which we will be dependent in wartime for resupply.[4]

For many years, armaments cooperation was discussed in terms of a "two-way street" between the United States and its European allies — that is, a more equal balance of transatlantic trade in defence items. Recent years have been marked, however, by a shift away from this concept. This is largely due to unprecedented reductions in America's traditional defence-trade surplus with Western Europe: current Department of Defense figures suggest a ratio of trade on a 1.6:1 basis with NATO allies, significantly down from 7:1 in the U.S. favour as recently as 1984.

Rather than trade, therefore, today's focus in arms cooperation emphasises coordination of weapons-systems development, from the earliest stages of research through procurement. It is this shift in emphasis that has the broadest implications, as Secretary Carlucci noted, for the future of the Alliance defence industrial base.

THE FOUNDATIONS OF COOPERATION

Armaments cooperation is, of course, not a new concept in NATO. Indeed, the Alliance has recognised the negative impact of the absence of a more effective and efficient process for developing and procuring weapons and other defence systems almost since its inception. What is impressive in the last few years is the extent to which the Alliance has given substance to rhetoric more than two decades old.

By 1974, the unacceptable conditions of Alliance defence procurement were dramatised by a report entitled "US/European Economic Cooperation in Military and Civil Technology" which received widespread attention in NATO councils. This report, called the "Callaghan Report" after its author, defence analyst Thomas Callaghan, highlighted the deleterious military impact produced by wasteful duplication of effort in the defence-industrial sector of the Alliance. Lack of interoperability, the incapacity of different national forces to communicate with one another, and the limited ability to service one another's equipment were only a few of the shortcomings. Callaghan recommended a strong move to standardised equipment, and he emphasised the building of a genuine two-way street in arms cooperation. Callaghan's recommendations were echoed in the Culver-Nunn amendments of 1975 and 1976 declaring the statutory policy of the United States to be weapons standardised, or at least interoperable, with those of the NATO allies, and emphasising the need to make the two-way street concept work better.

In 1975, President Ford told the third NATO Summit in Brussels that, "we must make more efficient, more effective use of our defense resources. We need to achieve our longstanding goals of common procedures on equipment. Our research and development efforts must be more than the sum of individual parts."[5] In that year, the Eurogroup Defence Ministers also called for a new institution that could become the European terminus of the two-way street — a call that led in February 1976 to the establishment of the Independent European Program Group.

The advent of the Carter administration promised renewed efforts at expanding Alliance cooperation. Ambassador Robert Komer was appointed NATO Adviser to Secretary of Defense Harold Brown, and together with Under Secretary Bill Perry, he gave new emphasis to the subject. At the fourth NATO Summit in London in 1977, the President promised a renewed effort to expand arms cooperation. At the next Summit Carter's new long-term defence (LTDP) program was approved.

Despite the initial enthusiasm for the LTDP, by 1979, American support for armaments cooperation had hit a new low. In that year the House Armed Services Subcommittee on NATO Standardization, Interoperability and Readiness issued a devastating report on the state of Alliance cooperation which found no redeeming political, economic, or military virtues in a two-way street with Europe. Armaments cooperation seemed "dead in the water" at a time when the leaders of the Alliance were finding themselves confronting the critical issues of nuclear modernisation and deployment of the Pershing II and cruise missiles.

It was not until the spring of 1982 that arms cooperation once more appeared on the Washington policy agenda. Congress led the way with the passage of the Roth-Glenn-Nunn Amendment in the Senate. This amendment called for Allied heads of government to agree on a strategy and a structure for improving Alliance arms cooperation, as well as policies that ended wasteful duplication and shared more equally the financial and economic burdens of the common defence.

That same spring the Reagan Administration also turned its attention to NATO Armaments cooperation. In April 1982, a Defense Science Board Task Force on International Industry-to-Industry Armaments Cooperation was established at the Pentagon, chaired by Malcolm Currie, who was charged with identifying ways for U.S. industry to work more effectively with Allied industry in development and procurement of armaments and other defence-related equipment. The Task Force's report concluded that American technological leadership was deteriorating, and that in order to foster economic and defensive strength, investment had to be increased for long-range research and development. The report also acknowledged a genuine trade-off within a strengthened Alliance, the prospect that increased technological sharing might help establish and inevitably bolster competition for U.S. industry.[6]

As this DOD Report was being completed, David Abshire was heading to NATO as the new U.S. Ambassador, committed to a revitalisation of Alliance arms-cooperation efforts. Abshire's Center for Strategic and International Studies had a record of promoting armaments cooperation that stretched over a decade. He made improvements in this area one of his four priorities upon taking the assignment despite the fact that many old "NATO hands" in Washington and in Europe told him he was foolish to waste his time on an issue that so many people had tried to tackle with a remarkable lack of success.

Ambassador Abshire has written that the December 1983 meeting of the Defence Planning Committee was a milestone in the efforts to revitalise NATO arms cooperation as part of a broader attempt to improve Alliance conventional forces.[7] Of special importance in this regard was the proposal made by West German Defence Minister Manfred Wörner to develop a Conceptual Military Framework (CMF) to bring order to the plethora of mostly U.S. initiatives with which NATO had been recently confronted (e.g., Emerging Technologies, Air Land Battle, and Follow on Forces Attack) and to guide NATO planning for 20 years rather than the six to eight years that then was the case. The CMF was to prove important not only for force planning; its impact ultimately was to be felt in the armaments planning area as well.

At about the same time in Washington, then Secretary of Defense Caspar Weinberger established a core management team — headed by his Deputies, first Paul Thayer and then William H. Taft, IV — to oversee the Pentagon's arms-cooperation efforts. Thus was born the DOD Steering Group for NATO Armaments Cooperation, the first step in institutionalising changing DOD attitudes toward the importance of the arms-cooperation issue. It also signalled DOD recognition that, even for the United States, arms cooperation was not a luxury but a necessity.

This Pentagon effort coincided with a renewed interest in arms cooperation on Capitol Hill. Senator Sam Nunn had sent a warning shot across the bow of NATO officials with his troop withdrawal amendment in the summer of 1984. This "bad" Nunn Amendment reflected his frustration with what he saw as a sense of complacency in NATO and an unwillingness to address some serious shortcomings that could lead to military disaster. By mid 1985, however, Nunn was impressed enough by the change in

Alliance attitudes and the sense of momentum behind conventional defence improvement efforts that he worked to craft an amendment to encourage further cooperative efforts to make better use of resources. The U.S. Mission in Brussels, the Office of the Deputy Secretary of Defense and the staffs of Senators Nunn, Roth, and Warner coordinated closely on the framing of the now familiar amendment to establish a NATO Cooperative Research and Development Program. The amendment stressed cooperation at both ends of the development process, with the bulk of the money being allocated for projects in the early R&D stages. Some funds, however, would also be available for side-by-side testing of competitive U.S. and European systems.

The 1985 Nunn-Roth-Warner amendment and the efforts of Senator Dan Quayle to cut through bureaucratic red tape provide new challenges to the U.S. Services and the NATO Allies to join in specific efforts to develop important weapons and equipment which address critical common military needs. Twelve international Memoranda of Understanding to begin cooperative NATO research and development have been signed since the passage of these important amendments to the 1986 Defense Authorization Act.

Figure 1.1: *NATO Cooperative Research and Development Projects*

Research and Development Projects	Participants										
	United States	Canada	United Kingdom	France	Germany	Netherlands	Denmark	Norway	Spain	Italy	Turkey
Ada Project Support Environments	●	●	●	●	●	●	●			●	
155mm Autonomous Precision Guided Munition	●	●		●	●	●			●	●	●
Modular Standoff Weapons (MSOW)	●	●	●	●	●				●	●	
Multifunctional Information Distribution System	●	●	●	●	●			●	●	●	
NATO Identification System (NIS)	●		●	●	●					●	
Standoff Airborne Radar Demonstration System (ARDS)	●		●	●							
Advanced Short Takeoff and Vertical Landing Technology	●		●								
Enhanced Fighter Maneuverability	●				●						
Advanced Sea Mine	●		●								
NATO Frigate Replacement -1990's	●	●	●	●	●	●			●	●	
Hawk Mobility Enhancement	●				●						
NATO Anti-air Warfare System	●	●	●		●	●				●	

as of November, 1987

Source: Frank Carlucci, *Annual Report to the Congress, Fiscal Year 1989*, Washington D.C., 1988

Congress has appropriated $445 million for the NATO Co-development Programs to date ($200 million more will be authorised for Fiscal Year 1989), and the Pentagon predicts the U.S. share of current development programs will reach $899.7 million. The allies are expected to contribute $1.77 billion to the co-development initiatives.[8]

The NATO Frigate Program is potentially the largest NATO cooperative venture in history, with eight countries planning to build 50 modern frigates with an estimated total value to the Alliance of $20 billion. An additional two dozen projects, including the development of a NATO tactical area-communications system and the upgrade of the F-16 fighter aircraft, are in various stages of negotiations to become cooperative programs. In total, the Pentagon has planned to dedicate nearly $3 billion through 1992 for this type of NATO cooperation.[9] The real importance of these so-called "Nunn Programs" is not just that they are cooperative efforts, but that they are linked to NATO's agreed critical deficiencies. Each cooperative program — whether it be the Modular Stand-off Weapon, the system to identify friendly and hostile aircraft, or the NATO Frigate of the 1990s — targets an identified Alliance military need. The transition, however, from joint development program to common procurement has yet to be made in any of these NATO efforts, and that remains a major challenge to the Alliance.

Another promising development in the armaments-cooperation field is the establishment of a Conventional Armaments Planning System (CAPS) at NATO Headquarters. NATO's force-planning process has made great strides in this decade; the Conceptual Military Framework increased the Alliance planning horizon from six to 20 years, and the Conventional Defence Improvement effort allowed NATO to evaluate how well individual allies were doing meeting mutually agreed critical deficiencies. Together, these innovations provided Alliance policy makers with important tools to identify and attack NATO's most serious military shortcomings. The next step, as Secretary General Lord Carrington correctly suggested, was to link NATO force goals more effectively with national armaments planning.

In mid 1987, Lord Carrington proposed the creation of an Alliance armaments planning system, arguing that a closer link between force planning and armaments decisions would "create optimal opportunities for enhanced cooperation."[10] Although some allies had reservations about parts of the Secretary General's proposal, at the December 1987 meetings of the Defence Planning Committee and North Atlantic Council, Alliance defence and foreign ministers approved a two-year trial period for a Conventional Armaments Planning System.

Under the chairmanship of Assistant Secretary General for Defence Support Mack Mattingly, a Conventional Armaments Review Committee (NCARC) will oversee a process which will analyse new national Armaments Goals and propose a NATO Conventional Armaments Plan (CAP). The purpose of the plan will be to identify specific opportunities for cooperative endeavours after a comparison of national armaments planning; and highlight areas in which NATO force goals are not being translated into national armaments goals.

Under the new system, NATO members will identify their need for an operational capability that might be met by the development, upgrade, modification, or other acquisition of military equipment. A reply to an Armaments Planning Questionnaire (APQ) is then submitted which describes national plans and programs to meet established Armaments Goals. The Review Committee oversees the analysis of the national submissions and the drafting of the CAP. In this manner, NATO is moving toward the linkage of force planning and armaments planning described in the chart below.

Figure 1.2: *Force Planning and Armaments Planning Interaction*

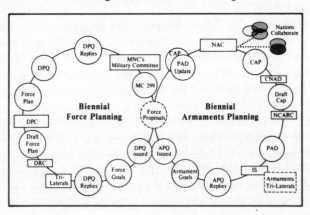

IS (International Staff) DPQ (Defense Planning Questionnaire)
PAD (Planning Analysis Department) DRC (Defense Review Committee)

Source: U.S. Department of Defense.

THE IMPACT OF IMPROVED ARMAMENTS
COOPERATION

Armaments cooperation within NATO is profoundly affecting the way allied governments and industry do business, forging what might be called the beginnings of an Alliance defence industrial base. Over the last five years, for example, 15 percent of the military equipment procured annually by the British Ministry of Defence has been collaboratively produced with the Allies. Another 10 percent of British military equipment is purchased directly from overseas industry.[11] Despite the declining U.S. defence trade surplus, the Pentagon's program of side-by-side testing of existing U.S. and European equipment is expanding rapidly. There are currently 49 Allied systems under evaluation in Pentagon test programs, and the Defense Department estimates that it will be evaluating 70 Allied systems in the next fiscal year.

Throughout the Alliance, defence industry response to the changing structure of the defence market has led to the creation of more efficient industrial consortia and the beginnings of a rationalisation of effort. To sense what progress is being made, one need only examine the latest Pentagon Selected Acquisition Report (SAR) on major weapons purchases to glimpse the increasing returns on joint industrial effort. Some $33 billion was planned for five trans-Atlantic purchases: the AV-8B Harrier (McDonnell Douglas, British Aerospace, and Rolls Royce); the Army Mobile Subscriber Equipment (GTE and Thomson-CSF); the T-5 trainer aircraft (McDonnell Douglas and BAe); the KC-135R re-engining program (Boeing and CFM International); and the Martin Marietta/Oerlikon system, which appears to have won the Army's forward area air-defence competition.[12]

Much of the progress in Washington can be traced directly to the efforts of the current Deputy Secretary of Defense, William H. Taft, IV. Chairing both the DOD Steering Group on NATO Armaments Cooperation and the Defense Resources Board, the Deputy Secretary has been able to press the Alliance cooperative agenda upon the sometimes-resistant military services with unprecedented success.

Taft's appearance at a 1985 "reinforced" North Atlantic Council meeting devoted specifically to armaments cooperation marked the first time since 1950 that Alliance Deputy Defense Ministers had so met. Most importantly, it was not a one-time event, but developed into a series of meetings which ensured that progress could be reviewed and outstanding issues addressed by political decision makers above the level of technical experts. Armaments cooperation was thus elevated to a priority position on the Alliance agenda.

THE FUTURE OF ALLIANCE ARMAMENT COOPERATION

Despite the historical commitment of NATO member states and impressive recent progress, trans-Atlantic armaments cooperation efforts are at a watershed; American programs to engage the Allies in co-development projects and Alliance attempts to institutionalise joint planning are facing growing challenges from commitments to intra-European cooperation, attempts on both sides of the Atlantic to protect the domestic industrial base, and pressure on the flow of advanced technologies.

The latter challenge, and the need it creates to develop a coherent technology-management strategy within the Alliance, is perhaps the most critical one facing NATO's efforts to expand armaments cooperation. This is so because it is crucial for the Alliance to translate the West's formidable advantage on the frontiers of technology to the conventional battlefield, thereby maintaining the Alliance-wide qualitative advantage in fielded weaponry — the advantage that has traditionally helped to balance the correlation of forces in Central Europe. As Senator Nunn has suggested, it is necessary to achieve greater coordination of Alliance research and development in the areas of most advanced technologies if we are to witness a "revolution" in conventional defence capability that is necessary to undermine the growing capability — quantitative and qualitative — of the potential adversary.[13]

To a certain extent, this was the focus of NATO's mid 1980s program on "Emerging Technologies/Long Term." While that effort produced some thoughtful ideas, the concepts derived have never been translated into action by the Alliance as a whole or by individual Allies. With this beginning of a conceptual framework already in place, however, NATO's examination of advanced technologies can and should be re-energised.

Yet, a new NATO initiative to coordinate military research and development efforts must scrupulously avoid becoming merely a technology identification process. Promising technologies abound in Allied laboratories; NATO's challenge is to bring critical new force multipliers to the battlefield in sufficient numbers to affect the balance of forces. As one defence analyst has suggested, key programming, budgeting, and planning decisions in the military R&D field must be driven more by today's military requirements, the "theatre demand," than by the momentum of rapid technological advance.[14]

The Pentagon's year-old Balanced Technology Initiative (BTI) is the current vehicle for just such a strengthening and focusing of American advanced technology research in conventional weapons systems and military equipment. An initiative of the Senate Armed Services Committee, BTI had its origins in the political debate of 1986 over the size of the military R&D budget devoted to strategic defence. In mandating a shift of resources toward basic research on conventional weapons systems and equipment, Senator Nunn's committee argued:

> if NATO is to find ways to reduce its current reliance on the threat of early use of nuclear weapons, it must harness its collective technological capabilities to counter quantitative advantages that provide the Soviet Union and its Warsaw Pact allies with a destabilizing capability for a short-warning conventional attack. The Balanced Technology Initiative is designed as a high priority response to this threat.[15]

Congress allocated $200 million in the 1987 defence budget for BTI, and the Pentagon selected 48 projects from 250 candidates nominated by OSD, the Defense Agencies, and the Services to begin the program. In 1988 Congress also appropriated $100 million to continue original BTI research programs and identify possible new starts. Prospects are good that the Pentagon's 1989 request for $238 million will emerge from the House/Senate budget conference unscathed.

The Pentagon, initially skeptical of Congressional commitment to this new initiative and unwilling to reorganise research and development efforts radically on the basis of a last-minute adjustment to the 1987 defence budget, has come to recognise the potential of this framework for defence R&D efforts which enjoys obvious support on Capitol Hill. In the President's 1989 budget request, BTI was identified for the first time as a line item in the Pentagon budget. Institutionally, the Office of the Undersecretary of Defense for Research and Advanced Technology has made remarkable progress in disciplining the selection of the promising projects in terms of the criteria of the 1987 legislation, which included focus on "smart" munitions and anti-armor technologies.

BTI research efforts are now organised into five broad technology areas: 1) Smart Weapons; 2) Armor/Anti-Armor; 3) Reconnaissance, Surveillance & Target Acquisition/Battle Management, Communications, Command & Control (RSTA/BMC3), addressing new technologies for obtaining, processing, and transmitting information essential on the modern battlefield; 4) High-Power Microwaves (HPM), an effort to understand the effects of HPM on U.S. weapons systems and place vulnerable enemy systems at risk; and 5) Special Technology Opportunities, a category that captures projects that might have important conventional impact such as the advanced cruise missile or high-energy lasers.[16]

Complementing the Balanced Technology Initiative as part of an American strategy to exploit emerging technologies is the Pentagon's Competitive Strategies Study. The Study's initial Task Force on Mid-to-High Intensity Conflict in Europe has produced the Department's first proposed strategy for matching the strengths of NATO's technologies and operational concepts against enduring Soviet/Warsaw Pact vulnerabilities on the battlefield of the future.

Competitive Strategies focuses on high-leverage changes in policy, doctrine, and technology to produce both peacetime and wartime impact on the actions of the Soviet Union. In peacetime, Competitive Strategies seeks to force Soviet and Warsaw Pact investment into areas of comparative disadvantage and reduce the adversary's flexibility to redirect defence resources. In wartime, Competitive Strategies is intended to provide the means to disrupt the sequence of Soviet offensive operations, allowing NATO the time it needs to mount a robust defence.

The Task Force's report, still classified, identified three priority areas for the application of new technologies in NATO: countering the Soviet air offensive, blunting enemy penetrations of NATO's forward defence, and disrupting East Bloc troop control.[17] The implications of these priorities for technology development programs are already clear. Countering Soviet concentration of manned aircraft and disruption of their main operating base tempo of operations is achievable through a greater reliance on unmanned/remotely piloted vehicles and stand-off weapons. Longer-range mass-fire systems and instantaneous mine-laying capability are required to halt deep penetrations of NATO's defences, and anti-radar systems and new warheads for NATO weapons are needed to target effectively Warsaw Pact strategic (theatre) command, communications, and control facilities.

The recommendations of the first Task Force report have been reviewed by the Office of the Secretary of Defense, the military services, and the operational commanders. A War Gaming Committee is now working to prepare recommendations on an operational concept for employing new technologies that could be fielded by the late 1990s. The development of this operational model will be the basis for a follow-on costing exercise and eventual impact on the budget formulation.

While the second phase of the Competitive Strategies Study will look at future non-nuclear strategic systems, the impact of this first phase of work on the future European battlefield is extremely important to the NATO allies. For the first time, the Pentagon has, with its Competitive Strategies approach, a new framework for translating emerging technologies into force multipliers in support of NATO doctrine. The challenge before NATO today is to begin a similar effort to pinpoint the most promising new technologies with highest potential payoffs for the conventional defence of Europe into the 1990s.

If the American Competitive Strategies effort and the Balanced Technology Initiative are to have a major impact on Alliance conventional defence capability, they must be placed within a NATO framework that engages America's European partners. For its part, the United States must review the range of its advanced R&D projects and identify specific technologies that could be most easily exploited cooperatively with the Allies under the BTI. Some new technologies will remain too sensitive to share even with our closest NATO allies, but the United States must identify areas for a freer flow of information and technology among NATO partners.

Regarding BTI in particular, an exciting new effort in NATO armaments cooperation can be driven by this creative American initiative if Alliance leadership is forthcoming. The idea of expanding the BTI program to include a NATO cooperative focus was first raised in a December 1987 study by the Washington Center for Strategic and International Studies which recommended to the Pentagon and Congress that a portion of BTI funding be earmarked for new collaborative programs with the Allies.[18] Appearing before the Senate Armed Services Committee on 7 October 1987, Deputy Secretary of Defense Taft stated that the DOD would have no difficulty with such an approach. This was affirmed in Secretary of Defense Carlucci's 1988 burdensharing report, which noted:

> The Balanced Technology Initiative is another new defense program that is addressing many problems of considerable importance to our

NATO allies. This program was explicitly established to support the development of technologies important to conventional defense.... In continuing the BTI program, we plan to establish cooperative technology development efforts with our NATO allies.[19]

Figure 1.3: *Cooperative Research and Development Percentage of RDT&E Budget*

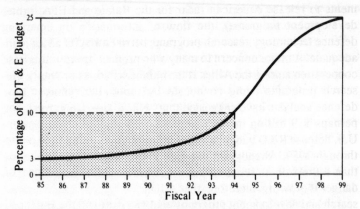

In fact, the creation of cooperative programs under the BTI rubric will be absolutely necessary if the Pentagon is to achieve its new goal of having 25 percent of its research, development, testing and evaluation budget devoted to international programs by 1999. The rapid expansion of cooperative R&D projected by the Defense Department shown in the graph below, from today's four percent to 10 percent of the total budget by 1994, will depend especially on success in coordinating advanced electronics development efforts. As the electronics components of U.S. military research rises to nearly half of the Pentagon's own RDT & E spending by the late 1990s, BTI programs to develop software-intensive battle management and intelligence gathering equipment should form the basis for expanding Alliance cooperation.[20]

Unfortunately, NATO as an institution is not in a position to act quickly on Secretary Carlucci's proposal to move armaments cooperation to areas of more advanced technologies. The systematic identification of new collaborative opportunities in advanced research and development, especially where impact on critical NATO requirements such as FOFA capability is maximised, has yet to be done. Further, the lack of a coherent policy on technology transfer and technology security clearly hampers planning for new NATO cooperative programs. A large measure of responsibility for the absence of such a framework rests with the American administration, whose inability to coordinate its internal policy on technology security has made a meaningful dialogue with the European allies extremely difficult.

While some important progress in this area has been achieved recently by a Pentagon effort to establish a new system for reviewing technology transfer cases (most notably, of course, the agreements to release American radar for the Rafale and EFA fighter development programs), the flow of information on emerging defence technology research programs between NATO allies is inadequate. A major concern to many who propose greatly expanded cooperation among the Allies is the number of secret or "black" research programs being conducted by the United States. Some defence analysts have suggested that "black" programs, funded at perhaps $19 billion in 1987, represent 25 percent of the current U.S. defense R&D budget and are projected to grow by 4.3 percent through 1989. Already, for example, the U.S. Air Force has more than a third of its research budget in classified programs.[21] The danger is growing, therefore, that Alliance efforts to merge new research and development programs could be derailed at some future date when the U.S. Army, Navy, or Air Force reveal the result of their own parallel, secret technology development program.

Vastly improved technology security arrangements will be necessary if transatlantic armaments cooperation is to transcend the current level of technology sharing. As a beginning, a major NATO conference, bringing together national governments and industry — with ministerial participation — is needed to address the broad agenda of technology protection policy and the structure of Alliance defence trade.

A profound handicap in forging any new Alliance arms cooperation initiative at the research and development stage is the continuing drain on scarce defence R&D resources produced by duplicative national efforts in Europe. As was suggested in the 1987 report of the Independent European Program Group (IEPG), "Towards a Stronger Europe," the lack of a common or coordinated European research program is one reason why NATO Europe is able to afford collectively only one-third as much military R&D as the United States, though the intra-European arms "market" is roughly 40 percent of U.S. procurement.[22] Indeed, the Report argued that it seems to be the case "that a nation will support the interests of Europe as a whole only when it is in their national interests to do so," and that support of existing employment levels or the preservation of technological capabilities are major motivations for sustaining uneconomical national production capabilities. A recent study of the U.S. National Academy of Sciences confirms this assessment, suggesting that duplication of effort by European defence industry costs $36 billion a year, or roughly just under a third of NATO Europe's arsenal defence spending.

Declining or stagnant defence budgets throughout the Alliance lend an urgency to finding a solution to this problem. In confronting it, however, the Europeans face a dilemma: go with cheaper options, generally weapons systems programs purchased directly from or developed in cooperation with the United States, or cooperate among themselves and safeguard Europe's defence industrial base, recognising that the costs are likely to be higher — considerably, in some cases.

CONCLUSION: CONFRONTING THE OBSTACLES

There are, of course, inherent tensions between a "European" approach and efforts to expand transatlantic cooperation. European Allies, especially those with larger populations, scientific establishments, and gross national products, are under mounting pressure to protect their national industrial bases as the world-wide market for sophisticated arms becomes more competitive. Increasingly, intra-European cooperation and the creation of an integrated European arms market is seen as the way out of this industrial dilemma. As the IEPG report argued, reflecting what is probably a broad and growing consensus in Europe, a vigorous program to expand intra-European arms cooperation is the first, necessary step toward a strong and independent "European Pillar" within NATO.

Some 20 all-European collaborative research and development programs are now sponsored by the IEPG. Among the most advanced of the European development programs are: a Franco-German anti-tank helicopter (total program cost: $5.4 billion); the British, French, and German effort to develop the next generation medium-range anti-armor missile; and a quadripartite program to build a transport helicopter for the 1990s. In Munich, a Joint Armaments Agency has been established to manage three intra-European cooperative ventures including the Franco-German helicopter program.

While intra-European cooperative programs have multiplied rapidly in the mid 1980s, the process of building the European Pillar in NATO is fraught with political barriers. Disagreement on operational requirements for military equipment, lack of information on national equipment replacement and modernisation schedules, and fragmented research and development efforts are only some of the barriers cited by the IEPG report to the creation of an integrated arms market in Europe.[23]

One of the most important, and almost axiomatically the most controversial, of the intra-European co-development programs underway now is the European Fighter Aircraft (EFA) effort. The EFA program has come to symbolise all of the tensions between intra-European and transatlantic cooperation. The European Fighter is being developed by a consortium of British, German, Italian, and Spanish industries at a probable cost of $9 to $10 billion for a total buy of some 750 planes.[24] The EFA project worries American defence planners, however. At twice the cost of upgrading the performance of the U.S. F-18 fighter, the EFA appears to the Pentagon to be a long-term wasteful drain on scarce European resources for conventional force improvements. It sees the "opportunity cost" of the EFA as enormous in light of all of the other conventional force improvements that are necessary but for which there will be, as a result of EFA, little money. The European allies counter that American offers of collaboration on upgrading the F-18 are no more than an attempt to destroy forever Allied capability to produce top-of-the-line fighter aircraft.[25]

A key issue in the debate over the EFA, but also in the larger context of the challenges of intra-European cooperation, is the degree to which today's major collaborative weapons development programs are becoming what Dennis Kloske, U.S. Deputy Under Secretary of Defense (Planning and Resources) has termed "industrial entitlements." Kloske's concern is that these major weapons programs are increasingly being designed to secure jobs or an advanced technology base, rather than as economically efficient responses to critical NATO military requirements. For example, the West German Defence Minister's final recommendation to the Cabinet on participation in EFA cited the program's critical role in fostering future German and European defence-aerospace industry competitiveness, but it made no mention of how it would meet military requirements. Moreover, German planning already reflects the trade-offs involved in the EFA purchase. According to press reports, some 100 other equipment programs, including the next generation, will be either cancelled or postponed to pay for the Federal Republic's 200 EFA aircraft.[26]

Another element of the tension between the NATO allies on issues of intra-European armaments cooperation is the possibility that the creation of a single European market, scheduled for 1992, will challenge the still fragile NATO framework for cooperation across the Atlantic. Recent moves by the European Economic Community appear to some to be harbingers of an effort to include defence industry in a single market protected from North American competition. The European Commission's consideration of a measure that would in effect require additional customs duties for imported American defence equipment is feared to be only the first step in this direction.[27]

Karl-Heinz Narjes, the EC Commissioner for Industry, has made little secret of his interest in expanding the Community's purview to include defence industry through the EC's ongoing industrial and information technology programs. Already, the ESPRIT informational technology research program accounts for one-third of Europe's pre-competitive research in the field.[28] Narjes has said that it is "unthinkable that military R&D and the production of weaponry should not be part of the whole process" of the 1992 internal market development. "We cannot deprive our defence industry," Narjes concludes, "of the benefits we seek for our civil industries."[29] U.S. defence industry has also begun to recognise that 1992 will change the shape of transatlantic trade by strengthening European industry's ability to compete.[30]

A strategy to expand Alliance armaments cooperation must establish an environment conducive to industry-to-industry initiatives. Defence industry remains far ahead of national governments in forging efficient international consortia. Consequently, reducing impediments to even greater international industrial cooperation and increasing industry input in government-to-government cooperative negotiations should be priorities for NATO defence planners. A crucial first step to unleashing private-industry cooperative initiative is a thorough review and reform of U.S. government technology-export licencing procedures. Other industry observations and complaints about the current structure of Alliance armaments cooperation efforts must be addressed. Critics of current arms cooperation point to the recent French withdrawal from the group of nations committed to producing a NATO Modular Standoff Weapon (MSOW), and the USAF exit from the cooperative program on part of NATO's Identification System (NIS) as evidence that existing transatlantic cooperation is poorly constructed, attempting to merge too many disparate national requirements. Skepticism about the actual economic efficiency of many NATO programs is another byproduct of industry experience with current co-development efforts.

In short, NATO governments must create the institutional framework for a more effective government-defence industry consultation on arms-cooperation issues. As the European allies move toward the inevitable merging of defence acquisition and the creation of a common armaments market, a forum is needed to provide input into the process for defence industry — European and American. The NATO Industrial Advisory Group exists in Brussels, and could be the focus of an Alliance effort to upgrade the defence industry role in NATO armaments cooperation planning. In a similar vein, in "Towards a Stronger Europe," the IEPG study team suggested that an advisory group of European industry representatives would be helpful in steering the course of intra-European cooperation.[31]

Alliance armaments cooperation efforts are at a watershed; recent important progress through American programs to engage the Allies in co-development projects and Alliance attempts to institutionalise joint planning are facing growing challenges from commitments to intra-European cooperation, attempts on both sides of the Atlantic to protect the domestic defence industrial base, and pressure on the flow of advanced technologies. Economic imperatives to forge industrial partnerships to increase return on collective defence investment and exploit the promise of advanced technologies are clear. The challenge before the Alliance today is to take the necessary further steps toward an Alliance industrial base by rationalising industrial effort at the research and development level.

Notes

[1]David Greenwood, "Economic Constraints and Program Choices for the 1990's," paper prepared for the Center for Strategic and International Studies (Washington, February 1988), p. 13.

[2]Helen Dewar, "Pentagon Budget Bill Approved," *Washington Post*, 14 November 1987, p. A1.

[3]For a discussion of Abshire's "defence investment strategy," see David M. Abshire, "A Resources Strategy for NATO," *NATO's Sixteen Nations*, October 1985; and also Abshire's testimony before the Senate Armed Services Committee, 27 January 1988.

[4]Frank C. Carlucci, "Report on Allied Contributions to the Common Defense," a Report to the U.S. Congress (Washington: Department of Defense, April 1988), p. 9.

[5]See David M. Abshire, "Arms Cooperation in NATO," *Armed Forces Journal International*, December 1985, p. 66.

[6]See "Industry-to-Industry International Armaments Cooperation, Phase 1, NATO Europe," a Report of the Science Board Task Force of the Department of Defense, June 1983.

[7]Abshire, "Arms Cooperation," p. 68.

[8]Frank C. Carlucci, "Support of NATO Strategy in the 1990s," a Report to the U.S. Congress in compliance with Public Law 100-180 (Washington: Department of Defense, January 1988), p. xv.

[9]News Release, Office of Assistant Secretary of Defense (Public Affairs), "DOD Announces Formation of Defense Cooperation Working Group," 21 January 1987, no. 34-87.

[10]The Right Honourable The Lord Carrington, "NATO Armaments Planning," a Memo to the Permanent Representatives (Council) of NATO, 13 May 1987, p. 2.

[11]"Statement on the Defence Estimates 1988, Part 1," presented to Parliament by the Secretary of State for Defence by Command of Her Majesty, London, 1988, p. 39.

[12]John F. Morton and Ben Schemmer, "Congress Backs Big Boosts in U.S. Two-Way Street Buys," *Armed Forces Journal*, December 1987, p. 72.

[13]See Senator Sam Nunn, "NATO Challenges and Opportunities: A Three-Track Approach," a speech to the DMS Symposium on Industrial Cooperation within NATO, Brussels, 13 April 1987.

[14]Anthony H. Cordesman, "Technology and the Search for Conventional Options: Religion Versus Reality," a Paper Presented to a Conference on "The Future of Strategic and Defense Technology," Wilson Center, Washington, 6 June 1988, p. 18.

[15]Report of Senate Armed Services Committee, National Defense Authorization Act for Fiscal Year 1988 and 1989, 100th Cong., 1st sess. (Washington: U.S. Government Printing Office), p. 124.

[16]See "Balanced Technology Initiative Program," materials prepared by William E. Snowden, Special Assistant to Deputy Under Secretary of Defense for Research, 1988, p. 8.

[17]Carlucci, "Support of NATO Strategy in the 1990s," p. III: 4.

[18]"NATO: Meeting the Coming Challenge, an Alliance Action Plan for Conventional Improvements and Armaments Cooperation," prepared by the Project on a Resources Strategy for the United States and Its Allies, The Center for Strategic and International Studies (Washington, 18 December 1987), p. 37.

[19]Frank C. Carlucci, Department of Defense, "Report on Allied Contributions to the Common Defense," p. 10.

[20]"Avionics Firms Increase Investments, But Market Growth Expected to Slow," *Aviation Week & Space Technology*, 30 May 1988, p. 72.

[21]Bruce D. Nordwall, "Electronic Technology to Dominate Next Generation of Weapons Systems," ibid., 6 June 1988, pp. 82-83.

[22]"Towards a Stronger Europe," a Report of the Independent Study Team of the Independent European Program Group, Brussels, December 1986, p. 1.

[23]Ibid., pp. 8-12.

[24]Jeffrey M. Lenorvitz and Keith Moroff, "European Fighter Funding Approval Sparks Opening of German Show," *Aviation Week & Space Technology*, 9 May 1988, p. 28.

[25]Tim Carrington, "Europe's Plan to Build New Fighter Plane Puts Western Firms on Cutthroat Course," *Wall Street Journal*, 23 May 1988, p. 16.

[26]Friedrich Thelen, "West Germany to Scratch Programs for EFA," *Defense News*, 30 May 1988, p. 1.

[27]Giovanni de Briganti, "EEC Mulls Tax on U.S. Hardware," ibid., 23 May 1988, p. 1.

[28]William Dawkins, "Keeping Europe on the I.T. Map," *Financial Times*, 18 May 1988.

[29]David Buchan, "West Europeans Are Inching Towards a Common Market in Arms," *Financial Times*, 15 April 1988.

[30]See remarks by Robert L. Kirk, Chairman and CEO of Allied-Signal Aerospace Company, to the Annual Meeting of the American Institute of Aeronautics and Astronautics, Arlington, Virginia, 4 May 1988.

[31]"Towards a Stronger Europe," p. 14.

2

The MRCA/Tornado: The Politics and Economics of Collaborative Procurement

Alistair Edgar

INTRODUCTION

The Panavia Tornado[1] has been thus far the most ambitious and controversial effort made by West European governments in the collaborative research, development, and production of an advanced military aircraft.[2] Disputes arose over alleged cost-escalation, claimed cost-saving benefits, apparent military-operational requirements, the place of such collaboration in the ongoing battle over the "two-way street" in transatlantic trade within NATO, and the aircraft's relation to the avowed NATO goal of increased equipment standardisation.[3] Its controversial status, however, may soon pale in comparison with another Euro-collaborative venture, the current European Fighter Aircraft (EFA) program, the brief existence of which already has demonstrated striking similarities.[4] Given its possible precedential significance for the EFA program, it is perhaps unfortunate that there should be such a dearth of analytical research and writing about the Tornado program.[5]

Collaboration is becoming an increasing feature of European defence procurement policies, as governments face rapidly escalating equipment costs and rising demands from public service sectors such as education, health, and social security. The spectre of structural disarmament merely adds further pressures towards more collaborative efforts. In this context, analysis of the Tornado program can shed light on the problems, costs, and potential benefits of collaboration. With regard to problems and costs, no doubt it is unhelpful to have "what is really testimony to the relevance of values and interests other than efficiency castigated as obstacles."[6] Nevertheless, constant tensions do exist between broader

46

international, national, or interest-group objectives on one hand, and the oft-touted goals of cost-savings benefits, and improved technological and military-operational capabilities on the other; and it is my purpose in this chapter to identify, describe, and analyse both those tensions and the potential benefits arising from collaboration. Clearly, as collaboration becomes entrenched within the West European defence industrial base, we will need to have a more complete understanding of its implications, both for scholarly and, increasingly, policy purposes.

I argue that a study of the Tornado case can contribute to this goal. In this case-study, I address five critical issues. The first section explores the international bargaining context as it became linked to the Tornado, and its effect upon the attitude and behaviour of the consortium's members. I next examine the national governments' domestic political and economic objectives that became associated with the project, and the impact (if any) of aerospace industries' views and party-political disputes. Following this, a more detailed analysis is given of how these varying demands shaped the work-sharing agreements that were signed regarding the engine, airframe, and avionics systems of the aircraft. I then evaluate the extent to which the Tornado obtained such avowed program goals as cost-savings benefits for consortium members, required national military-operational capabilities, and reliance on European technology. Finally, I conclude with a critical appraisal of the achievements of collaboration, and its potential future within the Atlantic alliance

INTERNATIONAL BARGAINING IN THE MRCA PROGRAM

The first hurdle facing a collaborative endeavour of this nature is a major one: the necessity of harmonising several frequently divergent national military-operational requirements and varying equipment-replacement schedules, to the reasonable satisfaction of each member. When, in mid 1968, the Memorandum of Understanding concerning the Multi-Role Aircraft for 1975 (MRA-75) — as it was originally entitled — was signed, six countries indicated interest in the project.[7] West Germany, Britain, Italy, Canada, Belgium, and the Netherlands all possessed ageing aircraft inventories that would require replacement in the next decade. Their intention was to examine the possibility of developing a single aircraft able to fulfil a wide variety of missions currently undertaken by a variety of planes.[8] Within a year of the MOU being signed, however, first Canada and Belgium, and finally the Netherlands, withdrew from the prospective effort before having to make any longer-term commitments. In each case, the decisions illustrate some of the problems that can arise in negotiating collaborative aircraft-production projects, and merit, therefore, some further comment here.

The decision of the Canadian government not to continue participation in the MRCA program clearly was a reflection of Ottawa's relative reorientation of its defence and foreign policy away from Western Europe. Shortly after it was taken, Canada's Minister of National Defence explained in Ottawa that the air element of the Canadian Forces in Europe was to be reduced to those squadrons of obsolescent CF-104s, intended for use in a conventionally armed ground-support role.[9] In the absence of strong political support, neither potential military nor economic advantages could have provided sufficient motivation for a continued Canadian participation. Following the initial MOU, however, it became apparent that, to Ottawa, it was questionable whether there might be military or economic benefits for Canada in the project. As one Canadian government official explained, "we withdrew because it looked as if we would not get sufficient attention paid to the Canadian requirements, because there appeared to be very little opportunity for Canadian manufacturing content, and because it showed signs of being very expensive."[10] West European governments' pressures to obtain a larger share of the MRCA work, as well as suspected Anglo-German compromises, were enough to persuade Ottawa to abandon the MRCA.

Soon after the Canadian withdrawal, the Belgian government announced that it was following suit. With its limited defence budget, it saw offset opportunities as an essential part of any major weapons purchase. Thus, while Anglo-German disagreements over project leadership were consuming several months in 1968 and 1969, France was offering Belgium excellent offset terms for the Dassault Mirage S, an aircraft ideally suited to the country's operational requirements.[11] Belgium never did buy the Mirage, but the French option contributed to the loss of another potential consortium member and its aircraft orders.[12]

Although the Canadian and Belgian decisions preceded the project definition phase, the Netherlands' government remained as a member until July 1969, by which time negotiations on aircraft specifications and work-sharing agreements were underway.

Nevertheless, government and military officials' comments reflect the earlier fears of the Belgian and Canadian critics. The Netherlands' Air Force originally had specified its requirement for a single-engine, highly manoeuvrable fighter aircraft with a maximum speed of Mach 1.8. In March 1969, the British and German governments — with the largest proposed aircraft orders — agreed to a twin-engine configuration, justified by their need to incorporate the long-range strike/interdiction role demanded by the RAF. Instead of the "fairly simple fighter plane with outstanding manoeuvrability" envisaged by Dutch Defence Minister Hendrikus J. de Toom, the MRCA was emerging as a vastly more complex aircraft with a minimum weight of 40,000 pounds.[13]

This was not the only concern expressed by the Dutch. Government officials privately vented their anger at the manner in which the administrative costs of the Panavia organisation, established to oversee the venture, had risen from 2.5 to 5 percent of total program costs.[14] In addition, the Anglo-German compromise raised the estimated unit price of the MRCA from the initial figure of $2.5 million to a new level of $4.8 million. Lieutenant-General Wolff, commander-in-chief of the Air Force and himself an advocate of collaboration, attacked the compromise, arguing that the Netherlands would obtain only "a limited capability [using the twin-engine design] for our needs, but we are paying for all the other compromises."[15] Finally, the new design agreement also resulted in the postponement of the intended delivery date for the MRCA, from the original target of 1975 to a new one of 1977/78. The Netherlands' national replacement schedule called for an aircraft available by the middle of the decade, and further MRCA delivery-slippages could not be ruled out.

The conclusion reached by Defence Minister de Toom was that the MRCA was too complicated, too costly, and technically unsuitable for the Air Force.[16] The Netherlands' defence budget, estimated and accepted on an annual basis, left little room for a long-term commitment to a program that offered an aircraft whose operational capabilities were seen as uncertain, with costs already escalating against the wishes of the government. The MRCA appeared as a poor military and financial risk, without offering any compensatory political benefits. Unable to negotiate an agreement satisfactory to the Netherlands, the consortium again lost a member and further production orders. The Netherlands instead turned to the United States, and negotiated licenced production of the F-16.

The above discussion highlights a significant contradiction facing collaborative aircraft development. Cost-savings benefits are maximised by high production orders, but a large number of partners creates greater divergence of requirements, thereby increasing political friction. What results is the withdrawal of some of the members, which may be necessary if the program is ever going to advance beyond the definition phase. However, this also decreases the domestic European market for aircraft sales, as alternative systems are obtained, and increases the need for export sales beyond Europe, in competition with U.S. products.

That Britain, West Germany, and Italy continued with their collaborative endeavours might be taken to indicate that these countries at least possessed common or compatible operational requirements. In fact, their original military needs differed considerably, with missions varying from long-range strike/interdiction, to close ground support, to air combat.[17] The Royal Air Force's requirements called for a twin-engine aircraft with a minimum range of 800 miles, and possessing advanced avionics systems for long-range, all-weather, low-level flight capability. To perform aircraft functions a two-man crew was necessary, consisting of a pilot and a systems operator. The Luftwaffe and Italian Air Force each sought a single-engine aircraft with a 200-mile range, avionics systems for Short Take-Off and Landing (STOL), with a single crew member. Ideal performance characteristics and weapons systems were different in each case.[18]

Such divergent requirements might have led to the abandonment of the MRCA in its earliest stages. Already, three states had departed the development consortium, and the main British and West German partners appeared to be locked in an ongoing dispute over project leadership. Italy, the third remaining member of the consortium, was left in a position similar to that which had precipitated the Dutch withdrawal, as Anglo-German bargaining seemed likely to dictate the final shape of the project without taking Italian views into account.

The March 1969 Anglo-German agreement on a common design for the MRCA appeared to optimise the aircraft for the RAF's primary mission, at least according to one leading defence journal, which reported that the "resulting twin-engine configuration represents a significant German compromise which very likely will put the [FRG's] $2.5 million flyaway price goal out of reach."[19] Bonn had signed the agreement despite the relatively advanced status of the NKF aircraft, ideally suited to Luftwaffe requirements and nationally developed by the industrial combine Entwicklungsring Sud (EWR). The MRCA, in contrast, already had been labelled as "a compromise aircraft to meet the requirements of all consortium members."[20] The West German government, apparently, was prepared to accept an aircraft project that certainly did not meet original price goals, and might not even achieve performance characteristics requested by the Luftwaffe.

Concessions in the 1969 agreement were made not only by the German partner. For the Royal Air Force, the MRCA design overlapped with the existing operational abilities of the Anglo-French Jaguar squadrons. In order to secure the collaborative agreement, the British government also was willing to accept an unnecessarily complicated — and hence expensive — aircraft design.[21]

With such operational and unit-cost compromises, it is perhaps less surprising that some of the original consortium members withdrew than that the development program managed to survive the initial negotiating processes. However, by this time deeper political and economic motivations were associated with its continuation; for collaboration regarding the MRCA was becoming an instrument of intra-European bargaining.

The importance of the Tornado project to Britain's application for membership in the European Economic Community was acknowledged by all the remaining members of the consortium. Faced with French opposition to his application, the project was a diplomatic symbol by which British Prime Minister Harold Wilson could demonstrate his resolve to other members of the Community. The Prime Minister's visits to Rome and Bonn in January and February 1967, to discuss the EEC issue and questions of technological cooperation between those three governments, coincided closely with their initial expressions of interest in the co-production of a new European combat aircraft.[22] "It was believed," noted one analyst some years later, "that the road to the Common Market passed through Bonn, not Paris."[23] The strong German support for the Rolls Royce RB.199 as the main power plant for the MRCA — discussed in more detail in the examination of work-sharing agreements, below — as well as the acceptance of the twin-engine configuration, was explained unofficially even at the time by the aircraft program "becoming deeply rooted in Germany's sponsorship of Britain's entry into the Common Market."[24]

German (and Italian) desire to see Britain become a member of the EEC was explained most explicitly in 1970 by former Italian Ambassador in Paris, Pietro Quaroni, in terms that indicate one of the ways in which international political bargaining can be associated with collaborative procurement. "The French," said Quaroni, "have never given up the hope of transforming the Common Market into a French sphere of influence... If my country and others [support the British application], it is because we believe that, in this way, the internal balance of power in Europe would be more assured."[25] The Italian government's willingness to accept Anglo-German compromises in the Tornado program — compromises made without its consultation — becomes more explicable in the context of this broader political objective.

Political and economic bargaining at the international level played an important role in determining the long-term membership of the Panavia Tornado consortium. The question of Britain's EEC application provided a broad and overriding motivation for the British and German partners to obtain a compromise agreement on aircraft design and on project leadership.[26] It also made the Italian government's acceptance of such compromises easier by providing the pretext of longer-term political advantages via a more balanced Community. However, the fear of cost-escalation and operational compromises drove three of the original interested parties — along with valuable domestic orders — to seek alternative sources. At one point, the Netherlands even considered a second European-based aircraft development project to rival the MRCA.[27] This failed to emerge, but the possibility of such increased internal competition is relevant especially as long as collaboration in military aerospace projects does not include the independent French industry with its valuable export markets.

The original design of the MRCA was based upon the differing missions of the various national air forces, yet international political and economic objectives provided vital incentives to reach compromise agreements when these missions proved difficult to reconcile. The following two sections provide more detailed analyses of national concerns and the specific administration and work-sharing agreements. The Anglo-German agreement of early 1969, however, clearly established the outline of the MRCA program, and set the general design parameters within which the aircraft would have to be developed. Whatever their longer-term impact upon program efficiency, cost-savings potentials, and the achievement of performance capabilities united to operational demands, these parameters were not based on specific military considerations. The concern must be whether such "political parameters" will prove detrimental to the end product, a more cost-effective and capable aircraft, by pushing design compromises in future programs against the limits of technology.

NATIONAL BARGAINING IN THE MRCA PROGRAM

The three national partners remaining in the MRCA program by 1970 — West Germany, Britain, and Italy — clearly possessed some common objectives that helped them to create and maintain their political will to cooperate. All three governments also sought domestic political and economic goals through the aircraft project. The question to be asked is how, or to what extent, pursuit of these governmental objectives influenced the development of the Tornado? The relationship between government policies, aerospace-related industries' views, and political party disputes during this period provides further insight into the nature of the powers at work shaping collaboration in the European defence industrial base.

The Defence Review that emerged from the Labour Government in Britain in 1964 reflected the increasing dilemma of rising equipment costs[28] in a defence budget that was being squeezed by the competing fiscal demands of public sector interests.[29] A number of decisions provided ample notice of future British procurement policy. The planned fifth Polaris submarine suffered cancellation, as did proposals for new Royal Navy attack carriers. The aerospace sector was cut similarly, with cancellation of three nationally based projects. The TSR-2, in particular, was underway already at a cost of £75 million, but nevertheless was closed. The research projects, the P-1154 and HS-681, were added to the list of cuts.[30] Defence Minister Healey announced that Britain no longer would compete "comprehensively and independently at the highest levels of arms technology."[31]

The alternatives to national aircraft development, given that the RAF faced increasing equipment obsolescence in its current inventory, were either direct purchase or licenced production of available U.S. aircraft, or else some form of intra-European collaboration. The option to purchase American F-111K systems "off-the-shelf" was scrapped in 1967, as Prime Minister Wilson pursued cooperation with Bonn and Rome. Healey, again, provided his government's case for collaboration in the proposed MRCA program, arguing that "by sharing the cost of developing and producing this aircraft, the European countries concerned will meet their defence needs much more cheaply [than several national

projects]... Technically it can help them to provide a solid foundation for the future of the aerospace industry in Europe..."[32] The
minister hoped that increased economies of scale would also
enable the MRCA consortium to compete for export markets with
the best U.S. products.

Potential overall cost-savings benefits, and the maintenance of
independent national research, development, and production capabilities, certainly provided valuable political arguments for use in
supporting the collaborative venture. The latter point has been an
important criticism of proposed "off-the shelf" buying of American aircraft.[33] However, British government and industry leaders
alike faced a growing crisis of excess production capacity in the
aerospace sector. Pressures to maintain employment levels in the
face of excess industrial capacity made collaboration an attractive
alternative.

As the MRCA program began to loom as a possibility in the later
1960s, the British government undertook an evaluation of the
needs of the aerospace industry. The direct relevance of this evaluation to the bargaining over project work-sharing was recognised
even before its findings were published, as the following commentary by a leading defence journal indicated:

> Another factor that has emerged in the engine competition is the ques-
> tion of where the British industry sees its most urgent need for work.
> If the assessment indicates that the airframe sector has more excess
> capacity...Britain could relax its strong push for the Rolls engine in
> exchange for a larger share of the airframe or even a combination of
> airframe and avionics.[34]

At its peak, the Tornado program was estimated to involve 36,000
jobs in aerospace-related industries. The government obviously
was concerned with where these jobs would be concentrated.

A brief evaluation of productivity figures for European aerospace industries illustrates the government's emphasis on employment rather than either efficiency or profits. Nationalised
following its bankruptcy in 1971, Rolls-Royce had a higher
employees-to-revenue ratio than other European aircraft engine
manufacturers; and only British Aerospace (another nationalised
company) and Aeritalia were less productive.[35] The power plant
competition for the MRCA is discussed in the next section;
however, here I should note that concerns over excess capacity lay
behind the governments' determined support for the experimental
RB.199, still on the drawing board as the MRCA program began,

against General Electric and Pratt & Whitney engines that involved fewer technical and developmental risks.

The domestic political and economic objectives being sought by the West German government, which subsequently became closely associated with collaborative defence procurement generally and the MRCA in particular, demonstrate similarities with, as well as some striking differences from, those pursued by its British counterpart. Most immediately, the MRCA was said to be favoured over the NKF aircraft of EWR because it provided cost-savings benefits, viz. the opportunity to split development costs, estimated at $250-500 million for each aircraft.[36] The concern with program cost-savings, nevertheless, may have been secondary to the broader political and economic objectives of developing national industrial capabilities. This concern with avoiding dependence on U.S. technology, reminiscent of the British Defence Minister's remarks, was expressed by Dr. Schomerus of the Economics Ministry since "aerospace is part of the infrastructure of any industrial region."[37] Europe, he argued, must be capable of producing and developing this infrastructure itself. Collaborative development of the MRCA was a step towards this long-term goal.

After having rejected offers of licenced production agreements for the McDonnell Douglas F-4E International Phantom, and also the French-designed Dassault Mirage G-2 (each well-suited to Luftwaffe requirements), the Parliamentary Defence Committee stated bluntly that "if we do not pay for research and development, we will be blacksmiths. The majority [of committee members] wants to keep the advanced part of the industry alive, even if it costs us a lot more."[38] General Johannes Steinhoff, commander-in-chief of the Luftwaffe, himself recognised the primary importance of improving West German aerospace-related capabilities.[39]

In contrast to the British government, with its emphasis on "make-work" policies, Bonn knew that excess capacity was not a problem facing West German industry. With an economy undergoing consistent growth, it was cautiously restrictive of rapid expansion in any sector so as to guard against future recessions.[40] However, the Brandt government did view the aerospace industry as both a growth leader in the economy, and as a potential source of valuable technological innovation. Its attitude to the MRCA program should be set against this background, particularly in the early stages of intergovernment bargaining.

The selection of the Rolls Royce RB.199 engine, supported by the German government, still offered the industrial combine

Motoren und Turbinen Union (MTU) excellent opportunities for expansion. Despite initially possessing a capacity for only 15 percent of the project's engine work in 1969, MTU was offered 52 percent by Rolls Royce.[41] For MTU, this meant investment in new tooling by its joint owners, MAN Turbo and Daimler-Benz. For Britain, the selection ensured obtaining the work it needed to maintain employment; while for West Germany, it meant carefully managed expansion and "a major infusion of high technology" to the aerospace industry.[42]

Along with the collaboratively developed Franco-German Alpha Jet, the MRCA was expected to provide 40 percent of West German aerospace industry work by the late 1970s. The government's design compromises and support for the RB.199, however, also served to address another problem, one unique to the Federal Republic among the consortium partners. In February 1967, Chancellor Kiesinger agreed to the purchase of 22 British Westland SH-3 helicopters to meet Germany's offset obligations regarding British troops stationed in the country.[43] After 1968, however, these payments would be settled through the MRCA program. The selection of the RB.199 engine was expected to "solve Germany's offset obligations to Great Britain for the next ten years."[44]

In common with its consortium partners, Italy viewed collaboration in the MRCA program as a means of pursuing domestic economic and political policies. In contrast, however, Rome's bargaining position was very weak, since it was placing the fewest orders for the aircraft and investing little in the initial definition phase. At least on the surface, one might assume that its willingness to accept MRCA design agreements — for instance, those made in March 1969, without any prior consultation by the two leading partners — indicates that these agreements met with Italian military requirements. In fact, such was not the case; instead, the Italian Air Force's interests were regarded as secondary to wider government objectives, although improvement in aerospace capabilities indirectly may have provided Air Force benefits.

Growth in the Italian aerospace sector had been slow following the Second World War, with the industry's capabilities remaining negligible until the late 1960s.[45] The creation of Aeritalia in 1969, following the Italian signature of the initial Memorandum of Understanding regarding the MRCA, was the first attempt by the government to provide stable political and financial support.[46] Premier Aldo Moro, head of the Christian Democrat/Republican Party coalition government in 1974, enunciated the reasoning behind efforts to rationalise the industry, when he argued that national economic recovery and industrial expansion could occur only in the context of international collaboration. Italian participation in collaborative efforts would be successful, he added, only if Italy "showed itself capable of reducing its own bureaucratic paralysis."[47]

The new company, resulting from the amalgamation of the airframe division of Fiat with the aerospace sector of Finmeccanica (itself a group of state-owned companies), was placed under the direction of the government-sponsored Instituto per la Riconstruzione Industriale (IRI). With IRI leadership, the activities of Aeritalia were to be tied to the government's policy "of shifting industry to underdeveloped regions in the southern part of the country."[48] A comparison of employment and productivity figures for Aeritalia with those of the nationalised British companies Rolls-Royce and British Aerospace provides striking similarities. Aeritalia, however, employing 30 percent of the Italian aerospace workforce, had productivity levels lower than the prime British MRCA contractors. The emphasis on "make-work" policies rather than efficiency is highlighted when one compares Aeritalia with the privately owned Agusta company, which obtained twice the level of sales per worker. [49]

The MRCA program offered the Italian government an excellent opportunity to attempt to alleviate regional unemployment problems, and possibly to reduce regional economic disparities. The development and improvement of the domestic aerospace industry's technological expertise and systems-management capability was a second domestic goal closely connected in both government and industry calculations with European collaboration. The relatively small scale of the aerospace sector in Italy meant that every major company was involved in some aspect of the co-production program.[50] As an Aeritalia official explained, "the Tornado has been important for Aeritalia not only from the airframe point of view, it also has provided work for subcontractors that supply electronics gear, systems and other hardware."[51] Though the Italian share of total program work on the Tornado was limited to 15 percent, Italy did have access to all technological aspects of the work, as well as a share in project management. The aerospace industry could expect to benefit by obtaining "a maximum of know-how at a minimum cost."[52]

The problem, or handicap, that faces collaborative development in these circumstances has been glimpsed in the earlier examples of British and West German bargaining over aircraft design and components. Such programs become entangled with broader considerations, often at the expense of more directly related concerns. As early as 1971, it was recognised that for the Italian partner "the MRCA is looked upon first as a means to develop aerospace technology, and second as a piece of military hardware."[53] However well or otherwise the scheme may have been managed and whatever the ultimate quality of the aircraft produced, program efficiency, cost, or military capabilities appear to have been regarded as secondary matters.

THE AEROSPACE INDUSTRY: LEADERS AND LOBBYING

Although exercising a significant influence in the national bargainng processes that helped shape the MRCA program — and that likely will influence future ventures — the objectives of the participating governments encompass only one aspect of those domestic interests concerned in the venture. Bargaining also included the calculations and goals of the various aerospace industries directly involved in the program, which therefore possessed an interest in design responsibility and work-sharing agreements. Moreover, each government also faced the possible eruption of budgetary disputes, especially given the high-technology, high-cost nature of this collaborative procurement.

A critical, or perhaps cynical, interpretation of the political "benefits"of collaborative efforts identifies the arguments over potential cost-savings benefits as providing merely an ex post rationalisation and justification for such policies. The real reason for collaboration, according to this view, is that such programs, once underway, increasingly involve government and industry prestige and thus become less likely to be abandoned by financially strapped governments than would be costly and inefficient national counterparts.[54] The cancellation of the TSR-2 certainly suggests that there may be some substance to the argument. One would expect, if such were the case, that aerospace industries facing work shortages and U.S. competition therefore would welcome collaboration, with relatively certain work guarantees and new technologies. However, examination of British industry's opinion of the MRCA — and collaboration in general — suggests that some modifications of this critical assessment may be in order.

Despite the reluctant recognition in 1970 by the Society of British Aerospace Companies (SBAC) that Britain "was being driven more and more into collaboration, whether we like it or not, [as the development costs of advanced high-technology aircraft increased] beyond the financial capabilities of any one country...," there still remained a strong consensus against the idea of involvement in European collaboration.[55] This sectoral consensus may have been partially a reflection of national industrial egoism and a continued belief that Britain should "go it alone," but it was generated as well by more relevant concerns.

The SBAC Report of 1972 openly criticised early MRCA agreements arranged between the British and German governments. It viewed with concern current collaborative arrangements, which it regarded with suspicion as having been presented to its members on decidedly non-commercial terms. British government compromises on design responsibilities and work-sharing also were held to be establishing future problems for the domestic aerospace sector. While employment levels were assured for the immediate future by the MRCA, the same could not be said of the longer term. The decision to cede design leadership for the MRCA to the less experienced West German industry — based on earlier political bargaining and the initially larger Luftwaffe order for aircraft — appeared to the SBAC to be a harbinger of further ground that would be lost by British industry. Rigid, politically based industrial agreements it saw as potentially detrimental, rather than beneficial as government objectives suggested.[56]

The focus of criticism, it bears emphasising, was not the MRCA program itself, but rather the policies pursued by the government and how these were seen to affect the program. In any case, the industry's opposition on this point could hardly be of great moment, in view of the enormous importance to it of government defence contracts, especially the lucrative MRCA ones. As one industry executive succinctly put it: "It has worked out to getting 2 percent of something or 100 percent of nothing, and we have gone for the 2 percent because we have no other choice if we are to stay in the [MRCA] game."[57]

Industrial opposition to government interests in the collaborative venture probably was further constrained by the nature of the primary British industrial contractors involved. Both British Aerospace and Rolls-Royce were recently nationalised companies, under the broad direction of the government's National Enterprise Board. Industry Secretary Anthony Benn argued that the problem with individual companies financing long-term development projects was such that public ownership was essential to guarantee firmer financial support and to ensure that jobs were not placed at risk.[58] A clear split seems to have developed within the aerospace sector as early as 1969 — one that pitted the nationalised companies against those in the private sector. Nevertheless, the continuation of the MRCA program, and new work-sharing agreements (discussed in the following section) based on political concerns, indicate that this split had little impact upon the program other than to exclude some potential subcontractors who were reluctant to become involved in the first place.

A clear contrast existed between British and West German aerospace industry leaders' attitudes towards collaborative projects. Rebuilding after the Second World War, the West German industry faced rapid cost-escalation problems with new advanced-technology aircraft. Their approach to this challenge was collaborative from the outset, with the aerospace sector being organised to participate in international development programs "first with the United States, largely as a result of offset payment problems, and second within European bilateral and multi-national" ventures.[59] Heavily dependent upon government contracts and state-sponsored research and development work due to strict export restrictions, the aerospace companies sought to cooperate closely with the government.[60] Industry leaders wanted new contracts to be planned and spread out carefully to ensure a steady workload and to avoid heavy redundancy payments to laid-off workers.[61] The cautiously restrictive planning policies of the federal German governments generally were met with support from industry leaders with similar preferences.

The convergence of interests was apparent in the 1960s, as aerospace companies readily acceded to government pressures for mergers in order to create a more competitive domestic industry. The link with the new MRCA proposals was obvious and immediate: when Messerschmidt and Boelkow merged in November 1968, it was anticipated that the merged company, which with 12,300 employees would be the largest in the country, would be granted the prime contract for the advanced fighter.[62] This is indeed what would happen; following an additional merger with Hamburger Flugzeugbau, owned by the Blohm group, the new MBB combine became the main contractor for West German work on the MRCA.

Whilst Messerschmidt-Boelkow-Blohm received its rewards, other major companies in the Federal Republic were also involved

heavily in MRCA development. Of the 10 largest aerospace contractors at the time, six took part in the collaborative project, including MBB. Together these six companies accounted for 60 to
65 percent of all domestic West German aerospace production.[63]
Given the dominant influence over the aerospace sector possessed
by these companies, had they opposed collaborative policies they
might well have created an insurmountable opposition for the
government. They did not, of course, and convergent views on
supporting international consortia — seen as being in each side's
best interests — precluded any friction in government-industry
relations.

Even *had* they opposed collaboration, the German industries'
ability to lobby the government would have been handicapped
greatly by sharp divisions within the Bundersverband der
Deutschen Luft-und Raumfahrtindustrie (BDLI), which with more
than 80 members was the largest aerospace lobby group. Disagreements arose between the larger electronics and microchip companies and smaller high-technology producers, especially over the
allotment by MBB of supply contracts for MRCA work. Under
these circumstances, the BDLI could not claim to represent the
general interests of its members. West German industrial interests
ironically may have been better represented in the MRCA program
by the willingness of the British government, the RAF, and British
Aerospace to make concessions in work-sharing agreements than
by any domestic industrial lobbying.[64]

The position of the Italian aerospace industry regarding collaboration suggested parallels with the situations in both Britain
and West Germany. The small post-war industry remained dependent upon government contracts for Italian Air Force work, which
provided it with limited room for manoeuvre should it have balked
at government policies.[65] However, as in Germany, so too in Italy
the relatively new industry, facing high development costs, would
view collaboration more positively than, for instance, would the
SBAC in Britain. According to one Italian aerospace executive,
"close air support is the only area in which we can consider a
national program. In other areas, such as air superiority and interceptor aircraft, the problems are such that we have to look toward
international collaboration to meet our requirements."[66] Moreover,
as was also the case in Britain, the prime Italian contractor in the
MRCA was government-controlled. Aeritalia, under the direction
of the IRI, looked very favourably upon collaborative projects,

which it took to be the only viable and acceptable alternative to in-dependent national projects.

Although the practical ability of the various domestic aerospace industries to affect significantly either the nature of the MRCA agreements or the progress of collaborative policies may have been limited uniformly in Britain, West Germany, and Italy, the desire to do so was not. In both the Federal Republic and Italy, relations between government and industry were marked by their parallel views in support of collaboration, though their specific motives re-garding the MRCA could and did differ. By contrast, in Britain, in-dustrial leaders' widespread concerns over collaboration and their open criticisms of the MRCA agreements were voiced loudly. Even in Britain the program developed unhindered, since both main domestic contractors were under government direction following nationalisation. However, a changing British political climate has led to de-nationalisation, or privatisation, which has been accom-panied by greater emphasis on productivity and profits and less concern about maintaining possibly artificial workforce levels. In this altered climate, one might expect to witness, and perhaps not only in Britain, either harder bargaining or outright reluctance to participate in future collaborative ventures. In the conclusion to this chapter I discuss this possibility as it has surfaced in the cur-rent collaborative project, the European Fighter Aircraft (EFA); I also make some general comments about the future of collabora-tive procurement policies in NATO Europe.[67]

POLITICAL PARTIES AND DEFENCE BUDGETS

The extended lead times for research and development of advanced-technology major weapons systems create difficulties with long-term funding requirements.[68] Such difficulties may be exacerbated by international cooperation, which "requires govern-ments to make long-term binding commitments to others on expen-diture."[69] Aside from the concerns over the political implications of such commitments, which perhaps ought not to be exaggerated, the nature of collaborative procurement opens up such programs to the swings in the fortunes of several governments in their domes-tic political arenas.[70]

The early history of the MRCA — again paralleled more recently in the EFA program[71] — indicates the potentially disruptive pres-sures that various budgetary disputes may exert upon the progress of collaborative efforts. Defence budget problems arose both in

Britain and in Italy, with criticism of the MRCA most apparent in the former. In West Germany, Defence Minister Leber in February 1973 was obliged to take to television and defend his government's expenditure on the project. The overall impact of these internal political debates is difficult to gauge, for the good reason that the sources of, and responses to, the criticisms varied widely between the partner countries.

Parliamentary debate in Britain over MRCA funding must be situated within the context of an ongoing tug-of-war over budgetary resources — a struggle that witnessed the defence sector losing steadily to the demands of social-welfare programs. Critiques of government defence-procurement policies, especially those originating from the Labour Party Defence Study Group, stressed alternative social-welfare applications for MRCA funds.[72] Nonetheless, the "make-work" aspect closely associated with MRCA contracts in Britain did provide a powerful political incentive for the project's continuation. Labour critics failed to produce effective responses to the growing fears of widespread aerospace-industry layoffs. Therefore, despite a shrinking defence budget, the wider concerns I noted earlier meant that MRCA funding would continue to receive priority under successive governments.

Rome's decision to support the development of the domestic aerospace industry, and to encourage its expansion in the underdeveloped southern regions, was accepted by most elements of Italy's political parties. Debate was minimised, first because the government was not required to make any expenditure commitments early in the program, and second because Italy's share of total development costs was a relatively small one of approximately $140 million. The main complication facing the MRCA in Italy was not opposition to collaboration or to specific project-related funding, but rather general political and economic instability. Social unrest constrained the government "to direct technological funds to politically acceptable but short-term welfare programs," the result of which was to "dilute both the impetus and prestige of the aerospace industry."[73] However, the limited importance of Italy to the initial phases of the MRCA program, and the cautious government policy to avoid public discussion of its participation, meant that internal upheavals or debates would have minimal effects upon the progress of the consortium.

The traditionally bipartisan nature of defence policy in West Germany added a large measure of stability to the MRCA program in that country. Indeed, the decision to insist upon co-production of the aircraft was made during the "Grand Coalition," or all-party, government. To be sure, the mood that occasioned the Defence Minister's 1973 television appearance was of concern to the MRCA consortium; but the resort to this medium had not been the result of party divisions over the principle of collaboration. Rather, the primary source of disquiet lay in the acrimonious relations between the defence and budget ministries over further, long-term financial commitments to the MRCA development phase. The aircraft's unit price had more than doubled, from an initial estimate of $3 million to $6.5 million. This, combined with the costs of the Franco-German Alpha Jet, would mean that fully 40 percent of the total national defence budget would be consumed by two aircraft projects, and for an extended time period. Leber defended the commitments on the basis of their assumed beneficial effect upon the development and expansion of the West German aerospace industry.[74] At about the same time, an outcry from the tiny left wing of the SPD — only some seven MPs — was generated by the failure of the government to release MRCA cost details, as it had promised to do in 1970. This in turn led the SPD to hold a secret ballot on the project, which resulted in 86 percent of the MPs voting in favour of continued German participation; in view of this, SPD criticisms would largely cease after 1974.

The anti-nuclear stance of the FDP in Germany led it to express concern over the long-range nuclear-bombing capability of the MRCA. Once again, however, the FDP had been a member of the Grand Coalition government in 1967 and had participated in the establishment of the project. Coupled with the party's traditional pro-industry leanings, this effectively stifled vocal opposition. Criticism from the CDU/CSU also was minimal, and for similar reasons. All in all, the Parliamentary critique of the MRCA program proved negligible in effect, although it did provide some parties' defence critics with public-relations exposure.[75]

In the cases mentioned above, the direct results for the MRCA of internal political debates may have been minimal, but the existence of identified pressures on national defence budgets would have some important consequences for the project. For instance, the initial West German aircraft order was to have been for 600 aircraft; but the rise in unit costs once the twin-engine design was adopted triggered a reconsideration of this order — a reconsideration that led to the order being reduced to 300 planes. This sharp decrease in base production orders, in return, added further to the unit price, by decreasing economies of scale and causing recalculation of production planning.[76]

WORK-SHARING AGREEMENTS IN THE MRCA PROGRAM

The assessment above of the international and national bargaining that attended the early phases of the MRCA indicates that the broad shape of the collaborative effort, and the design configuration of the aircraft itself, were both influenced much more by political pressures than by military requirements. Within the project itself, similar patterns of bargaining and compromise may be recognised. In this section, I examine the design leadership and work-sharing agreements of the MRCA, the basis on which contracts were allocated between states, and the relative importance of cost-savings benefits and military needs compared with political goals.

The first impediment to MRCA collaboration was the ongoing dispute between Britain and West Germany over project leadership. Britain argued that its domestic aerospace industry possessed considerable previous experience with advanced aircraft projects, having been occupied with research on the TSR-2, the AFVG, and the UKVG.[77] The West German industry had no such prior management experience. Bonn retorted that its (initially) anticipated order of 600 aircraft would be the largest placed by any consortium partner, and that by taking delivery of the aircraft first it also was taking the largest risk. Therefore, it deserved the role of lead agent.[78]

The case in favour of British leadership was weakened since one of the tacitly recognised objectives of the German government's continued participation was to redress precisely the deficiency in its aerospace sector that the British were stressing. Whitehall, concerned with West German support of its EEC application, and pressing its own interests in the engine competition, felt itself obliged to make some concessions. The upshot was yet another compromise, one that accorded weighted voting rights to each member of the Panavia consortium; as a result, Germany would hold 50 percent of the vote, Britain 30 percent, and Italy 20 percent. The compromise, making equity, rather than experience or efficiency, the major criterion for project leadership, enabled the collaborative efforts to proceed. Whether such compromises can prove attainable in future such projects may well depend upon the existence of similar overriding goals that can provide a basis for bargaining.[79]

Following the agreements on project management and design specifications, three main areas of work-sharing required settlement. Based upon the financial burden being borne by each partner, the division of labour was agreed at a general percentage split of 42.5/42.5/15 between Germany, Britain, and Italy respectively. Details of the engine, airframe, and avionics contracts, however, remained subject to further bargaining and competition. The competition for the MRCA's main powerplant contract initially attracted three entrants, the U.S.-designed General Electric GE-1 and Pratt & Whitney JTF16 engines, and the British Rolls Royce RB.199. The GE-1 was withdrawn from the competition early in 1969, ostensibly due to the short time-span given for submission of detailed bids (60 days), and a fear that proprietary data could be lost if Rolls Royce obtained its engine details.[80] Another reason for General Electric's decision, however, may have been related to the similar competition being carried out at that time for the A-300B Airbus. Industry commentators discussed a possible tacit compromise on the two projects; under the terms of a mooted "gentleman's agreement," the General Electric CF-6 was recognised to be the favoured entry in the A-300B tender, and the RB.199 that of the MRCA.[81]

The determination of the British government to support the RB.199 entry left the U.S. government reluctant to press the case for the remaining contender, the JTF16. Despite this reluctance, the German MBB combine favoured the Pratt & Whitney engine. Although the estimated price of the RB.199 compared favourably with that of the JTF16, the British engine still was in its experimental design stages. Development time for the JTF16 would be at least one year more advanced than for the Rolls Royce engine, and the U.S. Air Force was prepared to certify the technological capability of Pratt & Whitney to design and produce an engine that matched MRCA specifications. Bonn, however, supported the British contender for reasons unrelated to the details of competing engine designs.[82] Political manoeuvring led to the eventual acceptance of the RB.199 tender in September 1969, marked as it was by technological uncertainties and the potential for costly delays in development.

Compared with the drawn-out engine competition and the intrigues that surrounded its eventual resolution, the division of responsibility for development and production of the airframe for the MRCA was largely devoid of controversy. Only one development contract stirred much debate; but this too reflected the political horse-trading between the partners that has been noted elsewhere.

The allocation of responsibility for developing the new wing pivot for the variable-geometry MRCA, given to the West German partner, ignored previous British research experience on the variable-geometry projects (the AFVG and UKVG) as well as actual design work done on the TSR-2. Once again, existing or proven capabilities were set aside in favour of providing new research and development opportunities to an expanding industry, or to one requiring new work. In the event, the German MBB group turned to the United States for research assistance, since the U.S. industry had faced similar design questions in developing its F-111 and F-14 aircraft. Expertise in complex electron beam welding techniques was purchased from the Grumman company.[83] One of the most complicated airframe design problems thus was overcome not in Europe, but through importing U.S. patented technology — which the British government previously had striven hard to avoid.

The third main area of work-sharing agreements dealt with the technologically advanced avionics systems that would be required for the multi-role demands of the Tornado aircraft. The avionics package consisted of more than 50 subsystems, including flight control, navigation, STOL, and weapons-delivery and defensive aids. Altogether, avionics was estimated to make up over 40 percent of the total MRCA unit price. The importance of the avionics systems thus gave an impetus to the consortium members with contesting viewpoints.

The decision-making process that dealt with awards of avionics contracts proved almost as complicated as the technology itself. Each bidder was required to submit a two-part proposal, with one part covering technical data and the other dealing with price, delivery, and management details. Both sets of proposals had to be submitted to the three primary contractors — MBB, BAC, and Aeritalia — and to Avionica Systems Engineering GmbH, the group established to oversee this section of the project. Avionica then distributed the proposals to its three national partners, EASAMS of Britain, ESG of West Germany, and SIA of Italy. Finally, the technical proposals also were to be submitted to the three national defence ministries that would be receiving the aircraft.[84]

This administrative tangle, required to help co-ordinate the trinational venture,was complicated even more by the politically arranged requirement that the total program workload should be shared in the proportion of 42.5/42.5/15. Finally, the companies that offered bids were asked to submit additional proposals covering alternative equipment that did not comply with MRCA specifications but that might possess other attractions, such as lower price or better performance. Combined with the original problems of reconciling varying national military requirements, this selection process turned even the avionics bidding into a protracted and costly bureaucratic exercise.

Controversy over avionics contracts initially developed around the British goal of relying exclusively upon European technology for the MRCA. Following its exclusion from the engine contract, the U.S. exerted greater pressure to obtain part of the avionics package. British views clashed with those of the German government; for Bonn wished a close relationship with the U.S. in MRCA avionics. It expected to see competitive pricing, along with a chance for German industry to gain a manufacturing competence it did not possess. This latter goal was shared by the German avionics combine ESG, which sought to avoid having the contracts dominated by British companies.[85]

The choice of ground-mapping and terrain-following radars provides ample illustration of the avionics debate. The apparent subject of debate was the optimum operating frequency of the radars. The Luftwaffe sought a Ku-band for both subsystems, basing its requirement on the General Electric mapping radar and the Texas Instruments terrain-following radar, both of which had been installed in the F-111. The RAF specified a Ka-band mapping radar and an X-band system for terrain-following. Italy, which originally specified a third set of preferences, agreed to accept the Luftwaffe requirements as cost- escalation difficulties pushed the consortium towards seeking relatively cheaper off-the-shelf systems. When the British bids by Elliott Automation and Ferranti Ltd. emerged at twice the cost of comparable U.S.-developed systems, the West Germans insisted that the radar contracts be awarded to Texas Instruments.[86]

Within a year of the radar contracts being awarded, further avionics business was obtained by U.S. companies. Litton Industries, Honeywell, and the Astronautics Corporation respectively were awarded contracts for the Altitude Heading, Air Data, and Bearing computers, as European industries were unable to match U.S. costs for advanced avionics systems. Nevertheless, the complex bidding process and the disputes over types, and sources, of supply for various subsystems resulted in a five-month delay in the MRCA program, adding further to development costs. The inability of Avionica Systems Engineering to resolve the disputes and to settle the cost-escalation difficulties led to its dissolution in 1972, after which avionics management was led by EASAMS of Britain, perhaps a small consolation to the British government.

The work-sharing agreements suggest a curious and unfortunate blend of obstacles facing the MRCA program. The program-leadership dispute, though overcome, caused a delay of several months in the initiation of the definition phase. Voting rights were awarded on the basis of initial estimated orders, and although the German order was reduced considerably its management share remained at the original level. Its relatively inexperienced industry retained project leadership without making compensatory financial commitments. The powerplant contract was awarded largely on politically based criteria; later developmental problems were to cost the consortium both time and money. Meanwhile, the West German industry, obtaining airframe contracts based equally on political rather than technical criteria, turned to U.S.-developed technology against the specific desires of the British partner. Finally, the time-consuming and expensive avionics bidding process saw awards being made on the basis of least-cost supply and proven technological capability, but the disputes over the awards themselves caused delays and increased costs.

EVALUATION OF THE MRCA PROGRAM

The previous studies of the MRCA have typically proven to be inherently biased, either for or against collaborative procurement and/or defence spending in general. A more objective assessment, placing the benefits and problems into perspective, suggests that the MRCA program emerged as a mixed success, but with significant disadvantages and potential obstacles that likely will face follow-on ventures in collaboration. Two major concerns of the program, which together should provide the basic criteria for judging the achievements of the MRCA consortium, provide the focus of this evaluation. These are the military capabilities of the aircraft, and the cost-savings benefits (if any) obtained by collaboration. An assessment of these criteria will indicate whether the interference of the broader objectives discussed up to this point was detrimental to the project, or merely formed another set of constraints that were overcome by the Panavia group.

At least one evaluation of the military capabilities of the MRCA presents the aircraft as a model of achievement, meeting or approaching most of its test requirements.[87] This evaluation, however, failed to ask the more pertinent question, namely whether the compromise requirements initially were such that the aircraft could fulfil the variety of missions required by the three national air forces and the West German navy. Critics of the MRCA have been quick to cite this as a major problem, not only of the Tornado, but of all multi-purpose planes.[88]

The ability of the MRCA designers to provide an aircraft suited to the air- superiority/air-combat role appears to have been doubted by the participating governments as early as 1970. At the time, it was felt by some that the MRCA would lack manoeuvrability compared to other NATO aircraft such as the U.S.-designed F-15 and F-18, or even the F-4 Phantom,which had been proposed as an alternative by Washington. Although this problem has been either denied or de-emphasised by some recipients, there is good reason to conclude that the MRCA could not meet the original mission requirements of the Italian Air Force. However, as I noted earlier, meeting these requirements had been recognised for some time as only a secondary concern of the Italian government.

The German government's acceptance of the RAF's twin-engine, two-man crew design likewise was taken to indicate the secondary status of Luftwaffe military requirements. In this case, the development of *streuwaffen* (area bombs) for use against armoured formations helped to counter worries that operational requirements were being sacrificed. The heavier, long-range aircraft could still be used in a close-support role, and it now possessed a greater payload capacity. Nevertheless, one serious practical drawback remains evident: the relatively delicate and complex avionics systems required by the MRCA, and the high cost of the aircraft, make it a very expensive system for use in an environment where attrition rates inevitably will be high.

The role for which the MRCA appears to be optimised (perhaps as the Canadian and Dutch governments suspected) is the long-range strike/interdiction mission of the Royal Air Force. These were the "key characteristics" referred to in the report mentioned earlier. The MRCA fulfilled RAF requirements, and entrenched the bombing role that had come under increasing scrutiny. At the same time, it also opened up a new mission capability for the Luftwaffe, which possibly compensated for the emphasis on British design specifications.[89]

In addition to the common Interdiction Strike (IDS) variant of the MRCA, the RAF alone was to receive 165 of the F-3 Air Defence Variant (ADV) Tornado, to meet its air-defence mission. The ADV Tornado was criticised as being little better than the existing U.S. F-4 Phantoms then in service, although the latter could not match the ADV's weapon system and avionics.[90] An evaluation by the British government of the U.S. F-14, F-15, and F-16 aircraft as potential alternatives, however, concluded that "the F-14 was the closest substitute but that it was a costly aircraft, probably 50 percent more expensive than the Tornado."[91] Neither the F-15 nor the F-16 were felt to be able to meet the long-range, all-weather capability or the complex U.K. air-defence tasks required of the Tornado ADV.

Analysis of the original military requirements of the MRCA, and its eventual configuration and operational capabilities, suggests that the Royal Air Force obtained the greater degree of approximation to its needs. While the aircraft is capable of meeting Luftwaffe primary mission requirements, it is an expensive and complex system for use in such a high-attrition environment. The Luftwaffe may, nevertheless, benefit from obtaining additional operational capabilities. The least well-served of the recipients has been the Italian Air Force; in this case, the MRCA's shortfall was recognised and possibly accepted early in the program, since it was seen to offer alternative industrial and economic benefits to the domestic aerospace sector and to the government. Whether this is sufficient consolation for the air force, however, must be questionable.

Second to military criteria as a means of evaluating the MRCA program has been the achievement of significant cost-savings benefits; indeed, this criterion provides a measure of the success of the consortium. When one bears in mind the problems facing nationally based projects (which are also subject to escalatory pressure from a variety of sources), the MRCA program appears to have offered some benefits. Even assuming a cost-increase or "collaborative premium" of 40 percent on research and development and 10 percent on production, the Tornado has been estimated to offer the British government a cost-saving of £360 million compared to a similar national project. The only comparable national British effort, of course, was the ill-fated TSR-2. On the basis of the three nations' share in the project, total program cost savings may have been between £850 million and £1.9 billion (at 1976 prices).[92]

Logistic support costs for the Tornado aircraft, placed under the supervision of the Panavia Product Support Directorate, similarly benefit from comparison with national provisioning schemes. Common procedures, training programs for suppliers, and pooling of orders for spare parts have provided estimated savings of 40 to 50 percent per member.[93]

A comparison of cost-escalation in the MRCA program with that found in other joint ventures and independent national projects indicates that the Panavia consortium did achieve acceptable control over this aspect of the venture, even though cost-escalation became a target for criticism throughout the definition and development phases, and influenced decisions on the awarding of contracts. Despite this, the Tornado project compares favourably with the Anglo-French Lynx helicopter, or the civilian Anglo-French Concorde program; it fails, however, to match cost-controls on the Anglo-French Jaguar, which the Tornado was intended to replace. The U.S. F-111 and the British TSR-2 both compare unfavourably with the MRCA program.[94] The Dutch government's early complaints of rising costs perhaps should be seen in this later perspective, in which case the collaborative MRCA program appears better managed than originally was feared.

The analysis thus far has indicated that round condemnation of the military and cost-escalation aspects of the MRCA would be erroneous. The military case at worst is ambivalent, while collaboration has provided some financial advantages. However, problems and disadvantages have appeared in the program, which suggest some limitations of collaboration that must be addressed in the future.

The Anglo-German wrangling over project leadership during the early stages of the MRCA had been settled with the allocation of voting rights, established on the basis of intended orders for the aircraft. The subsequent decision of the West German government to cut its order from 600 to 324 aircraft was not matched by a concomitant reallocation of program control or work-sharing. By early 1985, the British industry was complaining bitterly that it required over $300 million of additional MRCA work to overcome losses resulting from rigid work-sharing agreements. A House of Commons Committee report concluded: "We expect the Ministry of Defence to have learned the work-sharing lessons provided by the Tornado project and to show themselves more robust in negotiation of memoranda of understanding [on future programs]."[95] In this case, political bargaining between the British and West German governments appears to have proven ultimately detrimental to the British industry. It is worth noting, however, that despite the House of Commons Committee's warnings, work-sharing agreements for the EFA program appear to be based once again on considerations of equity rather than efficiency, and on governments' announced intentions for aircraft orders.[96]

What may prove to be the most significant handicap arising from collaboration, however, is not connected directly either to cost concerns or to military requirements, although it affects both. The technical complexities of the multirole concept required to obtain the collaborative agreement, delays in reaching contractual agreements on work-sharing, problems with development of the experimental RB.199 engine, and stretching out of the MRCA production schedule by financially strapped governments, resulted in a development time for the aircraft of 12 years. The Tornado required more than twice as long as the U.S. F-111 and F-15 aircraft for development, and nearly four years more than the average development time for a British aircraft.[97] Originally intended for delivery to the national air forces in 1975, the Tornado did not reach operational deployment until 1980.

The extended development time for collaborative programs, if it is a general problem, has important implications. The task of coordinating, or creating, common procurement policies depends upon the aircraft's predicted availability. If expectations and requirements diverge too greatly, then obtaining either additional partners or export orders increasingly becomes unlikely. Alternatively, members of an existing collaborative consortium may be obliged to purchase intermediate systems, thereby incurring additional costs. In each case, American systems provide attractive alternatives, both in cost and availability.

Associated with the problems indicated above is the need to update avionics systems. Rapid advances in active and passive anti-aircraft defence technology may shorten the lifespan of the aircraft's existing systems. Eight years after its deployment began, the MRCA's recipients face the choice of accepting rapidly obsolescing avionics in the aircraft, or improving the avionics capabilities at a cost of several hundred million dollars.[98] Here again, U.S. alternatives may prove attractive, when compared with the uncertainties of collaboration, for the smaller European states or for the valuable potential export market. Indeed, additional orders for the Tornado from outside the consortium have been disappointing.[99]

The desire to exclude U.S. companies and technology from the MRCA project — expressed mainly by Britain — was connected to the goal of maximising the potential export market. By maintaining exclusively European participation, the consortium could avoid U.S. multilateral export controls, end-use clauses, and government-processing delays, all of which were regarded as placing unacceptable restrictions on overseas sales. The European governments and industries were not alone in viewing such obstacles as unacceptable; U.S.-based companies also faced similar restrictions by the Defense Department, and complained bitterly.[100]

Finally, by maintaining exclusively European participation, an independent aerospace industry could be nurtured as a "hedge against uncertainty" and fears over U.S. Congressional debates over burden-sharing in NATO. Reliance on American technology helped create and maintain European dependence; as one source put the dilemma, "a nation without an independent industrial base actually has no assured military force."[101] Such a situation was unacceptable politically to the West German, as well as the British, government.

In the event, it proved impossible successfully to exclude all U.S. technology from the project. West German technological inexperience led MBB to seek assistance with its wing-pivot contract, against British government opposition, and several avionics contracts crossed the Atlantic as the consortium sought least-cost suppliers. For the British Air Defence Version, avionics systems were obtained from GEC Avionics. The Tornado may have provided new technological capabilities to the European industries, but at least for this project the goal of exclusive European participation proved impossible.

CONCLUSION

This study of the MRCA program has demonstrated that bargaining over broader political and economic objectives at the international and national levels exerted a significant influence on the collaborative effort. Such bargaining determined the membership and structure of the consortium, the agreements on design specifications in the definition phase, the allocation of work-sharing ratios, and the awarding of specific, major MRCA contracts. Under these difficult constraints, with many key decisions taken out of its hands, the Panavia project management achieved moderate cost-saving benefits and produced an aircraft of varying utility for the national air forces. At all times, however, military and cost considerations were secondary to these broader objectives.

Any attempt to assess the success, or failure, of European collaborative defence procurement must bear in mind the value placed upon these interests by the participating governments. To criticise their existence, and relevance, would be of limited utility, since such interests are unlikely to disappear in the future. However, collaborative procurement must be judged by another criterion as well, that of its contribution to the North Atlantic alliance. European political and industrial cooperation in defence should be measured against the background of transatlantic relations and the NATO policy of standardisation of equipment within and between its forces. The MRCA and its successor project, the European Fighter Aircraft, have both engendered debate in this context.

Three main alternative policies arguably may be associated with European collaboration in the development of major weapon systems. The first option is that of creating an independent and more capable defence industry, partly to encourage greater competitiveness in equipment sales, and partly to provide some insurance against decreasing U.S. force commitments to Europe. The second option is the development of a more equal partnership in defence production between the U.S. and Europe through larger production runs, increased market size, and limited industrial rationalisation. As Gardiner Tucker notes, it is important to realise that neither the adversarial nor the cooperative interpretations suggested above are the same as the expressed NATO objective of standardisation.[102] In either case, rather than pursuing NATO policy, "collaboration could be defined as the pursuit of national goals through international means."[103]

The attempt to exclude the U.S. from participating in the MRCA, and repeated references to the need to develop a more capable indigenous European aerospace industry, indicate that the European governments may have seen collaboration as a political instrument for achieving an improved measure of independence in defence supplies. The desire to avoid problems with U.S. government restrictions on patented technology suggests that the MRCA was intended to provide viable competition to U.S. aircraft for export sales. When the "arms deal of the century" saw agreements for licenced production of the American F-16 being signed by

Belgium, the Netherlands, Denmark, and Norway, the adversarial nature of the U.S.-Europe aerospace competition became apparent. Observed one British aerospace executive, with some acerbity: "We in the U.K. do not regard the production of F-16s in Europe as an outstanding example of project-sharing.... This particular programme appears to be too much a benefit match for the U.S. industry and economy without equal technological reward for Europe or NATO."[104] The Belgian and Netherlands governments, of course, had been members of the original MRCA consortium, alienated by the compromises and increased costs that they saw as resulting from Anglo-German bargaining.

The European Fighter Aircraft program shows some signs that the nature of these relations may be altered very little with the newest European collaborative venture. On the subject of U.S. industrial participation, EFA consortium members' comments parallel earlier views: "We are not planning to favour European subcontractor companies, but our requirement is to be able to sell EFA for export. The Americans are welcome if there are no constraints on their equipment."[105] Complaints from the U.S. government and industry over alleged European subsidies for the civilian Airbus Industrie, and "protectionist" measures on EFA subcontractor bidding, illustrate how this adversarial relationship may undermine the greater cohesiveness and improved capabilities that the NATO standardisation policy is intended to enhance.[106] The European response to such complaints is that American interpretation of "fair negotiations" over such matters usually entails European acquiescence to Washington.[107] Such an outcome, of course, is politically unacceptable to the European governments.

In a 1984 article on the threat of structural disarmament in NATO, Thomas A. Callaghan, Jr., commenting on defence-procurement disputes, observed that the Alliance lacked an "overarching structure that would balance efficiency and equity over many projects, so that weapons could be exchanged at politically affordable costs."[108] European collaborative efforts to date including the Jaguar, Alpha Jet, Tornado, and now the EFA all have been pursued on an ad hoc basis, outside of a body such as the Independent European Programme Group. Current NATO efforts to coordinate national procurement policies, under the Conventional Armaments Planning System, will have to overcome considerable difficulties both in providing this structure and focus for European collaboration, and in reconciling the competing interests of U.S. and European governments and industries.[109] The obviously haphazard nature of European collaborative defence procurement policies to date, however, makes such co-ordination increasingly necessary. That the Tornado emerged as a capable aircraft is no guarantee that political imperatives will not in the future force similar but ever-more-costly projects against insurmountable technological limitations. Industrial efficiency and military-operational requirements need to be re-emphasised, especially in the context of such high-cost weapons systems.

Notes

[1] Panavia was the main administrative body within the MRCA program, responsible for overseeing all airframe and avionics work performed by the various national contractors.

[2] Collaborative procurement is taken to include cooperation in research, development, production, and logistical support.

[3] For more general studies on these questions, see for example Lawrence-S. Hagen, *Twisting Arms: Political, Military, and Economic Aspects of Arms Co-operation in the Atlantic Alliance*, National Security Series no. 3/80 (Kingston: Queen's University, Centre for International Relations, 1980); Keith Hartley, *NATO Arms Cooperation: A Study in Economics and Politics* (London: George Allen & Unwin, 1983).

[4] Disputes have arisen over EFA project management, with Britain and West Germany rejecting French demands for design and project-leadership; over delays due to West German budget difficulties; over design requirements; and also over U.S. industry allegations concerning unfair discrimination against American subcontractor bidding. See: *Flight International, Aviation Week and Space Technology*, AGARD Lecture Series, during 1987-88 for some idea of the continuing disputes. For an analysis of the EFA project, see the chapter by Andrew Latham in this volume.

[5] B. O. Heath, "MRCA Tornado: Achievement through International Collaboration," *Aeronautical Journal* 83 (September 1979): 329-43, presents the project as a model of achievement. Heath was a BAC Director closely associated with the project. Some harsh criticisms may be found in W.B. Walker, "The MRCA: A Case Study in European Collaboration," *Research Policy* 2 (January 1974): 280-305. More impartial studies include Hartley, *NATO Arms Cooperation*, and A. Mechtescheimer, *MRCA Tornado: Rustung und Politik in der Bundesrepublik* (Saarbruck: Osang Verlag, 1977). Both, however, present studies limited in scope to specific issues on a single nation.

[6] David C. Greenwood, "Allied Co-operation in Armaments Development, Production and Support," in *NATO: The Next Thirty Years*, ed. Kenneth A. Myers (London: Croom Helm, 1980), p. 323.

[7] MRA-75 became somewhat of an embarrassing title after time slippages made the original delivery date impossible. MRCA, or more commonly Tornado, soon became the project title.

[8]The MRCA was intended to replace the ageing inventory of three European allies' air forces, comprising F-104 Starfighters, F-4s, and F-86s in Italy and West Germany, and the Lightning, Vulcan, Buccaneer, and Canberra aircraft of the Royal Air Force.

[9]*Keesings Contemporary Archives*, 3-10 June 1970, p. 23753.

[10]Letter to author from George R. Lindsey, Operational Research and Analysis Establishment, Department of National Defence, Ottawa.

[11]*Aviation Week and Space Technology*, 2 June 1969, p. 160. (Hereafter cited *Aviation Week*.) However, Belgium finally opted for licenced production of the U.S. F-16 aircraft.

[12]The Belgian market was not inconsiderable; its later order for the F-16 amounted to 116 aircraft, for which it obtained offset contracts that exceeded the procurement costs of the aircraft to the value of $400 million. Ibid., 2 May 1977, p. 59.

[13]*Keesings*, 2-9 August 1969, p. 23492.

[14]*Aviation Week*, 5 May 1969, p. 27.

[15]Quoted in ibid., 2 June 1969, p. 160.

[16]*Keesings*, 2-9 August 1969, p. 23492.

[17]The full range of missions envisaged for the MRCA were: long-range strike/interdiction; land-based strike against maritime targets; close support/battlefield interdiction; air superiority/air combat; air-defence interception (by the RAF's ADV Tornado); reconnaissance; and training. See Dan Smith, *The Defence of the Realm in the 1980s* (London: Croom Helm, 1980), p. 133.

[18]See the tables on combat wing loading versus thrust-to-weight ratio, and combat spar span loading versus thrust-to-weight ratio in Heath, "MRCA Tornado," p. 332. The tables compare the Tornado's performance characteristics with those of more specialised aircraft.

[19]*Aviation Week*, 7 April 1969, p. 23.

[20]Ibid., 4 November 1968, p. 22.

[21]See Walker, "The MRCA," p. 285. Even this compromise design, however, did not comply fully with the specifications required by the RAF for the role of air-defence interception. In this case, the F-2 and F-3 Air Defence Variants of the common GR.7 Tornado had to be designed to fulfil RAF operational needs, although the ADV had a 90-percent commonality with the GR.7 aircraft.

[22]*Keesings*, 19-26 August 1967, pp. 22205-6.

[23]Walker, "The MRCA," p. 286.

[24]*Aviation Week*, 7 April 1969, p. 23.

[25]Pietro Quaroni, "European Integration: An Italian View," *Survival* 12 (December 1970): 402.

[26]The leadership dispute was solved through awarding each country voting rights in Panavia on the basis of their original aircraft orders. The

inability of the EFA participants to reach a similar compromise arrangement suggests that there have not existed broader incentives sufficiently strong to overcome initial obstacles of particular national interests.

[27]The "mini-MRCA" project foundered as the U.S. F-16 deal emerged. However, a parallel can be seen now in the French Rafale project, which may detract from export sales of the EFA should both projects be completed.

[28]Capital production costs of military weapons systems are estimated to rise at six to 10 percent per annum after allowing for inflation.

[29]For a summary of the defence budget squeeze in this period, see David Greenwood, "Defence and National Priorities since 1945," in *British Defence Policy in a Changing World,* ed. John Baylis (London: Croom Helm,1977), pp. 174-208.

[30]Taken from Roy Mason, "Britain's Security Interests," *Survival* 17 (September 1975): 218-24.

[31]Greenwood, "Defence and National Priorities," p. 200.

[32]Quoted in *Keesings,* 14-21 June 1969, p. 23406.

[33]Trevor Taylor discusses the argument that "production of American equipment represents a rapid road to dependence on the U.S." See his *Defence, Technology and International Integration* (London: Frances Pinter, 1982), p. 155. R. W. Dean similarly raises the concern of European defence industries being transformed into "the step child of U.S. industry." See R. W. Dean, "The Future of Collaborative Weapons Acquisition," in *European Security: Prospects for the 1980s,* ed. Derek Leebaert (Lexington, Mass.: Lexington Books, 1979), p. 97.

[34]*Aviation Week,* 9 June 1969, p. 32.

[35]Tabulated figures on sales and productivity for major companies, and across countries, in NATO are given in Hartley, *NATO Arms Cooperation,* pp. 29, 108.

[36]Unidentified German sources quoted in *Aviation Week,* 4 November 1968, p. 22.

[37]Ibid., 24 April 1972, p. 39.

[38]Ibid., 7 April 1969, p. 23.

[39]Steinhoff argued that "the competence of the West German industry is a definite asset, and it is important that the industry exploit its potential as a developer as well as a producer of aircraft."

[40]Despite this policy, employment in aerospace-related industries rose from 16,000 in 1960 to 50,000 by 1970, although the total required by the late 1970s was estimated to be 40,000. *Aviation Week,* 24 April 1972, p. 34.

[41]Ibid., 10 January 1972, p. 19.

[42]Ibid., 1 September 1980, p. 117, for a list of West German companies involved in the MRCA program.

[43]Reported in *Keesings,* 30 March-6 April 1968, p. 22618.

[44]*Aviation Week*, 8 September 1969, p. 19.

[45]The Italian aerospace workforce was the smallest of any industrialised nation in relation to the total national population — 18 to 20 thousand full-time workers in a population of 55 million, with only seven percent of them working in R&D compared to the norm of 15 to 20 percent elsewhere. Ibid., 5 June 1972, p. 32.

[46]The move towards rationalising national aerospace industries was occurring in Britain and West Germany at the same time, with the nationalisation of British Aerospace and the creation of the MBB combine.

[47]*Aviation Week*, 5 June 1972, p. 32.

[48]Ibid.

[49]See tables in Hartley, *NATO Arms Cooperation*, especially p.108.

[50]A summary of Italian companies involved is provided in *Aviation Week*, 5 June 1980. They included Aeritalia as the prime contractor, plus Macchi, Piaggio, SACA, Siai, Fiat Aviazione, and Alfa Romeo.

[51]Unnamed Aeritalia company manager: "Italy Hopes Current International Efforts Will Lead to New Joint Programs," ibid., 15 June 1987, p. 171.

[52] Ibid., 28 April 1975, p. 26.

[53]Ibid., 8 March 1971, p. 29.

[54]This argument is discussed in most assessments of aerospace procurement policies. See for example Mary Kaldor, *Democratic Socialism and the Cost of Defence* (London: Croom Helm, 1979); Smith, *Defence of the Realm;* Hartley, *NATO Arms Cooperation*; and Taylor, *Defence, Technology.*

[55]Sir Richard Smeeton, Director of the Society of British Aerospace Companies, quoted in *Aviation Week*, 7 September 1970, p. 14.

[56]SBAC Report 1972, reported in ibid., 10 January 1972, p. 19.

[57]Sir George Edwards, former director of BAC, quoted in ibid., 7 September 1970, p. 14.

[58]Difficulties with the civil aerospace engine RB.211 project had recently forced Rolls-Royce into bankruptcy. Ibid., 11 November 1974, p. 23.

[59]Ibid., 24 April 1972, p. 8.

[60]For an analysis of these export restrictions, see Bernd Huebner's chapter in this volume.

[61]Mechtescheimer, *MRCA Tornado*, p. 164.

[62]*Aviation Week*, 23 September 1968, p. 17.

[63]The risk companies were: MBB, Siemens, VFW-Fokker, AEG Telefunken, MTU, and Industriewerke-Karlsruhe. From Mechtescheimer, *MRCA Tornado*, p. 166.

[64]A list of aerospace industry interests ignored by the federal government includes cancellation of national R&D work on STOL aircraft; purchasing U.S. F-4s as interim aircraft for the 1970s, thereby reducing money available to industry for the MRCA program; and the continued enforcement of the tightest military exports restrictions amongst NATO European governments. Ibid., pp. 167-68.

[65]Approximately 70 percent of aerospace contracts came from the government. The MRCA program was viewed as a potential means of breaking this cycle of dependency through an improved export market. To date, this hope has been disappointed.

[66]Unidentified official for Aeritalia's Combat Aircraft Division, quoted in *Aviation Week*, 23 January 1978, p. 60.

[67]This prospect appears pertinent to the EFA program in both Britain and West Germany. In Britain, the Managing Director of British Aerospace, Sir Raymond Lygo, clearly expressed his company's concern with collaboration:

> Are consortia the right way to go? People are beginning to look at the cost of collaboration. Time is money and collaborative efforts all go at the pace of the slowest partner.

From David A. Brown, "British Industry Scrutinizes Worth of Collaborative Projects," ibid., p. 147. Sir George Edwards, predecessor to Lygo, commented wryly that "the beauty of two countries cooperating on a weapons project and sharing everything 50-50, is that it only costs each two-thirds." Pressures for equity are seen invariably to cause inefficiency. Thomas A. Callaghan, Jr., "The Structural Disarmament of NATO," *NATO Review*, no. 3 (June 1984), p. 22. The West German government apparently shared this view in the EFA program, which was delayed while the Minister of State for Arms Procurement refused to approve the FRG's role in the project until the German share of costs was reduced by over $2 billion. Even after the agreement was reached, the new costs have to be approved by the parliamentary budget committee, which has voiced some earlier criticisms of program costs. For a fuller discussion of these difficulties, see Graham Clark, "Germany Cuts Billions from Share of EFA Costs," *Defense News*, 7 March 1988, pp. 1, 51.

[68]The Tornado required funding commitments for 12 years; further modifications to the avionics systems continue to make demands on defence budgets. Production of the EFA similarly is scheduled to begin in 1995, and initial deployment in 1997; already, however, the West German government has reduced its initial order from 250 aircraft to 200.

[69]Taylor, *Defence, Technology*, p. 7.

[70]Although the European NATO states accept the need for cooperation in defence production, they have avoided commitment to principles. Each project is regarded as individual and separate. See Trevor Taylor, "Standardization: The Dimensions and Implications of a Policy Issue," *Journal of International Studies* 7 (Autumn 1978): 111-23.

[71]See for example Clark, "Germany Cuts Billions."

[72]See Mary Kaldor and Dan Smith, *Disarming Europe* (London: Molin Press, 1982); and Mary Kaldor, *The Baroque Arsenal* (London: Andre Deutsch, 1982).

[73]*Aviation Week*, 5 June 1972, p. 9.

[74]Ibid., 26 February 1973, pp. 21-22.

[75]Mechtescheimer, *MRCA Tornado*, p. 183.

[76]In his examination of the F-14 production, Trevor Taylor cites the claim by Grumman that cutting the production rate from three to two aircraft per month would increase the unit costs from $23.9 million to $28.9 million. See Taylor, *Defence, Technology*, p. 52.

[77]Following the demise of the TSR-2, the Anglo-French Variable Geometry project and the UKVG (which continued after AFVG's cancellation) sought to maintain the British aerospace industry's R&D capabilities until a new collaborative venture could be established.

[78]*Aviation Week*, 23 September 1968, p. 17.

[79]Despite official French government comments to the contrary, which emphasise the failure of the aircraft to match its air force's specifications, the intractable dispute in the early stages of the EFA program over project leadership was a major factor in the decision of West Germany, Britain, Italy, and Spain to continue the project-definition and development phases even if this meant France's withdrawal. See *Flight International* or *Aviation Week*, various issues 1986, 1987, 1988. Also see David A. Yost, "Franco-German Defence Cooperation," *Washington Quarterly* 11 (Spring 1988): 177.

[80]*Aviation Week*, 19 May 1969, p. 25.

[81]Ibid., 7 September 1969, p. 23.

[82]The German government tacitly acknowledged the political motives behind their choice of engine:

> Our concern for the Rolls Royce engine...is purely political. The Common Market will dry out unless the British come in. We are now forced to work with the British in fields not covered by the Common Market, and advanced technology is one of them.

Unidentified West German government defence official, quoted by Edward Kolkum, *Aviation Week*, 7 April 1969, p. 23. Of course, West Germany obtained excellent work-sharing proposals from Rolls Royce despite MTU's limited capacity. The mutually beneficial pattern of this arrangement is not difficult to recognise.

[83]Taylor, *Defence, Technology*, p. 179.

[84]*Aviation Week*, 26 April 1971, p. 55.

[85]Ibid., 7 September 1970, p. 78.

[86]Ibid., 16 August 1971, p. 64.

[87]Heath, "MRCA Tornado." Heath clearly possessed a vested interest in pressing the case in favour of the MRCA project's achievements.

[88]"There is one problem with multi-role aircraft...: they tend to do each task less efficiently than aircraft specialized for that task." Smith, *Defence of the Realm*, p. 133.

[89]"What the RAF has got, what it has wanted and been fighting for ever since the 1957 defence White Paper threatened the future of manned bombrs, is a modern, ...high-speed, low-level bomber. [In addition]...for the FRG Tornado is a back-door entry to the long-range bombing missions..." Ibid.,p. 134. Whether this is the case remains uncertain, since area bombs do permit the Tornado to meet Luftwaffe requirements. The comment on the aircraft's price and delicate avionics nevertheless suggests Smith's argument has some validity.

[90]The Foxhunter radar designed by GEC Avionics for the F-3 interceptor ADV Tornado remains plagued by production and performance difficulties. The 50 F-3s delivered to the RAF by mid 1987 in fact had to be installed with ballast in place of the radars until the technical problems could be overcome. See "British Set Date to Change Tornado Radar Contract," *Aviation Week,* 6 April 1987, p. 26.

[91]Unit costs for the aircraft have been estimated at £13.1 million for the F-14; £8.2 million for the F-15; £3.1 million for the F-16; and £8.5 million for the Tornado. Hartley, *NATO Arms Cooperation*, pp. 172-73.

[92]For Britain, Hartley estimates that co-production of the Tornado offered Britain cost-savings of some £360 million as opposed to the potential costs of a comparable national program, even with the collaborative premiums on R&D and production. Ibid., p. 161.

[93]Taylor, *Defence, Technology*, p. 162.

[94]See the table on cost control in joint projects provided by Hartley, *NATO Arms Cooperation*, p. 170.

[95]*Aviation Week,* 18 February 1985, p. 17. The committee's report followed the news that British industry required over $300 million of additional work on the MRCA to overcome losses said to result from the rigid original work-sharing allocations. It should be remembered that West Germany's sharp cut in MRCA orders was not matched by cuts in the work-sharing levels. Whether this will re-emerge in the EFA program remains to be seen; however, the British government's early hope of benefiting its domestic aerospace industry via the MRCA work may be brought into question if such losses continue.

[96]Development work for the EFA is to be split 33/33/21/13 percent between British Aerospace (GB), MBB and Domier (FRG), Aeritalia (Italy), and CASA (Spain). Production work "...is to be shared equitably in relation to the number of units ordered by each country...". Development, production, and engine work details are provided in Clark, "Germany Cuts Billions."

[97]Hartley, *NATO Arms Cooperation*, p. 166.

[98]Such improvements, it is claimed, would extend the operational lifespan of the Tornado through to the late 1990s. The need to update avionics systems in particular may be a significant problem with advanced-technology aircraft, which take excessive time to reach deployment stage.

[99]Eight of the F-3s were sold to Oman by Britain in August 1985; 24 F.3s and 48 GR.1s also have been ordered by Saudi Arabia. Altogether, these figures do not make up the original orders lost when either Canada or Belgium withdrew from the project.

[100]The frustrations of attempting to overcome the legal, administrative,and political obstacles which the U.S. Defense Department can create are summed up amply by these comments from George Kachajian, Chairman of Silicon Technology Corporation:

> After six years of trying to make this [export licencing] process work, I come away with the sense that this regime is not one of laws but of men, powered by the motors of secret political agendas and intrigues, and operating with unpublished rules and decisional principles totally alien and inimical to fundamental concepts of administrative due process.

Quoted by James K. Gordon, "Commerce Decontrols Technology Because of Foreign Availability," *Aviation Week*, 24 November 1986, p. 63. More recently, the proposed Canadian purchase of British nuclear-powered *Trafalgar*-class submarines is being hampered by U.S. reluctance to approve the transfer of restricted American technology. By contrast, despite its strict export controls on the domestic aerospace industry, the West German government decided not to question the sale of the Tornado to Oman and Saudi Arabia. For a discussion of U.S. export-control policy, see the chapter by David Haglund in this volume.

[101]"The 1970s: Challenge in the Marketplace," *Aviation Week*, 2 June 1969.

[102]Gardiner Tucker, *Towards Nationalizing Allied Weapons Production* (Paris: Atlantic Institute, 1976), p. 48. The broad aims of NATO standardisation are to increase the combined military-operational effectiveness of the Alliance's armed forces, and to improve the general efficiency of the use of NATO defence resources.

[103]Dean, "Future of Collaborative Weapons Acquisition," p. 80.

[104]Quoted in B. Burrows and G. Edwards, *The Defence of Western Europe* (London: Butterworth Scientific, 1982), p. 67.

[105]Unidentified Aeritalia company manager, quoted in "Italy Hopes....," *Aviation Week*, 15 June 1987, p. 171.

[106]On the subject of American allegations of European protectionist measures and subsidies, U.S. Ambassador to West Germany Richard Burt stated that trade protection on either side of the Atlantic damaged both sides' defence industries, and that "equally important, serious frictions in our economic relations could spill over into the political realm and undermine the cohesion of the alliance." Reported in Michael Feajel, "NATO Arms Cooperation...," ibid., 9 March 1987, p. 77.

[107]Kenneth Moss, "The Next Step in U.S.-European Relations," *Washington Quarterly* 11 (Spring 1988): 106-7.

[108]Callaghan, "Structural Disarmament of NATO," p. 23.

[109]A two-year test of the Conventional Armaments Planning System(CAPS), which aims to reduce the level of duplication of R&D and procurement in NATO, began in early 1988. See Giovanni de Briganti, "NATO Review Board Begins Work on Plan to Coordinate Arms Procurement," *Defense News*, 7 March 1988, p. 6.

3

Conflict and Competition over the NATO Defence Industrial Base: The Case of the European Fighter Aircraft

Andrew Latham

INTRODUCTION

As many observers have argued, the military and economic consequences of a NATO-wide free-trade area in defence goods would be highly beneficial to member states faced with rapidly rising defence costs and fixed or declining budgetary resources.[1] At its simplest, this argument suggests that under ideal conditions, specialisation based on comparative advantage could be expected to enhance inter-Allied equipment commonality and compatibility, and reduce the costs and uncertainties typically associated with large defence-related development projects. In short, Alliance-wide free trade in defence goods would allow NATO to deploy more and better military equipment (e.g. aircraft, tanks, warships) without increasing the budgetary resources its members allocate to military preparedness.

As far as NATO is concerned, however, it would seem that there is decidedly little possibility of achieving anything even remotely approximating such a free-trade arrangement. While Allied governments generally acknowledge that specialisation and international exchange are mutually advantageous, they continue to argue that the close relationship between military power and sovereignty puts defence-related trade in a unique and separate category. Moreover, particularly in the case of the high-technology defence industries, there are substantial European reservations regarding the broader economic implications of unrestricted competition in the defence marketplace. It is part of the conventional wisdom in this respect that in an unregulated trade environment whole sectors of the European industrial base would fall victim to the competition of larger, more productive, American firms. As

Europe is counting on many of these threatened industries (particularly aerospace, electronics, and informatics) to assure its future international competitiveness, it is not surprising that European political leaders evince little in the way of concrete support for more liberalised trade arrangements within the Atlantic Alliance. Indeed, together with U.S. congressional opposition (based on fears of regional economic dislocation) and the more or less natural predisposition to defence-industrial autarky, European economic concerns constitute something of an insuperable barrier to specialisation through free trade.

The improbability of pure and unfettered free trade, however, has not meant that NATO members have been entirely unwilling or unable to undertake significant initiatives aimed at enhancing specialisation and rationalisation within the Alliance. What it *does* mean is that NATO has been forced to promote specialisation through politically negotiated industrial coordination rather than simply by relying on market forces.[2] In this connection, the various bilateral Memoranda of Understanding (MOUs) and the "family-of-weapons" initiative (undertaken pursuant to U.S. DOD Directive 2010.6) are but two examples of negotiated arrangements that are intended to enhance the overall rationalisation and specialisation of the Alliance's defence industrial base without violating the political or economic parameters established by governments on both sides of the Atlantic.[3]

It is important to realise, however, that while managed specialisation of this sort promises on the one hand to enhance greatly the military preparedness of the NATO allies, on the other it contains the seeds of significant transatlantic disharmony and conflict; for the very policies that are prerequisite to the long-term objective of managed specialisation within NATO are also incompatible with some of the more immediate and fundamental goals of both the U.S. government and American industry. If a politically negotiated division of labour is to become a reality within NATO, simple economic logic and U.S. procurement legislation require that the European development and production effort be re-organised in order to match American capitalisation rates and scale economies — that is, along (inter)continental rather than strictly national lines.[4] However, as the active presence of U.S. defence firms in the European market is one of the chief impediments to this type of re-organisation, this transformation of the European defence industrial base from a collection of relatively small-scale competing national firms to a truly competitive continental effort is likely to involve exactly the type of state-led industrial policy that the U.S. finds so distasteful, namely, tariff and non-tariff barriers to American participation in European defence projects.

Given the importance of foreign military sales to both the Defense Department and a great many American industrial concerns, it seems likely that should U.S. manufacturers indeed find themselves shut out of the lucrative European market (and possibly other export markets as well as a result of greater international competition from European firms), both government and industry in the United States will begin to question the importance and workability of continued transatlantic armaments cooperation. Indeed, if past trade conflicts in the civilian sector are any indication, the exclusion of U.S. defence goods from the European market might even trigger a costly and highly destructive cycle of economic sanction and counter-sanction. In the final analysis, although one can only speculate as to the outcome of such a train of events, one cannot dismiss the possibility that conflict and competition over the Alliance's defence industrial base will ultimately result in a significant reduction in transatlantic defence trade, and perhaps even a partial dissolution of the Atlantic Alliance.[5]

In summary, then, the inner logic of politically directed rationalisation belies the appearance that it is a relatively risk-free solution to the West's defence industrial problems; for over the long run, managed specialisation threatens to generate dangerous and sustained centrifugal forces that will likely prove highly deleterious to the workability (and, indeed, the viability) of NATO. To put it directly, the "two-pillar" approach to rationalisation is not practicable because the immediate pre-condition for such an arrangement, a reasonably competitive European defence industry, is impossible to establish without the use of protectionist economic measures — measures that are likely to result in the exclusion of U.S. firms from the European military equipment market, and so cause substantial American resentment toward Europe. Under these conditions, and contrary to the original intent, attempts to promote the rationalisation of the European defence industrial base (as part of a broader Allied effort) could contribute to a further deterioration in Alliance cohesion, and ultimately a reduction in the West's collective preparedness effort.

In this chapter I seek to demonstrate the dynamics of this process in connection with the European military aerospace industry, and particularly in connection with the European Fighter Aircraft program. Aerospace and the EFA were chosen for several reasons:

1. They illustrate the basic conflict between the short-term requirements of a healthy European defence industrial base and the long-term requirements of a healthy Alliance defence industrial-base;

2. They demonstrate the importance of protectionism and expanded sales markets to European competitiveness;

3. They illustrate the potentially divisive tensions that exist between Europe and the United States; and

4. They demonstrate the political limits even to strictly European industrial collaboration. The *ad hoc* nature of the EFA program suggests that European nations have other, more important, goals than simple economic efficiency, and that structural re-organisation of the sort advocated by several EC studies (including the 1978 Klepsch Report, and the 1983 Fergusson Report) is not politically feasible at the present time.

Thus, a study of the European Fighter Aircraft program provides evidence regarding my central assertion that the rationalisation (even on an *ad hoc* basis) of the European defence industrial base is simultaneously pre-requisite to, yet incompatible with, the broader goal of Alliance-wide specialisation and rationalisation. As we have already seen, managed specialisation (or, indeed, specialisation through free trade) requires that Europe begin producing defence goods that are commercially competitive with those of its American rivals. What remains to be demonstrated in a concrete way is that policies and programs aimed at achieving that goal are more likely than not to undermine transatlantic industrial rationalisation and contribute materially to the centrifugal forces already operating within the Alliance. A starting point in this connection is a model of the European aerospace industry that outlines both the importance of market consolidation and expansion, and the role of American aircraft firms in impeding this.

THE STRUCTURE OF THE EUROPEAN AEROSPACE MARKET

The demand for competitive aerospace equipment, of course, suggests the need for substantial restructuring and re-organisation within the European defence industrial base; for as things stand, Europe's disparate national aerospace industries enjoy neither the market scale nor the capitalisation rates required to make them truly competitive with the American giants. Stripped of its details, this line of reasoning suggests that if European firms are to have any chance of competing with U.S. manufacturers it is essential that European development and production be organised along continental, rather than strictly national, lines. As many observers on both sides of the Atlantic have noted, Europe must effectively "get itself together" industrially (i.e. coordinate demand and cooperate on supply) before there is any genuine possibility of realising a more equitable balance of traffic on the two-way street.

Essentially, the realisation of a more competitive European aerospace industry requires two fundamental changes in the structure of the European market. First, if European firms are to produce aircraft and component systems that are qualitatively competitive with those of their American rivals, it is absolutely essential that NATO Europe reform its highly under-capitalised and unnecessarily duplicative research and development infrastructure along American lines. As one team of experts put it:

> The need for a considerably greater effort in research and development (R&D)... is self-evident... [N]ot only are the European members devoting considerably fewer resources to it than the United States — European publicly funded R&D is only 31% that of its transatlantic partner — but it is fragmented, duplicated and thus highly wasteful.[6]

In short, the compartmentalisation and disaggregation of the European military aerospace industry (particularly in comparison to that of the U.S.) has tended to undermine the technological verve and vitality of the NATO European allies. Combined with consistently low levels of capital funding, over time this has resulted in generally inferior European product and production technology — and an inability on the part of European firms to compete qualitatively with their American counterparts.[7] Clearly, this requires not only higher levels of funding, but also a basic restructuring of the European R&D effort.

Second, if the Europeans are to manufacture aerospace goods that are commercially competitive with respect to price, it is necessary to re-arrange production so as to secure the benefits commonly associated with servicing a large consolidated market. At present, of course, such a market does not exist; the NATO European defence industry consists of a collection of discrete and disparate national production efforts operating within a largely uncoordinated and disaggregated market environment. As a result, European prices are high while productivity tends to be relatively low. In sum, the limited nature of the national (and even the regional) market in Europe effectively undermines Europe's ability to compete with American firms.

The key variable in this equation, of course, is the relative inadequacy of a European defence market that lacks both the scope and capital intensity required to sustain a truly efficient and competitive aerospace industry. This being the case, the most obvious solution to Europe's current defence-industrial malaise would seem to consist largely in a two-pronged policy of systematically consolidating and expanding demand for European aerospace goods (through the harmonisation of national procurement schedules and a more aggressive extra-regional export strategy) while at the same time rationalising the European research and development effort (thus reducing duplication and overlap and allowing a greater aggregation of capital in support of a dangerously underfunded industrial sector). To put the point only slightly too starkly, a larger and less-fragmented European defence market would provide European industry with many of the advantages currently enjoyed exclusively by American manufacturers — including, most importantly, a virile and efficient R&D sector, and the production economies associated with large orders and long production runs.

More precisely, this two-pronged approach would improve European competitiveness in three ways. First, joint research and development would provide an effective means of overcoming the limitations imposed by relatively small national R&D budgets. Broadly, joint ventures allow firms and governments to pool their resources, resulting in the elimination of purely duplicative research (and the diversion of saved resources to additional research), economies of scale (the realisation of a critical mass of researchers and equipment), and diversity (several approaches to the same problem).[8]

Second, a less fractured regional market would substantially increase the size of the average domestic order placed with European firms. For example, whereas under the present structure a large European aircraft order tends to be somewhere in the neighbourhood of 400 units, in an integrated aerospace market the average would more typically be in the region of 800 plus. For a sophisticated combat aircraft (say the American F-18 or the European Tornado) the scale and learning economies associated with a production increase of this magnitude translate into significant price reductions. Indeed, given an 85-percent learning curve (not unreasonable in the aerospace sector), doubling output from 400 to 800 units would lower unit costs by as much as 15 percent.[9]

Finally, an increase in extra-European sales could also be expected to result in significant cost reductions. Assuming the same learning curve as above, for example, if an 800-unit European effort were to be expanded through export sales to 1200 units, individual aircraft costs would drop by a further 13 percent. In short, under ideal conditions, a larger and less-fractured European defence market promises to generate significant production economies, resulting in substantially lower prices, and over the long run producing technologically superior and more competitive goods.[10]

This, of course, is not to argue that the NATO European allies would ever be able to realise all the economies associated with large orders and capital-intensive production arrangements; clearly the often substantial cost-premia attached to *ad hoc* collaborative efforts threaten to preclude this. It is, however, to suggest that European defence firms, if they are to become more competitive with their American rivals, require access to a far broader market than they currently enjoy. In connection with the aerospace industry (although the logic applies to other sectors as well), Trevor Taylor offers perhaps the most succinct expression of this type of economic logic when he argues that "there is little hope of aircraft manufacturers in Europe competing successfully against an American firm backed by a large U.S. government order unless they too enjoy a large base order."[11] In the final analysis, it seems that Europe's future competitiveness in the aerospace sector hinges largely on its ability to begin producing to a continental (even intercontinental) scale.

THE ROLE OF U.S. AEROSPACE FIRMS

Historically, there appear to have been two major reasons for the collective inability of the various European aerospace industries to consolidate and expand their markets and so realise the scale economies required for commercially competitive production. On the one hand, rationalisation was (and is) impeded by European concerns regarding the potential political, economic, and strategic implications of regional industrial re-organisation.[12] In this connection, the conventional wisdom suggests that there are three barriers to a full-scale integration of the European aerospace sector. First, assuming — and this is not unreasonable — that rationalisation would result in a large-scale re-allocation of production capital within Europe, all nations would be faced with staggering, possibly overwhelming, adjustment problems. Given the relative immobility of European labour and capital, this would mean greater unemployment, substantial loss of tax revenue, and a worsening balance-of-payments situation.

Second, as the aerospace industry is characterised by advanced technologies, there is a general fear that the loss of national aerospace capacity would undermine future economic competitiveness. In a world in which Europe can no longer compete in certain labour-intensive industrial sectors, "commanding heights" industries such as aerospace have assumed an enhancedsignificance, and European governments have become particularly loathe to abandon them — even in pursuit of long-term regional development. Third, national governments are naturally concerned that the loss of a national aerospace capacity would leave them at the mercy of foreign suppliers, possibly leading to reduced political independence, higher life-cycle costs, and inappropriate weapons systems. While it is true that these considerations will probably continue to act as constraints on any movement toward comprehensive structural integration in the aerospace industry, recent history suggests that the Europeans have been able at least to partly address many of these problems by means of *ad hoc* collaborative projects and joint ventures (such as the MRCA Tornado).

On the other hand, and perhaps more importantly, the active commercial presence of many of the American aerospace giants in NATO Europe continues to pose a serious impediment to efforts to enhance the competitiveness of the European aerospace industry. For a variety of reasons this problem has proven less amenable to political negotiation than intra-European concerns, and continues to constitute the chief barrier to the realisation of an internationally competitive European aerospace sector. Essentially, the presence of U.S. defence firms in Western Europe undermines European competitiveness in two respects. To begin with, the availability of American military systems and sub-systems in Europe (often of superior quality and at relatively low prices) effectively "steals" market share from European firms, preventing them from realising the economies typically associated with large orders and long production runs. In connection with the aerospace sector, for example, U.S.-designed and/or-manufactured aircraft currently account for approximately 35 percent of the value of the combined NATO military airfleets. [13]

While in itself the loss of nearly a third of the potential European regional market constitutes a serious handicap for the national European aircraft industries, American market penetration further aggravates Europe's competitive weakness in that it tends to reinforce the already highly fractured and disaggregated structure of the European aerospace market by making it difficult for European manufacturers (operating either independently or collaboratively) to sell their products to other European countries. In this respect, of course, the F-16 case is particularly instructive in that it demonstrates how the sale of an American aircraft to Belgium, Denmark, Norway, and the Netherlands (the so-called EPG nations), allowed General Dynamics effectively to shut a European-designed aircraft (the collaboratively produced Tornado) out of almost 20 percent of the European aerospace market — in the process undermining the commercial viability of a European project designed specifically to improve European competitiveness by consolidating regional demand and coordinating supply.[14] Under these conditions, it would seem that even when the European allies enter into collaborative development and production projects, American competition means that European firms are often faced with the prospect of a regional sales market that is too small financially to sustain either advanced R&D or efficient, capital-intensive production arrangements.

In addition, the participation of U.S. firms in the European aerospace market tends to undermine European efforts to realise greater scale economies through increased foreign sales. Exports, of course, are often an important variable in determining the viability of any given industrial project; indeed, in the words of one European defence-industry executive, they are "the swing factor between a profitable and an unprofitable arrangement."[15] American participation in European aerospace projects, however, almost invariably results in a failure to exploit potential export markets. Broadly, to the degree that European firms produce or utilise American-designed systems or sub-systems, European export sales are subject to the extra-territorial application of U.S. trade and export-control legislation — that is, to political regulation by the American government.[16]

While this is clearly offensive to the European allies on political grounds (it is often perceived as an unwarranted violation of national and regional prerogatives to control and regulate domestic economic affairs), European governments also find it loathsome in that, to the extent that it can be used to undermine European export initiatives, American trade and technology control legislation clearly has a purely commercial (as opposed to security) application.[17] As Joseph Rallo argues, U.S. export control legislation can be used to limit the Western European share of the global market, in the process severely undermining Europe's "ability to maintain an efficient domestic industrial base," and ultimately compromising the capacity of European firms to "compete on equal terms with American MNEs in global commercial competition."[18]

The active presence of U.S. defence firms in Europe, then, can be seen to constitute a serious impediment to the development of a truly efficient and competitive European aerospace industry. Perhaps nothing reveals this impediment as much as an analysis of one particular European aerospace project, the contemporary European Fighter Aircraft program, to which I now turn.

THE EUROPEAN FIGHTER AIRCRAFT PROGRAM

Prosaically, the European Fighter Aircraft has been described as a "canard delta, twin-engined fighter optimised for the air-to-air combat role with a secondary mission of air-to-ground and air defence."[19] Despite the disarming simplicity of this description, the EFA is unquestionably the most sophisticated and technologically advanced aircraft yet to be attempted by European industry, either nationally or collaboratively. Essentially, the EFA is what is known as an active control technology or fly-by-wire (FBW) aircraft; in other words, it is an aerodynamically "unstable" design requiring a computerised flight-control system in order to fly. As such, it is dependent on sensors that monitor internal and external conditions and relay this information to an onboard computer, which then adjusts the control surfaces so that the aircraft remains in stable flight. The chief advantage of the FBW system is that it can achieve higher levels of manoeuvrability than is possible for conventional aircraft, presumably resulting in superior combat performance.

At the heart of the EFA is an avionics system that necessarily stretches the current state of the art to its limits. The Eurofighter has been conceived as a fully FBW system with no mechanical back-up — that is, the aircraft is entirely dependent on its hardware and software packages not only to enable it to fly, but to ensure that no matter how the control column is manipulated the aircraft never exceeds its cleared flight envelope boundaries. Also included in the avionics system are a revolutionary new "intelligent" fuel-management system, an advanced three-dimensional tactical display, and possibly an integrated multi-purpose aircraft and weapons-management processing unit built directly into the plane's structure to maximise the efficient use of space and cooling resources.[20]

Similarly, the new power plant for the Eurofighter will also be at the cuttingedge of aerospace high-technology. While the new engine will not be ready in time for the first prototype aircraft (to be powered by either a Rolls Royce RB199 or a General Electric F404) upon completion it will incorporate some of the latest developments in aero-engine technology including, *inter alia*, single crystal turbine blades, powder metallurgy, and full-authority digital engine control.[21] Overall, the new engine design, advanced avionics, innovative construction materials, and sophisticated fly-by-wire techniques incorporated into the European Fighter Aircraft represent a quantum leap forward in aerospace and related technologies.

Organisationally, the EFAP is very similar to the collaborative MRCA project, the intent being to draw on the Tornado experience for guidance and direction, and so avoid some of the shortcomings associated with the Panavia/NAMMA management structure.[22] The government steering organisation for the Eurofighter, for example, has been modelled on NAMMA (the Tornado state management agency). Called simply the NATO European Fighter Management Agency (NEFMA), this body represents the governments involved in the EFA and is charged with the task of overall project management and supervision, particularly in connection with the allocation of development and production responsibilities. NEFMA has a multi-national staff (including a manager, deputy, technical director, and commercial director) which is responsible to a Board of Directors composed of senior officials from each of the participating countries' defence ministries. The agency is headquartered in Munich and will share existing facilities with NAMMA.

Parallelling the government organisation, the four participating aerospace firms — AIT, CASA, BAe, and MBB/Dornier — have formed a joint company known as Eurofighter-Jagdflugzeug GmbH (limited liability company) to act as the prime contractor for airframe, ground, and avionics equipment. Work-sharing and development costs for the initial production of 800 units are to be shared 33 percent each for the UK and FRG, 21 percent for Italy, and 13 percent for Spain, reflecting the proportion of initial output each country will take. Engines are to be produced on a similar basis by another international firm known as Turbo Eurojet Engines GmbH (Eurojet). This company — formed by Rolls Royce of the UK, Motoren- und Turbinen Union (MTU) of Germany, Fiat Aviazione of Italy, and Sener of Spain — has been established specifically to develop and produce the power plant for the EFA. The allocation of development and production work will correspond to that on the airframe side; with each industrial partner responsible for research, design, and production of specific engine sub-systems.

In establishing the industrial organisation for Eurofighter, the participating firms attempted to integrate the best features of MRCA management while avoiding some of the more serious errors. In this connection, elements of continuity are apparent not only in the organisational structure of the EFA program, but also in the management and research personnel associated with Eurofighter GmbH and Eurojet. For example, many of the project managers (including — among others — the managing director of Eurofighter GmbH, Gerrie Willox of BAe, and departmental directors Piero Scarafiotti of AIT, and Martin Friemer of MBB) have had a long professional association with the Tornado project, and presumably will bring to the EFA some of their experience regarding the vagaries and caprices peculiar to international collaborative ventures. In one sense then, Eurofighter can be said to be exploiting the advantages associated with institutional learning. To be sure, the Tornado and EFA programs have been kept institutionally distinct (although at one point there was talk of merging the two). However, the continuity in personnel (among other things), means that the organisational experience gained on the Tornado project has been largely transferred to the Eurofighter, sparing the latter the need to "re-invent the wheel" in connection with collaborative aerospace development and production. *Ceteris paribus*, this can be expected to reduce the number of delays typically associated with joint ventures, resulting in fewer collaboration premia, lower unit costs, and ultimately a more price-competitive final product.

Building on the Tornado experience, the Eurofighter program also involves a number of practices that diverge sharply from the MRCA model, particularly in connection with the level of concern regarding product support and maintenance, as well as the level of American participation in the program. Unlike the MRCA, Eurofighter GmbH has a product support director responsible for the maximisation of the aircraft's maintainability during the design and development phases, and for product support at the time of introduction into service. The product support group is functionally similar to FFV Maintenance in the Swedish Gripen program, and is intended not only to enhance the combat effectiveness of the Eurofighter (the aircraft can be serviced, refuelled, and re-armed in 30 minutes), but also to improve export prospects by lowering life-cycle and maintenance costs (resulting in fewer aircraft being required for a particular task). Perhaps more importantly, the EFA also differs from Tornado in that, whereas Tornado involved significant American participation at the sub-systems level, efforts are being made to exclude American firms from any participation in the Eurofighter program.[23] While not mentioning the United States explicitly, the EFA consortium wants firm guarantees from subcontractors that the aircraft can be sold to any buyer, and has established bidding rules that insist on freedom to export all component systems and parts. As U.S. government export and technology controls often prohibit American firms from making such a commitment, there is little European enthusiasm for U.S. involvement, and the likelihood of American firms participating in the Eurofighter program is near nil.

EFAP and European competitiveness

How, and to what extent, is this project likely to enhance the international competitiveness of the European aerospace industry? If one were to view the issue in terms of European cooperation to meet a U.S. economic and technological challenge, rather than simply as a military matter, the specific shape or configuration of the European Fighter Aircraft program would appear to have been determined by two principal factors. On the one hand, the program is quite clearly intended to support a more technologically robust and cost-efficient European aerospace sector, enhancing the international competitiveness of the various aerospace-related industries (including, *inter alia*, avionics, informatics, airframes, and engines), and helping to minimise the European military-preparedness burden. To this end, the project is aimed at coordinating demand and rationalising supply so that R&D costs can be shared and scale economies realised.

On the other hand, and equally importantly, the program's objectives are of necessity being pursued within a very definite set of political constraints. At this juncture, of course, these limits would appear to preclude the pursuit of structural reform as an approach to European defence-industrial rationalisation, primarily because no European government is willing to sacrifice jobs and high-technology industrial capacity for the seemingly rather distant benefits associated with regional economic development (from which they may derive little immediate benefit).[24] Far more common is the type of *ad hoc* cooperative approach employed in connection with the Tornado project; for in the past this approach has delivered a reasonably satisfactory trade-off between the commercial objectives related to cost and quality and other national objectives related to jobs, technology, and industrial prestige.

Ad hoc collaboration, however, while reasonably effective in the strictly European context, is far from being a perfect solution to the Alliance's transatlantic defence-industrial problems. To be sure, it does allow competing and conflicting European interests to be managed satisfactorily, reducing costs through relatively painless cooperation and work-sharing. The problem is that American economic interests cannot be introduced into the equation without rendering it unworkable. In short, even within the context of *ad hoc* collaboration, it seems to be impossible to accommodate both European and American interests; suggesting, of course, that perhaps these interests are in some sense mutually exclusive — that is, that European and American objectives are irreconcilable within the Alliance as it is currently configured. If this is so, NATO would seem to be approaching a point in its history at which a decision will have to be made regarding its very structure and direction, particularly as these relate to transatlantic armaments cooperation and defence-industrial rationalisation.

More specifically, the EFAP is intended to improve the international competitiveness of the European aerospace industry by exploiting the benefits typically associated with both collaborative R&D and economies of scale and learning. With respect to the former, the conventional wisdom suggests that collaborative ventures such as the Eurofighter are likely to have an important and positive impact on the technological competitiveness of participating firms, largely because they allow for the pooling of research and development resources and the sharing of costs. In this respect, while it is true that international collaboration tends to result in higher overall research and development expenditure (due to so-called "collaboration premia") the typical cost penalty is often substantially less than 20 percent and has been falling as Europeans have become more experienced at joint ventures.[25] On the plus side, in return for this extra expenditure, joint projects allow European firms to aggregate "scarce" investment capital in support of the historically underfunded aerospace sector, improving both productivity and technological quality. Moreover, this type of aggregation tends to produce more research than would several discrete projects totalling the same expenditure, simply because duplication and overlap are reduced and a critical mass of researchers can be assembled.

A charge commonly made by those opposed to joint ventures is that full specialisation of R&D is never realised (there are invariably duplicate testing facilities and too many expensive prototypes), and that this necessarily results in higher costs and less bang for the research buck. As was the case with the Tornado, the Eurofighter program is particularly open to such charges in that it does indeed involve several flight-test centres and a number of expensive developmental prototypes. However, it should be noted in this respect that whereas the Tornado project involved 15 development aircraft, the EFA will require only eight (two of which are two-seat training aircraft). Presumably this will result in less cost-inflation.[26] Moreover, it would appear that the Eurofighter program, building on the experience gained during the MRCA project, will in fact involve little if any duplication of R&D work. From the initial stages of the program, both Eurofighter and Eurojet have assigned each participating firm responsibility for a particular set of technological problems and for the development, design, and (usually) production of specific sections of the airframe and engine. For example, the Spanish firm, CASA, is exclusively responsible for the EFA's twin tail segment.[27]

The result of these arrangements is that during testing there will be little in the way of duplicate rigs or tooling, and both consortia, therefore, can expect to exploit the gains associated with specialisation. Nor should it be forgotten that — as is so often the case in business — in the aerospace industry, time equals money. Thus duplicate test centres, to the extent that they facilitate the rapid evaluation of new product technology, may actually reduce overall R&D costs. All in all, then, the projections are that collaborative R&D work associated with the Eurofighter will probably result in a technologically superior final product at marginally higher total costs.

In connection with the production side of the equation, supporters of collaboration also claim that joint ventures improve competitiveness in that they reduce production costs by exploiting the scale and learning economies associated with large orders. In this respect, the Eurofighter program has two objectives. The first is to consolidate regional demand by generating a base order approaching the scale commonly enjoyed by U.S. firms. On the EFA, as on the Tornado, each firm specialises in the manufacture of specific parts for all 800 aircraft, allowing companies to employ labour and capital more efficiently, and to spread the costs of R&D, physical plant and administration over more units than if they were building to a national scale.[28] Usually, this allows firms to move further down their learning and unit cost curves and to achieve cheaper production. Moreover, large base orders mean that the most efficient and capital-intensive plant and machinery can be installed, reducing unit costs even further. Drawing on evidence provided by the Tornado experience, this suggests that a base order of 800 aircraft could result in unit savings of 10 percent for the UK, 15 percent for the FRG, and as much as 30 percent for Italy and Spain.[29] According to this logic, savings would be increased substantially if the Eurofighter consortium managed to further coordinate demand with other European nations; and this might largely explain recent European efforts to persuade Belgium and other EPG nations to join the venture.

Collaborative production, of course, is not without its cost penalties. All four participating countries plan to establish their own final assembly lines, and this will necessarily tend to reduce the benefits derived from specialisation. However, as final assembly typically accounts for only about 10 percent of European production costs, the collaboration premia associated with duplication can be as little as 1 to 2 percent of final production expenditures.[30] Considering both the benefits derived from scale and learning economies and the penalties associated with duplication, it would seem that a base order of 800 units for the EFA program could be expected to reduce unit costs by as much as 30 percent of the cost of a national program (although 15 to 20 percent is perhaps a more reasonable estimate).[31]

A second objective of the Eurofighter program is to reduce production costs even further by vigorously exploiting the export potential of the non-NATO military aerospace market, particularly (but not exclusively) in the form of sales to the Middle East and Asia. Assuming the same learning curve as above, if an 800-unit European effort were to be expanded through export sales to a total of 1200 units, individual aircraft costs could be expected to drop by a further 13 percent.[32] Clearly, this indicates the significance of foreign sales to any effort to reform the European aerospace industry so that it can compete commercially with its U.S. counterpart; for in the absence of substantial foreign markets and the associated scale and learning economies it will indeed be difficult for the Europeans to amortise their R&D investment or keep unit costs competitive with those of their American rivals.

The importance of exportability to the Europeans, and, as noted above, the belief that the incorporation of U.S. technology will give the American government a veto over any proposed foreign sales, has meant that there has been considerable European resistance to American participation in the EFA program.[33] Although to date no firm decisions have been made, it appears likely that this resistance will result in two American firms being denied important sub-contracts on the Eurofighter. First, it is unlikely that Hughes Aircraft Co. will be successful in its bid for work on the EFA's airborne radar system. Hughes has teamed with AEG of Germany, GEC-Marconi of the UK, Fiar of Italy, and INISEL of Spain to produce an upgraded version of the U.S.-designed AN/APG 65 radar (known as Multi-mode Silent Digital or MSD-2000) for inclusion in the Eurofighter. The other competitor for the contract is an all-European consortium led by Ferranti of the UK (and again including Fiar of Italy and INISEL of Spain). The Ferranti team is proposing a derivative of the Marconi Blue Vixen radar (the ECR-90), which it is arguing would be unaffected by U.S. export controls and which would ultimately prevent the U.S. from squeezing Western Europe out of the high-technology airborne radar field. While it is true that the FRG and Spain are thought to prefer the AN/APG 65 in order to control costs, maintain interoperability within their respective airforces, and (in the German case) because AEG is to be the prime contractor on Hughes project, the ability to market the ECR-90 internationally without regard to U.S. export or technology controls has already become a key consideration in the competition between the two consortia — and will likely result in the all-European radar being chosen over the American design.[34]

Similarly, the U.S.-designed GE F404 aircraft engine is also likely to be excluded from the EFA program, primarily because it too is subject to regulation by Washington. The long-term intention of the Eurofighter consortium is that later prototypes and production aircraft will be powered by a jointly developed engine based on the Rolls Royce XG 40 (to be known as the EJ 200). Until this power plant is developed and in production, however, the plan is to rely on an existing interim design — either the Rolls Royce RB 199 or the General Electric F404. European fears that, once included, economic constraints would incline NEFMA to retain the relatively inexpensive F404 in later production models (and that this would impede EFA export sales and undermine the commercial viability of the European aero-engine industry) have disposed the consortium members to favour the RB 199 until the EJ 200 is introduced into service.[35]

As Trevor Taylor has argued, then, the Eurofighter program has placed the Europeans in the position of "giving either contracts or offence to the U.S."[36] Considering the importance of exports to the future of the European aerospace industry, it is difficult to imagine that this dilemma will be resolved to the satisfaction of the Americans as long as Washington continues to regulate the re-export of the high-technology goods in question. Moreover, considering the importance of the European market to the U.S. aerospace industry, and in particular the fact that the EFA radar and engine contracts are worth a total of $1.5 billion, the offence offered to the Americans if they are excluded from participating in the program will likely be serious indeed. It remains to be assessed at this point precisely how Washington is reacting to the possibility of non-participation in the EFAP, what this suggests about the possible future U.S. response if American technology is excluded from Europe, and what this might mean in terms of the long-term prospects for NATO-wide defence-industrial rationalisation.

THE AMERICAN RESPONSE

Initially, efforts to rationalise the various European defence industries were conceived with the intent of improving Europe's international competitiveness and so generating a more equitable flow of traffic on the so-called two-way street. As a regional goal, of course, rationalisation was important to the Europeans as a means of redressing the increasingly unacceptable transatlantic defence-related trade imbalance and generally strengthening Europe's industrial infrastructure. As an Alliance goal, too, European rationalisation was considered important, primarily because it allowed the European allies to play a larger role in their own defence and also because it allowed for greater European armaments cooperation with the United States (thus reducing the latter's preparedness burden). Increasingly, however, European efforts to rationalise their collective defence industrial base have become something of an irritant to the Americans. What has changed in this respect is not so much the logic underpinning the European efforts, but rather the effect those efforts are having (or threatening to have) on the American defence industry, above all in connection with the military aerospace sector.

Perhaps the most pressing American concerns regarding the Eurofighter program are related to the potentially deleterious effect European collaboration and protectionism (an essential element of European rationalisation) will have on U.S. aerospace exports, to Europe particularly, but also to other traditional American customers outside the NATO European market. Foreign military sales (FMS), of course, are important to the U.S. for a variety of reasons. First, while it is true that the American economy as a whole is not appreciably dependent on arms exports, certain key indicators of economic health are indeed significantly influenced by the balance of defence trade. For example, a Congressional Budget Office study tabled in 1976 concluded that for every $1 billion in FMS 42,000 U.S. jobs were created.[37] If we apply this rule of thumb to the five top DOD aerospace contractors, we find that a decade ago foreign military sales generated more than 125,000 American jobs.[38] Given that liberal democratic governments are naturally concerned with the political ramifications of such gross economic statistics, some idea of the national (and partisan political) importance of aerospace exports begins to emerge.[39] Second, foreign military sales are important as a means of reducing U.S. DOD budget expenditures. In this regard, it has been estimated that for every $8 billion in arms exported by American firms, the U.S. DOD realises $560 million in budgetary savings, primarily as a result of recouped R&D outlays and production economies (resulting in cheaper weapons being available in the U.S.). Moreover, savings may be even greater in connection with the aerospace sector. To quote another CBO report, the most substantial budgetary savings accruing to the DOD can be expected in the area of "recently developed, high technology systems — particularly fighter aircraft and missiles."[40]

The third major reason why foreign military sales are important to the U.S. is that certain security-active firms rely heavily on exports for both revenue and the large base orders that generate production economies and underpin the international competitiveness of the U.S. industry. Although it is true that the export market typically accounts for a relatively small percentage of the military sales of American aerospace firms, there are still a number of companies that are dependent on foreign orders for a substantial proportion of their total military sales. For example, no fewer than five of the top 10 U.S. aerospace firms derive 20 percent or more of their defence-related business from foreign military sales, with some (notably Textron and Northrop) deriving almost half their business from this source.[41] Nor should one underestimate the importance of export sales in maintaining the international comparative advantage enjoyed by U.S. aerospace firms. In this respect, the CBO is again instructive, suggesting in one of its reports that foreign military sales are a significant contributing factor to the commercial competitiveness of the American industry, and citing four sources of potential savings in this connection (viz., recouped R&D, learning-curve effects, economies of scale, and production-line stability).[42]

At minimum, then, it would seem that foreign military sales are of considerable interest to both the U.S. government and the American aerospace industry. Not only do exports improve corporate competitiveness and profitability (by generating production economies), they also improve the cost-effectiveness of the Department of Defense (by reducing procurement costs) and promote national economic stability (by maintaining employment levels and helping with the balance of payments). Given the importance of FMS, then, it is perhaps not too surprising to find Washington vigorously opposing foreign efforts to restrict and regulate America's export markets. Nor is it particularly surprising that the U.S. is finally waking up to the transatlantic economic implications of successful European armaments cooperation; for Europe, once largely an American-dominated market, is increasingly becoming hostile to U.S. defence goods. In the context of an American defence budget that is unlikely to grow substantially in the next few years, the possibility that armaments cooperation among the European allies could significantly reduce U.S. exports to Europe and elsewhere naturally bodes ill for American interests; and understandably, U.S. policy makers are beginning to react to this perceived threat. In this connection, the Eurofighter program provides an interesting case in point.

Given the political and economic importance of aerospace exports to the Americans, it is difficult to see how a program like the Eurofighter (with its promises of greater protectionism and increased international competition) could not generate significant conflict between Washington and the European capitals. All told, the Americans see the EFA project as posing a three-fold threat to their interests. First, the Americans feel that, because of the Eurofighter consortium's bidding rules, U.S. manufacturers will be excluded from participating in the program itself and will not therefore have a share in a project that should sell well in Europe and beyond. American fears in this respect, of course, have been reinforced by the near-certain failure of Hughes Aircraft and General Electric to secure up to $1.5 billion worth of engine and avionics contracts, and by the European refusal to accept Secretary Weinberger's suggestion that the U.S. contribute to EFA with a share of about 10 percent of the total project. Should the Americans fail to gain access to the Eurofighter program, they are concerned that they will be permanently shut out of the fighter-aircraft market in the four EFA-consortium nations.

Second, the Americans feel that if the Eurofighter is commercially successful (that is, competitive in terms of price and quality with U.S. products) there is a strong possibility that they will eventually be excluded from the broader European military aerospace market. Naturally enough, this concern is partly underpinned by ongoing Eurofighter efforts to persuade the EPG (F-16) nations to enter the EFA-consortium as full partners — efforts that may prove irresistible to European nations dissatisfied with licenced production under American export controls. If Eurofighter GmbH proves successful in its bid to attract more European participants, then U.S. firms do indeed face "being frozen out of the vital European export market."[43] As some calculations suggest that by the turn of the century as many as 2000 U.S.-designed European aircraft will be approaching the end of their operational life-cycles, and that their replacement value will be around $30 billion, such a development would be a substantial blow indeed to U.S. industry.[44]

A third American fear regarding the Eurofighter program is that a commercially competitive European aircraft might well challenge the U.S. stranglehold on the global (non-Soviet) military aerospace market. Currently, American designs account for about 85 percent of the aircraft in service outside of NATO, while the European share is closer to five percent.[45] However, if European collaboration and protection succeed in producing a combat aircraft that is reasonably priced, of good quality, and not subject to U.S. export controls, then there is a good chance that Eurofighter might sell 200 or more aircraft to foreign buyers. To be sure, given the magnitude of the numbers involved, the sale abroad of 200 aircraft would not appreciably alter existing European market share (at least not immediately). That would require far more exports than are currently projected. However, a successful EFA, incorporating exclusively European technology and know-how, may prove to be the first step toward establishing not only a more balanced two-way transatlantic street, but also a more equitable division of the global aerospace market.

Given the significance of the Eurofighter program to the future-viability (and profitability) of the American aerospace industry, it is perhaps not too surprising to find that Washington's response to the EFAP has been one of unambiguous and vigorous opposition — both to the program itself, and more particularly to the bidding arrangements that threaten to exclude U.S. firms from participating in it. Broadly, the Americans have reacted to the project in the form of three general policy initiatives, each designed to undermine the commercial viability of (and political support for) a wholly European developed and produced combat aircraft. First, both the Administration and Congress have reacted to European protectionism by attempting to persuade and entice the NATO European allies to participate in more *transatlantic* (as opposed to strictly European) collaborative armaments programs. In this connection, former Secretary of Defense Weinberger, former U.S. Ambassador to NATO David Abshire, and Deputy Secretary of Defense William Taft recently spearheaded an American effort to convince the European allies that NATO needed to make the best use of its available defence resources, and that U.S.-European industrial teaming was the most effective means to that end. Moreover, in recent months the Administration has made an effort-to facilitate the transfer of American technology to Europe and to relax American re-export controls in connection with the EFAP. In late May 1988, for example, Defense Secretary Frank Carlucci approved a draft MOU expressing American willingness to provide the technology to develop the MSD-2000 radar for the Eurofighter, and suggesting that DOD would be willing to negotiate the future re-export of that technology to non-EFA parties.[46] While the guarantees offered in the MOU remained inadequate to satisfy European doubts regarding technology-transfer issues, the document nevertheless represented a significant American effort to avoid being totally excluded from the Eurofighter program.

Similarly, the legislative branch has also responded to the EFA by pursuing a relatively constructive, non-confrontational policy designed to bring the Europeans back into the American fold by means of incentive rather than threat; and to this end has amended the 1986 Defense Authorization Act in order to provide funds for U.S.-European collaborative projects and further reduce some of the formal (and obstinately irritating) legal barriers to European participation in the U.S. market. In addition to the $125 million for U.S.-European co-development projects allocated by this amendment, subsequent legislation has since sweetened the pot by earmarking a further $3 billion for collaborative transatlantic research and development.[47]

The second American initiative has been to approach the Eurofighter "problem" by occasionally applying political pressure to the Europeans with the intent of convincing them that it would not be in anyone's best interest to exclude U.S. aircraft and subsystems from their aerospace market. In this connection, Washington has periodically assumed a somewhat less than congenial posture toward the EFA countries, and has even threatened to respond to "unfair" Eurofighter bidding rules with political pressure and retaliatory legislation designed to highlight the potential costs of such a course of action. Indeed, in early 1987 the Defense Department went so far as to issue a note to the EFA countries declaring that protectionist measures undertaken in connection with the Eurofighter program were in violation of some of the various Memoranda of Understanding that existed between the U.S. and NATO Europe. This note indicated that failure to amend the EFA bidding requirements so that U.S. firms could participate in the project would result in additional restrictions being placed on the transfer of American military technology to Europe and a loss of European procurement opportunities in the American defence market — moves that would effectively signal the end of meaningful transatlantic armaments cooperation.[48]

The third, and increasingly favoured, element of Washington's response to the Eurofighter initiative has been to depend on the commercial competitiveness of American aircraft and components to convince financially constrained European governments to eschew the exclusively European EFAP in favour of a co-developed transatlantic (i.e. predominantly American) aircraft.[49] In this connection, the Pentagon has been engaged in a vigorous public relations campaign designed to raise the profile of U.S. aerospace technology among relevant European political decision-makers, and to transmit the message that transatlantic armaments cooperation is the most effective means of utilising Alliance defence-industrial resources.

More specifically, over the past year DOD has made several concerted efforts to persuade the Europeans that in American aerospace systems they would be getting qualitatively superior products at considerably lower prices than would be possible in a wholly

European effort. In early 1988, for example, DOD dispatched Dennis Kloske, the Department's Trade and Cooperation Advocate, to Bonn in a bid to persuade the European governments to consider the F-18 derived Hornet 2000 as an alternative to the EFA. Kloske and his team emphasised the financial benefits associated with the joint development plan, particularly the fact that the United States was willing to allocate 60 percent of the codevelopment and production work on the Hornet 2000 to Europe; they also stressed that total development costs would amount to only $3.5 billion (as opposed to $8 to 10 billion for the Eurofighter).[50] The delegation also pressed the argument that if the Europeans and the U.S. Navy were to consolidate their requirements, the initial Hornet 2000 order would be for 1,265 aircraft at a fly-away unit cost of approximately $21 million — or less than half the projected cost of the EFA.

The Pentagon also announced that it would be willing to enter into a joint U.S.-European program to upgrade collaboratively both the F-16 Agile Falcon and the Hornet 2000 with technology (particularly avionics and engines) from the U.S. Air Forces's Advanced Tactical Fighter program.[51] Once again DOD emphasised the cost and quality advantages associated with transatlantic codevelopment, arguing that the new upgrades would make the American aircraft superior to the EFA in beyond visual range combat and that unit costs ($17 million for the Agile Falcon; $26 to 28 million for the Hornet 2000) would still be substantially lower than those projected for the Eurofighter ($50 million).

Finally, DOD made a serious effort to ensure some form of U.S. participation in the European aerospace sector (in the form of subsystems and components), even in the event that the Europeans rejected the U.S. co-development bids and the EFA program went ahead as planned. Initially, as mentioned above, this effort took the form of Secretary Weinberger's offer to contribute 10 percent of the development costs to the Eurofighter project in return for guaranteed access to the program for U.S. subcontractors — an offer that the Europeans rejected because of the possible impact of technology controls on future export prospects. Recently, however, this initiative has increasingly manifested itself in the form of greater DOD support for U.S. manufacturers in an effort to out-compete their European rivals. In this connection, Paul H. Kennard, vice-president of Hughes Radar Systems, points out that the Defense Department has offered repeated assurances to both Hughes and the EFA consortium that there will be no legal complications involved in transferring the AN/APG 65 radar technology to the Europeans (although some time-phased release restrictions will still be in effect), and that a State Department advisory opinion covering 24 countries (including all NATO members) has suggested that future re-export of the Hughes radar will be unlikely to contravene U.S. transfer legislation.[52]

Thus far, American efforts to persuade the Europeans to abandon the EFA or incorporate major U.S. subsystems into the Eurofighter project have been wholly unsuccessful: the F-16/F-18 co-development schemes seem to have come to nothing, and, although no firm decisions have yet been made, it appears unlikely that the Hughes radar or General Electric engine will find acceptance with NEFMA. Still, neither American industry nor government appear to have lost hope and (at least for the present) both are continuing to rely on aggressive sales techniques rather than political arm-twisting to secure continued access to the European fighter aircraft market. The depth and intensity of the overall American effort to prevent the development of an exclusively European designed and produced fighter aircraft, however, suggests that the stakes involved in this transatlantic conflict are high, and that failure to resolve the dispute could have serious implications for future U.S.-European armaments cooperation and the long-term rationalisation of the Alliance defence industrial base. While it is still too early to forecast what these implications might be, it seems likely that the future of the European-American defence industrial connection will ultimately be determined largely by the degree to which the U.S. is successful in selling transatlantic co-development and production to the Europeans.

Should the Europeans accept the invitation to participate in the Agile Falcon or Hornet 2000 projects, or even include American subsystems in the EFA, then Washington will obviously be only too happy to refrain from taking retaliatory or punitive action against Europe. Conversely, however, should the Europeans continue to reject the U.S. offers, and persist in pursuing regional defence industrial development at the expense of American industry, then it is clear that the United States will feel constrained to begin protecting its own economic interests — to the near-certain detriment of further industrial collaboration between Europe and America. Indeed, one only has to look as far as the Defense Department's February 1987 warning note in order to develop some feeling for possible implications of greater European protectionism. At the very least, the American note suggests that exclusion from the EFAP will likely sour the willingness of both the U.S. aerospace industry and the American government to collaborate with Europe on other projects, or even to allow the Europeans significant procurement opportunities within the United States. At worst, of course, the long-term effects of such a conflict could be much more destructive; for if the EFAP does represent a new attitude toward American participation in the European defence market, it is likely that it will trigger greater industrial unilateralism and protectionism in the U.S., and possibly even cause the Americans to reappraise their material commitment to the security of Western Europe.

CONCLUSION

The central argument of this chapter is that efforts to rationalise the European defence industrial base are both pre-requisite to and incompatible with the broader goal of Alliance-wide specialisation and rationalisation, at least within NATO as it is currently configured. Broadly, the contention is that rising weapons costs in the context of stable or shrinking defence budgets are moving the NATO alliance inexorably toward structural disarmament — that is, to the point at which the trend curves for national defence budgets and the cost curves for relatively minor purchases of military equipment intersect. In response to this development, the Alliance has been forced to consider means of reforming its duplicative and highly wasteful defence industrial effort so that development and production costs can be controlled, and the price of military preparedness can be kept within reasonable limits. From a simple economic perspective, of course, the creation of a NATO-wide free-trade regime in defence goods would seem to be the optimal approach to this problem as it promises the most comprehensive rationalisation and the most effective cost reductions. Free trade, however, is fraught with political hazards that make it largely unacceptable to most Alliance governments.

An apparently attainable alternative to free trade in this connection is "managed specialisation," or rationalisation according to a politically negotiated division of labour. Within Alliance circles managed specialisation has long been considered more realistic, and therefore more attainable, than free trade, largely because it minimised Allied fears that industrial reorganisation would be painful and traumatic. In short, as Lawrence Hagen pointed out, "[managed specialisation] offered the benefits of collaboration in the context of current production patterns — integration without tears."

Managed specialisation, however, proved not to be the panacea many had expected. "Current production patterns," heavily favouring the U.S., were considered largely unacceptable to a Western Europe that was increasingly inclined to economic competition, as well as military cooperation, with the Americans. Consequently, the European allies made it clear from the start that any specialisation within the Alliance would have to be based on the prior realisation of a more equitable flow of traffic on the transatlantic two-way street. In short, the Europeans established as a precondition for NATO-wide defence industrial rationalisation greater access for their goods to the U.S. domestic defence market.

This precondition, unavoidable and perfectly legitimate from a European perspective, has proven in large measure to be at the root of the Alliance's current defence industrial dilemma; for if the Europeans want to enter the American defence market, U.S. trade and procurement legislation requires that they do so on the basis of commercial competitiveness, and that means that Europe must first of all "get itself together" industrially and begin producing top-quality equipment at reasonable prices. However, because this is likely to require greater European intervention and protectionism (and because it ultimately suggests that Europe will begin to offer the U.S. more global competition), there is every possibility that, ironically, European efforts to rationalise their pillar of the NATO defence industrial base will increase rather than reduce the Alliance's military preparedness burden.

It is perhaps going too far to suggest that the current conflict and competition over the defence industrial base will herald the ultimate demise of the Atlantic Alliance; NATO has weathered too many potentially divisive crises in the past to permit one uncritically to suppose that it will not prove capable of "muddling through" this time as well. It does seem reasonable, however, to suggest that if NATO is to survive into the twenty-first century it cannot continue to handle defence industrial issues as it does now; for as matters now stand, the Alliance permits neither the United States nor Europe to pursue their common goal of defence industrial rationalisation simultaneously with their respective, and increasingly divergent, regional and national economic goals. Nor would it appear that the types of market-oriented policies proposed in recent years offer much in the way of workable alternatives. This clearly implies that some form of political-economic structure is needed that would allow the Allies to accommodate one another's interests without unduly sacrificing efficiency in weapons development and production. While it is unclear at present precisely how NATO should create such a structure (or even if such a structure is possible), it is nevertheless obvious that some effort must be made in this direction. For, in the context of skyrocketing defence costs and limited industrial and budgetary resources, the current conflict over the EFA serves only to further diffuse and fracture the Alliance's already dangerously uncoordinated collective preparedness effort.

Notes

[1] See Thomas A. Callaghan, Jr., *US/European Co-operation in Military and Civil Technology*, rev. ed. (Washington: Center for Strategic and International Studies, 1977).

[2] Jan Feldman, "Collaborative Production of Defense Equipment within NATO," *Journal of Strategic Studies* 7 (March 1984): 283.

[3] Lawrence Hagen, *Twisting Arms: Political, Military, and Economic Aspects of Arms Cooperation in the Atlantic Alliance* (Kingston: Queen's Centre for International Relations, 1980), pp. 98-99.

[4] U.S. defence procurement legislation generally requires that goods must be purchased on the basis of price and quality. Even under the terms of the various MOUs, firms located in qualifying countries are not guaranteed contracts, only the opportunity to compete. See "Bright Future for the MOU," *Jane's Defence Weekly*, 3 October 1987.

[5] While not suggesting that competition over the defence industrial base will in itself lead to a dissolution of the Alliance, within the context of a broader malaise such conflict may contribute to a long-term fracturing. At the every least, defence industrial competition threatens to make transatlantic arms co-operation decidedly more difficult than is presently the case. For a discussion of the concept of the "widening Atlantic" see Ralf Dahrendorf, "The Europeanization of Europe," in *A Widening Atlantic? Domestic Change and Foreign Policy*, ed. Andrew J. Pierre (New York: Council on Foreign Relations, 1986).

[6] Frederick Bonnart, "The Open Market: The Way Ahead For the European Defence Industry," *NATO's Sixteen Nations* 32 (July 1987). In the mid 1980s the IEPG commissioned a group of experts to identify and analyse shortcomings in the structure of the European defence industry. The final report of this panel (The European Defence Industry Study Team) was tabled 22 June 1987. In brief, the report demonstrated that the crux of Europe's defence-industrial weakness was that (a) European R&D was severely underfunded by U.S. standards, and (b) that Europe lacked a single procurement agency with the authority to act as such. To redress these shortcomings, the Team recommended that a common R&D program be

established, and that the IEPG create a permanent secretariat to handle acquisition.

[7]In 1975, for example, America's assistance to its aerospace industry totalled about $US 8.8 billion (1975 dollars). For the same period aggregate European aid totalled only about $US 2.9 billion (1975 dollars). See Joseph C. Rallo, *Defending Europe in the 1990s: The New Divide of High Technology* (London: Francis Pinter, 1986), pp. 59-60.

[8]M. J. Peck, "Microelectronics and Computer Technology Corporation," *Research Policy* 15 (October 1986): 222.

[9]Trevor Taylor, *Defence, Technology and International Integration* (London: St. Martin's Press, 1982), p. 89.

[10]This is assuming, of course, that at least some of the savings generated by scale economies would be redirected to R&D. Even in connection with *ad hoc* collaborative production this promises to result in some technological improvement.

[11]Taylor, *Defence, Technology*, p. 89.

[12]For an analysis of these concerns, in the context of aerospace procurement efforts, see the chapter by Alistair Edgar in this volume.

[13]See Hagen, *Twisting Arms*, p. 153; and Keith Hartley, *NATO Arms Cooperation* (London: Allen & Unwin, 1983), p. 103.

[14]The development and production savings that would have resulted from the sale of Tornado to the EPG nations would probably have been in the region of 10-15 percent. See Taylor, *Defence, Technology*, pp. 89-90.

[15]Count Corrado Agusta, quoted in *Meeting Report, International Symposium on NATO Standardization and Interoperability*, American Defense Preparedness Association, March 1978, pp. 77-83 (as quoted in Hagen, *Twisting Arms*, p. 83).

[16]On this problem, see the chapter by David Haglund in this volume.

[17]Existing U.S. policy (particularly the Arms Export and Control Act, and the Export Administration Act) prohibits the unauthorised sale of defence systems or sub-systems designed in the United States. Under the provisions of this legislation, Washington has disallowed proposed sales of the Swedish Viggen (containing an American engine) to India, and the co-produced F-16 to Jordan. See Hagen, *Twisting Arms*, pp. 82-85.

[18]Rallo, *Defending Europe in the 1990s*, p. 73.

[19]"Eurofighter Organisation Takes Shape," *NATO's Sixteen Nations* 31 (July 1986): 90.

[20]For a discussion of the enabling technologies and a technical analysis of the EFA see B. Wanstall, "Manufacturers Prepare for Europe's New Fighters," *Interavia*, no. 10, 1985, pp. 1133-36; S. Broadbent, "EAP: A Step Up the Ladder of Advanced Technologies," *Jane's Defence Weekly*, 21 March 1987, pp. 510-11; and idem, "EFA and Beyond: A Giant Leap for Avionic Software," ibid., 28 March 1987, pp. 560-62.

[21]"Eurofighter Organisation Takes Shape," p. 90.

[22]For a discussion of the organisational aspects of the EFA see "Europe's Fighter Prospects," *Jane's Defence Weekly*, 31 August 1986, pp. 379-81; and Frederick Bonnart, "The European Fighter Aircraft: An Update," *NATO's Sixteen Nations* 31 (November 1986): 58-60.

[23]W. B. Walker, "The Multi-Role Combat Aircraft (MRCA): A Case Study in European Collaboration," *Research Policy* 2 (1974): 291.

[24]By "structural reform" is meant the more or less comprehensive re-allocation and re-organisation of production capital along continental lines, as opposed to *ad hoc* rationalisation that is project specific.

[25]Hartley, *NATO Arms Cooperation*, p. 150.

[26]"Eurofighter Organisation Takes Shape," p. 90.

[27]X. I. Taibo, "EFA is a First for Spain," *Jane's Defence Weekly*, 30 August 1986, p. 381.

[28]Trevor Taylor, "European Armaments Cooperation: Competition for Resources," *Defence Yearbook 1987* (London: Brassey's Defence Publishers, 1987), p. 145.

[29]Hartley, *NATO Arms Cooperation*, p. 152.

[30]Ibid., p. 153.

[31]Ibid.; and Taylor, "European Armaments Co-operation," p. 145.

[32]Based on an assumed 85-percent learning curve. See Taylor, *Defence, Technology*, pp. 89-90.

[33]Thus the Europeans rejected Secretary Weinberger's suggestion (made in the autumn of 1985) that the U.S. be allocated a 10-percent share in the EFA program. The Europeans feared that this would contribute to the fracturing of the regional aerospace market, and impede their efforts to sell the Eurofighter on the wider world market.

[34]F. Clifton Berry, Jr., "The British Are Coming," *Airforce Magazine*, June 1987, p. 76.

[35]For a discussion of the American bids for the radar and engine components of the EFA see ibid.; and Taylor, "European Armaments Co-operation," pp. 146-47.

[36]Ibid., p. 147.

[37]U.S. Government, Congressional Budget Office, "The Effect of Foreign Military Sales on the U.S. Economy," Staff Working Paper, 23 July 1976, p. 1

[38]See H. Tuomi and R. Vayrynen, *Transnational Corporations, Armaments, and Development* (New York: St. Martin's Press, 1982), p. 29.

[39] Congressmen, too, are concerned with employment — particularly-as it affects their district. Thus, Congressmen for whom loss of exports means a loss of jobs in their constituency are unlikely to favour foreign protectionism or increased international competition.

[40]U.S. Government, Congressional Budget Office, "Budgetary Cost Savings to the DOD Resulting from Foreign Military Sales," Staff Working Paper, 24 May 1976, p. ix.

[41]Tuomi and Vayrynen, *Transnational Corporations*, p. 30.

[42]CBO, "Effects of Foreign Military Sales," p. 181. Also see Jacques Gansler, *The Defense Industry* (Cambridge, Mass.: MIT Press, 1980), p. 214.

[43]See "The Battle for a European Fighter," *Jane's Defence Weekly*, 20 June 1987, p. 1278.

[44]Pierre Condon, *Interavia*, no. 4 (1986), p. 379.

[45]Hartley, *NATO Arms Cooperation*, p. 103.

[46]See "Carlucci Letter Backs Supplying Radar Technology for EFA," *Aviation Week and Space Technology*, 16 May 1988; and "Pentagon Outlines Terms for Transfer of Radar Technology," ibid., 23 May 1988.

[47]Taylor, "European Armaments Co-operation," p. 151; Ted Hooton, "Europe's Fight for US Contracts," *Jane's Defence Weekly*, 3 October 1987, p. 754.

[48]*Washington Times*, 2 March 1987, p. 2.

[49]See Michael Mecham, "Congress Advised Not to Pressure Allies on Agile Falcon, Hornet 2000," *Aviation Week and Space Technology*, 18 April 1988.

[50]See Nick Cook, "Tempting Europe with the Hornet 2000," *Jane's Defence Weekly*, 23 January 1988; "USA Makes Late Hornet 2000 Bid," ibid., 12 March 1988; and "European Fighter Project Partners Cool to US Hornet 2000 Proposal," *Aviation Week and Space Technology*, 26 March 1988.

[51]See Hugh Lucas, "New U.S. Bid to End Eurofighter Development," *Jane's Defence Weekly*, 23 April 1988.

[52]See "Hughes Counters Ferranti on Radar Technology Issues," *Aviation Week and Space Technology*, 11 April 1988.

PART TWO

The Dilemmas of Preserving a Defence Industrial Base

4

The Importance of Arms Exports and Armament Cooperation for the West German Defence Industrial Base

Bernd Huebner

INTRODUCTION

Those who examine German arms exports, and their importance for Germany today, will observe a double phenomenon. In all Western military magazines the German defence industries advertise their products and "know-how" with glossy photos and glowing descriptions, as though anyone could become a customer and gain a decisive advantage simply by buying German defence products. For example, between 10 and 15 advertisements are to be seen in each issue of the Bundeswehr-sponsored magazine called *Soldat und Technik*. Open and aggressive information and advertising has also been demanded by the State Secretary responsible for armaments who has declared: "protection of German industry's interests must be significantly improved by military people in international bodies and integrated staffs, so that we have no disadvantage in competition, both in NATO and in third world countries as long as there are no export limitations because of political considerations."[1]

On the other hand, those who seek information on the importance and the background of German arms exports will find that open information quickly becomes limited. In the course of research for this chapter, I surveyed 26 companies, all of whom advertise their products, but only 11 replied. Moreover, only four really gave direct answers; the others simply replied in the same vein as one big company that said, "this subject is both politically and economically explosive." This is understandable, considering that the former Federal Minister of Defence, Dr. Manfred Wörner once declared, when asked about exporting arms, "I am a member of the Federal Government and am urgently against making this subject an item of public dispute."[2]

Because of the limited information available, the problems of arms exports and their importance for Germany can only be shown by example. Further complicating the chore facing the analyst is the fact that officially there is no independent defence industry. As a result, analysts must consider all companies that "either produce weapons and equipment which are capable and destined to inflict losses to an enemy during martial actions, or which produce equipment which are destined for use in the armed forces according to their technical skills and were in no civil market."[3]

Such well-known observers of the arms-export market as the U.S. Arms Control and Disarmament Agency (ACDA) and the Stockholm International Peace Research Institute (SIPRI) have for years considered the Federal Republic as one of the most important arms exporters to countries of the Third World.[4] For their part, the Germans like to be seen as a country with very limited arms exports.[5] The question has never been discussed in principle, but it does arise from time to time; for example, with sales of tanks to Saudi Arabia or submarines to South Africa and Chile.

In this chapter I intend to discuss the arms-export role of the Federal Republic, concentrating on both its legal limitations and its objectives. The impact of arms exports on German industry and the country's defence-industrial base will be traced and a comparison drawn between illusion and reality. Finally, I will offer some policy recommendations.

THE STATE AND ARMS: THE WAR WEAPONS CONTROL ACT AND THE FOREIGN TRADE ACT

The Federal Republic of Germany is in principle committed to a restrictive arms-export policy. The basic law, the German constitution, demands the following in Article 26, entitled *Ban on War of Aggression*: "Acts tending to and undertaken with the intent to disturb peaceful relations between nations, especially to prepare for aggressive war, shall be unconstitutional. They shall be made a punishable offence. Weapons designed for warfare may not be manufactured, transported or marketed except with the permission of the Federal Government. Details shall be regulated by a Federal law."[6]

This restrictive arms-export policy as a "peace-political rule"[7] is part of the constitution and the "commission and decision monopoly"[8] is delegated to the Federal Government, as opposed to an export-willing defence industry. The Government, therefore, takes over the political and, in some cases, commercial responsibility for arms sales abroad. A change of these constitutional principles is not likely, since it would require a two-thirds majority in Parliament. However, it is conceivable that a final judgment could be demanded, and obtained, from the Federal Constitutional Court with the aim of limiting the freedom of action the government now exercises in this area.

To better define the demands made by the constitution, two laws were enacted in the early 1960s, the War Weapons Control Act (KWKG) of 20 April 1961, and the Foreign Trade Act (AWG) of 28 April 1961. These laws were enacted at a time when awareness of the problems involved was not particularly well-developed.[9]

The purpose of the KWKG is to prevent weapons being used in military conflicts outside the control of the Federal Government; hence the manufacture, acquisition, transfer, and transportation of military weapons are strictly controlled by the Act. Since 1978 a contract of agreement and brokerage must specifically permit weapons transfers outside German borders.[10] Because the limitation only refers to war weapons, such weapons are named in the "war-weapons list," an appendix to the KWKG which is revised periodically. It deals primarily with heavy weapons such as tanks, armoured vehicles, artillery pieces, heavy infantry weapons, war ships, missiles, combat aircraft, and their components, but not with smaller weapons such as pistols and rifles. According to Article 6 of the KWKG, the government *must* deny the export, if:

1. danger exists that the war weapons will be used in an act that will disturb the peace, especially in a war of aggression; and,

2. there is reason to assume that issuing the permit would conflict with the obligations of the Federal Republic under international law.

Beyond that the government *can* deny the export licence "if giving permission would be against the interests of the FRG in maintaining good relations with other countries."[11]

Originally the purpose of the AWG was to regulate the export of goods to the Soviet Union and its allies. Today it serves to control the export of all defence-related material to all countries.[12] The goods intended to be controlled by the Act are recorded in the so-called "export list" (Ausfuhrliste), an appendix to the "Foreign Trade Decree" (Aussenwirtschaftsverordnung) issued by the government on 22 August 1961, and modified on 21 December 1982. The export list contains three categories: defence products, nuclear material, and strategic goods. It also includes the embargo list agreed to by COCOM (Coordinating Committee for Multi-lateral Export Controls) and the war-weapons list of the KWKG. As well, it serves to control designs, workshop drawings, and other production documents.[13] The export of all goods registered in the export list may be permitted by the government. "Exports [can] be limited to guarantee the security of the Federal Republic of Germany, to prevent a disturbance of the peaceful life of nations, and to prevent a disturbance in the foreign relations of the Federal Republic of Germany."[14] The government has also taken into account the principle of free trade as a competing factor. There-fore, decisions made by the administration based on the KWKG can only be challenged in court; according to the AWG, the court has to decide in weighing the different interests, whether *consider-able* damage to the Federal Republic by non-denial can be ex-pected. Despite the remarkably limited discretion of the administration with regard to the KWKG, no case is known in which industry brought court action for export licences.[15] It could be argued either that the German administration grants licences very liberally or that it has always acted properly; in any event, in-dustry knows that it depends on the government, and it does not welcome questions on these issues. Should it wish to export its defence products, it must "take part in the competition under a state monopoly; it must execute orders and commissions silently in the background."[16]

The additional legal restrictions imposed on the Federal Republic by reason of its membership in the Western European Union (WEU) are meaningless in practice. There has never been any thought of building up industrial capacities for nuclear, bio-logical, or chemical weapons, and all the other limitations (for ex-ample, tonnage of submarines) have been cancelled.[17]

Because of the sensitivity of arms exports, the law demands the predominance of political factors over free trade, delegates the control function to the government, and bans peace-disturbing actions. The government's policy does not allow the unrestricted sale of arms, as is perhaps the case in some other countries, if this comment by Israeli senior statesman Abba Eban serves as any guide: "If an Iranian regime is friendly, we let them have arms to celebrate friendship. But if it is hostile, we let them have arms to mitigate the hostility. We end up in a situation where selling arms is the only constant."[18] Rather, the export of arms demands a clear political decision on a state's values. As Tanzanian president Julius Nyrere phrased it, "The selling of arms is something which a country does only when it wants to support and strengthen the regime or group to whom the sale is made."[19] By law the federal government is the only responsible agent in the FRG; therefore, it has to suffer the "economic and political costs" of the arms trade.[20] Thus, Bonn's restrictive export policy has to be understood in the broad context of foreign policy, and not merely, as some argue, in the narrow one of defence policy.[21]

KWKG and AWG give the government both the capability and rationale for strict control. The reasons for denial of sales are stated in broad terms and the export lists, a principal item of the laws, are laid down by the government itself. It is the declared intention of the current Christian-Democrat leadership that there be no principal change in the export policy;[22] therefore, alteration of the laws cannot be expected until at least 1991. This might provide an explanation of why there has been no new draft of the 25-year-old laws, although there have been arguments about governmental decisions such as the sale of tanks to Saudi Arabia, and warships to Chile and South Africa. The only possibility of limiting the freedom of action of the government will be by judicial judgement.

The "Political principles of the Federal Government for the export of war weapons and other defence products"

The "political principles of the Federal Government for the export of war weapons and other defence products"[23] of 28 April 1982, otherwise referred to as "export principles 82", have been said to have nearly attained the importance of law.[24] In fact, these principles are no more than a declaration by the Federal Government as to how it will exercise its legal freedom of action.[25] How little (or much) this declaration has meant can be inferred from the fact that its predecessor declaration, of 16 June 1971, was never even officially published; it appeared in print in the magazine *Wehrdienst* nearly six years later. The Social-Liberal government of Helmut Schmidt was forced to admit that weapons (warships and boats) had been delivered to so-called "areas of tension," which was permissible in accordance with the KWKG, although the term "area of tension" might have signalled a prohibition of their delivery, given that the government assumed that "peace-disturbing actions," in a broad sense, had not taken place at sea since World War II.[26]

On the other hand, the "export principles 82" have survived the change of government from Social-Liberal to Christian-Liberal, and Bundesminister Schauble has declared them obligatory until 1991.[27] They are published by the government and serve as a guideline to the administration, industry, and potential customers. Therefore, a close look at the principles and the allowances they make is warranted.

The 1982 export principles stipulate the intention "to orientate [exports] to the security needs and the interest of foreign policy of the Federal Republic of Germany." They also commit the government to make "a contribution to secure peace by limitation and control" of arms exports. Bonn further pledges "to take into account the resolutions of international institutions" without having to explain what that means in detail. The current government evaluates the previous arms-exports policy as "approved restrictive," so it can be assumed that it has followed and will follow the pattern in place since 1969. The export principles distinguish among recipient countries as NATO countries, non-NATO countries, and communist countries in accordance with the COCOM list, which specifies that arms exports are not permitted without the agreement of all COCOM members.

The classification of defence goods as war weapons by the KWKG and defence products by the AWG has been extended to a third category, "war-weapons-like defence products," which means "installations and documents to produce war weapons." Normally these items are included in defence products and are therefore licenced under the rules of the AWG. However, they are now considered similar to war weapons and handled under the much stricter rules of the KWKG. Thus a legal loophole utilised by the industry has been closed. For example, the German standard rifle Cr3 from Heckler and Koch is rebuilt by 14 countries, 7 of them in the Third World,[28] and can be seen daily on television as a sign of expansive German exportpolicy.

The export of war weapons and other defence products to NATO countries "is not to be limited on principle unless a limitation is demanded by special political reasons," because the Federal Republic gives highest priority to the standardisation of NATO equipment. It requires an end-user certificate from NATO countries to prohibit anybody from violating its restrictions. While for defence products, exporters and importers in NATO countries have only to verify their intentions, Bonn insists that war weapons and "war-weapons-like defence products" can only be exported again with a "written accord of the Federal Government." This different handling indicates that the government is not sure that its own restrictions work. For example, an Italian company bought parts for the 105 mm tank gun, officially to be used as spare parts for Italy's own Leopard tanks, and then sold them directly to Argentina.[29]

Although cooperation based on governmental agreements is in the interest of the alliance, total harmonisation of arms-exports-policies with Germany's main partners, the U.S., France, and Great Britain, is not possible. Nevertheless, Bonn has made a clear decision in cases where interests conflict "to give priority to the cooperation interest." Further, it has refused to place limitations on the trade of foreign war weapons. It has declared, "if these parts are integrated in the weapons system by solid mounting, manufacture in the partner country confirms a new origin of the good in an export sense." The government limits the declared flexibility of its own restrictive policy by holding "consultation proceedings on principle," for the purposes of making objections to intended exports.

Altogether it is clear that Bonn gives such high priority to NATO cooperation that it accepts some contravention of its own policy. For that it has been rebuked by some critics; at the same time, industry has been quick to take advantage of this situation. The government seems to have adopted a sensible approach for the short term, but it must show that it is willing to fight for this approach. In view of the historical record, some doubt must be permitted on this score; for instance, in the early 1970s the government violated its own principles by delivering blueprints for submarines to the Vickers Yard in Great Britain, knowing that the boats were being built for Israel.[30]

The 1982 export principles state that exports of war weapons "are not permitted" to countries outside NATO. This strong statement is modified, however, by the fact that the government may exercise discretion to decide differently in particular cases. For example, export is considered suitable to most of the European neutrals, Australia, and Japan, as well as when vital interests of the Federal Republic (that is, "foreign-policy and security-policy interests under consideration of Alliance-interests") are involved. Therefore, one can no longer distinguish a qualitative difference between arms exports to NATO or non-NATO countries. To be sure, a quantitative difference apparently continues to exist. Industry can always hope for a favourable decision in a particular case, but will never have the certainty it would like to develop far-reaching plans. For example, it has been reported by a former government spokesman that the Social-Democratic-Liberal government was willing to sell armoured vehicles to Saudi Arabia in 1980/81, but was hindered by the publicity engendered by the issue of exporting submarines to Chile.[31] More to the point, perhaps, the present government has not permitted export of the battle tank Leopard 2 to Saudi Arabia.[32]

Export licences for "war-weapons-like defence products" are only given "in the interest of protecting the security of the peaceful living of the nations or if foreign relations are not endangered." As with war weapons, they are an important trade good; up to 1982 a quarter of all arms exports to the Third World were defence products.[33]

The export of other defence products is allowed by the rules of the AWG, which are not very strict. The difference between war weapons and "war-weapons-like defence products" on the one hand and defence products on the other hand, as explained by an official of the shipyard industry, is as follows: nearly all the parts of a minesweeper can be exported without restriction because they are not weapons or parts of weapons; the total system, however, often will not be licenced for export as a weapons system. This example indicates a major dilemma of export policy, that is, the artificial distinction between war weapons and defence products.

Bonn's ambiguous export policy can be said to have imposed further restrictions on both the country's foreign politics and its domestic affairs. For example, it seems to be the case that jobs are created or saved by exports.[34] There are between 30 and 40 thousand permanent working places in the defence industry;[35] and Defence Minister Wörner argued in 1981, as an opposition politician, that the export boom of the shipyard industry had its roots in employment policy.[36] Other industries have experienced similar effects; and it is very clear that because of the export market the number of employees in the submarine business increased.[37]

The declared arms-export policy of the governments of the last 15 years has been characterised repeatedly by its restrictive nature, save in the important instance of membership in NATO, which has meant that arms exports to the allies have been construed ideally as domestic trade. By the same token, it is considered absurd to deliver weapons or other defence products to the countries of the Warsaw Pact, in spite of Lenin's having observed that the capitalist can be expected to sell the rope on which he will be hanged. For all other countries, however, war weapons and "war-weapons-like defence products" will not be delivered in principle, while all goods classified as defence products may be delivered around the world except when the security of the Federal Republic, its foreign relations, or the peaceful existence of these nations is endangered.

The policy in practice: where do the weapons go?

The assumption that the export of defence material flows primarily to NATO countries is contradicted by the statistics; for the Federal Republic exports more than three times as many defence products to non-NATO than to NATO countries.

Table 4.1: *Arms Transfer Deliveries and Agreements 1973-1984*

	(in Billions of 1985 Dollars)			
	1973-76	1977-80	1981-84	Total
NATO	1.3	1.3	1.7	4.3
WTO	0.0	0.0	0.0	0.0
Non-NATO	2.3	5.5	5.5	13.3
Total	3.6	6.8	7.2	17.6

Source: U.S. Arms Control and Disarmament Agency (ACDA), "World Military Expenditures and Arms Transfers 1985." Extract from Table B. (It includes war weapons and other defence products.)

What are the reasons for this imbalance? No doubt, the NATO arms market has a limited ability to absorb German exports. However, the strong distinction Bonn makes between war weapons and all the other "not-so- deadly" defence products is also highly relevant. In truth, the question of what is necessary for the conduct of fighting is difficult to decide.[38] Some might consider trouser buttons to be almost a weapon because without them the soldier would be unable to use his hands for fighting; while others might not consider a tank-engine as a deadly spare part or believe that modern command, control and communication (C^3) systems could possibly be belligerent. Even the German export lists are inconsistent because, to take one example, minesweepers are counted as war weapons even though the criteria for war weapons are injury or destruction of humans or material, and the purpose of a mine-sweeper is to destroy a weapon (mine) that itself injures or kills humans and damages material. One whose view is only directed at a single defence good might, perhaps, be able to think in terms of the relative danger provided by that item. On the other hand, one who regards defence goods as part of the system's "war machinery" might not follow this logic. For example, a C^3 system can be much more effective in winning a war than a few tanks at the same price. These examples are simply another way of saying that the difference between war weapons and other defence products does not seem particularly helpful if one is trying to construct a credible, morally based arms-export policy. (Nor, as I argue below, is the distinction between "offensive" and "defensive" weapons easily drawn.)

The relative concentration of exports to non-NATO countries shows up most in the category of trade in war weapons.[39] These statistics do not include all non-NATO countries, but provide a clear illustration that the export of war weapons to non-NATO countries is more than an exception. Nor was I able to find any sources stating that "vital foreign-political and security-political interests" are the reason for this pattern. Traditionally Germany's military reputation has been based on its land forces, but the export success to non-NATO countries has been accomplished primarily through building warships: from 1975 to 1980, export licences were given to a total value of 3.768 billion DM; of this amount 3.315 billion DM were directed to exporting warships.[40] This trend can be seen in current SIPRI documents, and that it will likely continue is indicated in this comment by one adviser to the Chancellor, who was comparing the export of warships with that of armoured vehicles: "What swims, runs; what runs, doesn't run."[41]

It is very clear that, official documents apart, the government does make distinctions between naval war material and other war material. It does so on the basis that since World War II there have been few large-scale actions at sea, and thus there is a small risk in that environment of "peace-disturbing actions."[42] Furthermore, it is argued that ships cannot become involved in domestic struggles. The principal response to this argument is that all weapons support an existing government and their non-use only indicates the success of the balance of power. With the Falklands War of 1982, and the current naval combat in the Persian Gulf, it

Table 4.2: *Value of total major weapons export of the FRG in comparison to export to countries in Middle East, North Africa, South Asia, Far East (ex. Vietnam), South America, Sub-Saharan Africa, Central America, South Africa, Oceania*

(in million constant 1975 dollars)							
Years	1978	1979	1980	1981	1982	1983	1984
Total	553	488	316	435	250	613	746
In special regions	41	229	136	291	93	371	549
% of Total	9	46	43	66	39	52	74

Source: Stockholm International Peace Research Institute (SIPR) Yearbook 1984, "World Armaments and Disarmaments." Extract from Table 11.1, 11.A.1, 11.A.2

seems illusory to imagine that future wars at sea are unlikely. If an armed conflict between Pakistan and India comes to pass, the German-built Indian submarine will obviously figure in the fighting. Thus, the differences between naval war material and other war material are rather artificial and are supported by an assumption that we sell something for which there is no real need. This, in turn causes German export policy to lose credibility.

During the debate over exporting weapons to Saudi Arabia a new criterion was introduced for land-warfare material. The leader of the Christian-Socialists, Franz-Josef Strauss, confirmed that three hundred GEPARD anti-aircraft tanks were being exported "in order to compensate for the denial of Leopard tanks in 1983."[43] Apparently, Bonn believes itself able to differentiate between "offensive" and "defensive" weapons and to deliver arms that do not give the customer an aggressive capacity. Does the marketplace really allow such a differentiation? After all, an armoured, mobile air-defence system, which can be bought everywhere, only makes sense to protect armoured troops. Thus, a German air-defence system will decrease the Israeli air capability and increase the offensive capability of the Saudi forces. More importantly, a difference between offensive and defensive weapons is simply not very useful in principle. For example, a typical defensive weapon such as the sea-mine can be used to mine harbours aggressively, as shown by the U.S. in Nicaragua;[44] ABM systems protecting ICBM fields can improve their offensive capacity; and anti-tank guided missiles provided the conditions for the Egyptians to attack across the Canal. Significantly, Clausewitz did not try to make such a distinction when he discussed the "relationship between branches of the service." To him, a major distinction is unthinkable because "the defensive form of war is not a simple shield but a shield made up of well-directed blows."[45] That corresponds with German military thinking,[46] as well as with that of the Soviets — the other Clausewitzians — who "regularly emphasize the reciprocal interaction of offence and defence, which is characterised as a dialectical unity of opposites; the defence is at once a form of offence just as offence can and necessarily does serve defensive purposes."[47]

The administration and politics of arms exports

Because of the freedom of action they possess, it is worthwhile here to add a word about those bureaucratic actors responsible for administering arms-export policy. One salient aspect of arms-export administration in the Federal Republic is that it can be very time-consuming. Lack of documentation prevents me answering fully the question of whether the bureaucracy's decisions are always in time, from an industrial point of view; suffice it to note that some industrial officials have reported shortcomings. Examples of this can be found in the licence quarrel surrounding the sale of the Leopard 2 tank to Saudi Arabia from 1982 to 1986, as well as in the delivery of armoured vehicles initially without turret weapons to Malaysia two years or so ago.[48]

The political or administrative bureaucracy does not contact the customer officially, unless the issue is military aid, which I discuss below. The customer, normally a foreign government, negotiates directly with the German firm, although the latter often has no export licence at that time. It has been observed that such a procedure can lead to a competitive disadvantage; nevertheless, the government appears to like to talk directly and seeks to obtain early decisions.[49]

The agency responsible for granting export approval is the Ministry of Economics, which delegates routine matters to a subordinate agency. The Ministry of Defence and the Foreign Office always participate as experts, and the judgement of the Foreign Office is most important in evaluating the foreign-political interest in the deal. The primacy of politics is guaranteed in that the final decision is made by the Federal Security Council, a cabinet committee.[50] It is often involved because of the lack of guidelines and because of the financial implications, especially in the ship-export cases.[51] Despite this framework, the possibility of political misjudgement cannot be excluded, as for example, in the evaluation of the Argentinian military junta in 1982, or the attempt to use arms exports as a political weapon to preserve the claim of exclusive representation for the whole of Germany, by the Federal Republic.[52]

The Federal Republic's seesaw arms-export policy (for that is what it is) seems to have been influenced by the experience of Germany's having waged two world wars in a period of 30 years.[53] While Germany's rearmament was discussed publicly and is now accepted widely by the German population, its arms-export policy has never been the subject of broad interest. Rather, it has been considered taboo by the political parties, and is only questioned in special cases, such as Saudi Arabia or Chile. The problem of the morality of arms exports has never been settled in public. All parties represented in Parliament agree that a restrictive arms-export policy is required, but it appears that they mean different things by that term. While the Greens would rigorously prohibit arms exports, the views of the other parties are less clear, and seem to be shaped more by individual politicians than by party consensus. Although a party resolution of the Liberals demands the limitation of arms exports to NATO countries,[54] a member of that party and Minister of the Federal Government, Mr. Moellemann, has sought approval for exports to Saudi Arabia.[55] The Christian-Democrats have stated that they would continue to follow their old policies, whatever they might be.[56] The ideas of the Social-Democrats do not seem to be defined at the moment, but will probably be more restrictive than the policies followed by their own former government. Only the leader of the Christian-Socialists, Strauss, speaking on behalf of his party, openly advocates more freedom to export. He would protect the security of the free world in concert with other nations by arms exports that meet the following criteria:

1. protection of employment in high-technology industry;
2. guarantee of the development and production capacities of industry indispensable to Germany's own defence capacity;
3. export of military installations for the benefit of German industry and employment;
4. gaining of political influence that could be exercised in the interest of peace and stability.[57]

Thus, only the Greens and the Christian-Socialists have clear policies on arms exports.

While German industry is largely uncommunicative in public, other politically relevant organisations such as churches and labour unions speak out in favour of a restrictive policy. The unified conference of the Churches (both Catholic and Protestant) has, for moral reasons, declared that restrictions on arms exports should not be loosened.[58] Similarly, a proclamation for "peace and disarmament" has been issued by the unions,[59] which decided in favour of a moral stand only after becoming persuaded that the costs would not be decisive for the overall economy.[60]

The German Democratic Republic has attacked the Federal Republic as ruled by a "rapacious, extreme aggressive group," the so-called "military/industrial complex" — a special form of the *Monopolcapitalism* which creates an immoral policy of "imperialism" and "neo-colonialism."[61] Using facts and figures provided by the Federal Republic, the GDR delights in commenting upon the differences between the declared and the real policies. However, while it damns the Federal Republic, it paints a more positive picture of the communist military aid program. As defined in the GDR military encyclopedia, military aid consists of:

> Help during the build-up of forces or conduct of military operations in war by means of giving credits, delivery of weapons, military technology and military equipment in exchange for cash or on loan; dispatch of military specialists and instructors, training of military cadres and participation of volunteers or mercenaries as regular troops and units in a war or conflict on the side of the favoured country. Military aid can be different in purpose and pattern. The Soviet state carries out military aid ... loyally as part of its international responsibility. ... The character and aims of the military aid of the imperialistic countries are different in principle. [They] look out for their expansive and aggressive purposes.[62]

Therefore, both countries follow similar policies; but the GDR denies that they could be pursuing similar moral and political aims as two powerful and self-interested countries (albeit with different value systems).

Little is known about the influence of other western governments on Bonn's policy. It can only be assumed that a restrictive policy must be viewed favourably by potential competitors. Military aid is arranged through the United States to Turkey, Greece, and parts of Africa.[63] The Federal Republic was the target of considerable pressure from the Israeli government after it heard of German intentions to export weapons to Saudi Arabia. The Israeli Prime Minister threatened to mobilise American public opinion,[64] which may not seem entirely logical given that the U.S. itself is the main supplier of arms in the Middle East and Israel has not been exactly prudish in its own weapons trade. However, the threat was effective, given Germany's sensitivity on this issue.

To sum up, the German public has not decided to what extent arms exports are morally acceptable, but strong emotional reservations have been expressed. In international politics it is necessary to take into account the burden of German history and the difference between the declared policy on, and the reality of, arms exports.

THE IMPORTANCE OF THE DEFENCE INDUSTRY TO THE FEDERAL REPUBLIC

The previous sections have sought to show that Germany's arms-exports policy constitutes a real burden to the government, making it necessary to ask what the government's intentions really are with regard to the maintenance of a national defence industrial base. As Regina Cowen has demonstrated, the build-up of the country's defence industrial base occurred to satisfy the needs of the Bundeswehr; and its growth was accompanied by strong pressure from government to counter the influence of industry. Despite changes in the parties forming the government, the justification and demands for a national defence industry have remained unaltered since 1970, as can be seen in the statements below, gleaned from a succession of defence White Papers. Altogether, there are five basic principles contained in these various defence-policy papers.[65]

First, the Federal Republic does not aspire to autarky in armaments. Therefore, it will avoid undesirable domestic dependencies.[66] It will also prevent the growth of surplus capacity, which must later be subsidised or otherwise supported.[67] In 1963, 55 percent of defence expenditures for military research and development, procurement, and maintenance were allocated to German industry.[68] The current figure is 85 percent,[69] denoting a long upward trend, and calling into some question the avowed goal of avoiding autarky.

The second principle is that defence-production capacities in the Federal Republic be integrated into the market economy.[70]

They are "imbedded in the private economy"[71]; therefore an "isolated defence economy is unthinkable."[72] However, is this really the case? In accordance with the principle of free competition, there are many firms who are sellers; but on the buyer's side, there is only the government. Thus the government rules the market because its extent and structure is directed by the requirements of the Bundeswehr, and not ideally by "the possibilities and chances of arms export."[73] However, Bonn insists that it "cannot and does not intend to assume entrepreneurial responsibility," nor will it take over employment or contract guarantees, "although it endeavours to maintain such defence production as is indispensable for the Bundeswehr."[74] A conflict in principle is bound to result, because the self-interested industry will not provide capacity for defence and political reasons, but rather, as will be argued later, for reasons of profit generated in all markets.

The third principle is that a national defence industry "creates opportunities to have a voice and to influence developments in the Alliance."[75] Partnership in the Alliance, it is held, demands "independent ability."[76] Bonn, therefore, seeks "to participate in international cooperation as an equal."[77]

Fourth, it is maintained that defence technology research, development, and production at the advanced technological levels required for military equipment can and do provide important stimuli for civilian industry.[78] Therefore, the production of armaments with high technical innovation is to be encouraged at home.[79] For that reason, to cite one example, the new European fighter aircraft will feature a substantial amount of German production.[80]

Finally, defence capacities are needed "for production and maintenance"[81] of Bundeswehr material to create the personnel and materiel conditions for national logistics required by NATO.[82] Therefore the need exists for defence-industrial-base capacities in peace and war, especially for a conceivably longer war in Europe with conventional forces. The difference between the volumes of defence products needed in peace and war is not known, but exports could close the gap between the low requirements for peace and the higher volumes needed in war. In this latter regard, a crucially important factor seems to be the liability of a supplier in wartime. NATO countries — Germany included — must ponder whether German industry can supply them while parts of the country are the battlefield. Non-NATO countries as well can be expected to evince concern about this potential political liability, because defence procurements bind a nation for a long time.

MILITARY AID AS SUPPORT TO ARMS EXPORTS

Officially, the term "military aid" is not used, but I shall apply it here to embrace defence aid, equipment aid, and training aid. *Defence aid* is proof of the solidarity of the Federal Republic with NATO. Since 1964, shipments of defence material from Germany have been made to Turkey, Greece, and Portugal without payment. To some extent, this material has been surplus to the needs of the Bundeswehr, but it has still meant money out of the German budget.

In total, 3.4 billion DM were so disbursed up to 1983. In addition, funds totalling 130 million DM are being given to Turkey, 70 million DM to Greece, and 45 million DM to Portugal in the current fiscal year. German industry profits directly from such transfers, because 80 percent of the goods are new products and only 20 percent are surplus. The deliveries consist of weapons, military equipment, and spare parts as well as manufacturing and maintenance facilities.[83] Even if the amounts involved are relatively small, German industry acquires reliable customers, particularly if Bonn is able to exert some influence upon the recipients. There is no question but that the delivery of Leopard I tanks to Turkey and Greece brought benefits to the struggling tank industry. The hypothesis that defence aid has the ability to open other markets cannot be proved, however, for Turkey bought a British rather than a German air-defence missile system.[84] German industry built air force maintenance facilities, factories for small arms, and navy installations. The tank-maintenance plant in Turkey demonstrates how that country's forces can move toward a posture of less dependence on foreigners; for Turkey now produces spare parts, optics, and tracks for different types of tanks, both for its own tanks as well as to compete in the international market. Eventually, Turkey hopes to develop the know-how to begin its own tank production.[85] Thus, the political aim of strengthening one's ally economically may only convey a short-lived advantage upon German industry, which likely will lose a customer and gain a competitor. But then, German industry itself developed in the same pattern after World War II.

The provision of *equipment and training aid* occurs in the context of cultivating Germany's foreign political relations, broadly conceived in terms of fostering the peaceful lives of nations. In states whose form of government, structure and stage of development give special functions to the military and police, "our own ideas of democracy and political values can be demonstrated in that way."[86] Therefore, equipment aid is an "instrument of foreign and peace policy." Although it is kept secret, the main effort is directed toward Africa, where publicity has surfaced regarding German assistance in constructing communication systems in Ruanda and Zaire, military hospitals in Zaire, Congo, and Burundi, and an air transport system in Malawi. Weapons and ammunition, as well as the machines and installations to produce them, are not part of equipment aid. Thus, only other defence products can be exported in accordance with the AWG. Some 40-60 million DM will be spent annually by the government. A strategy of developing markets cannot be demonstrated, but seems unlikely as there is no arms export and the military is supported more as a domestic power than as a fighting force.

Training aid is not directly related to German arms exports. In 1985, soldiers of 19 African, 19 Asiatic, and six South American countries, as well as soldiers from Australia, Yugoslavia, and Switzerland, received exposure to German military doctrine, which could stimulate future demand for German defence products.[87]

In summary, military aid makes for sometimes good but often ambiguous politics.[88] It can assist a government, but not necessarily make it an ally, as has been shown most dramatically by the relationship between Egypt and the Soviet Union.

THE IMPORTANCE OF EXPORTS TO THE GERMAN DEFENCE INDUSTRY

The defence industry produces defence goods as a complement to civil goods and accounts, on average, for not more than 3.4 percent of the total value produced by all German industry. Of the firms producing defence products, military goods account for only seven percent of total output. In the automobile industry, this share drops to between one and two percent; in the shipbuilding industry, it is 10 percent. Only the aerospace industry and the weapons and ammunition industries have defence shares of more than 50 percent.[89] To conclude that the economic impact of defence industries can be neglected would be unwise, since 3.4 percent of total value, as well as the importance of the 10 biggest defence-material producing companies, is hardly negligible. (Appendix 4.1)

Furthermore, it can be argued that the economic dependence of small and medium-sized businesses producing defence goods is high because 13 percent of all Bundeswehr contracts go to them. Their participation as subcontractors and suppliers for larger Bundeswehr contracts is not included in this figure.[90]

Officially, some 250,000 jobs are related to defence contracts. While this might be a conservative calculation,[91] it is not a trivial figure, as was acknowledged by Chancellor Kohl when he pointed to the creation of 600,000 jobs in 1982-86 as a major success of the government.

The importance of a national defence industry can be seen in the fact that Germany spent a constant 3.4 percent of its GNP for defence between 1981 and 1984; 23 percent of this expenditure was in capital equipment, and 85 percent of that amount went to German industry.[92]

The total economic importance of arms exports is shown by table 4.3. It can be noted that the value of the exports has been continually increasing since 1973 (except for 1982) and has become 10 times larger in a period of 10 years (1974-1984).

Shares of the GNP and of total exports have demonstrated a rising trend, but have not achieved the proportions reached in other European nations, as can be seen in table 4.4.

Generally, the conclusion may be drawn that arms exports simply reflect the normal economic trends followed by the German economy in the world market. Over a 10-year period (1973-83) the defence product share of 4.3 percent of the world's arms deliveries was relatively constant.[93]

The market structure of the defence industry is totally atypical of a free-market economy because the State is a monopoly buyer and industry is essentially an oligopoly. The response of the industry has been to concentrate its efforts in joint ventures under only a few large consortiums,[94] although the government has attempted to counter this move by passing business to mid-sized enterprises.[95] In general, however, the government reduces the risks to the industry, resulting from its awkward position in the market, by guaranteeing defence capacities for the requirements of the Bundeswehr.[96] The NATO Long-Term Defence Program and

Table 4.3: *Arms Exports*

Year	Arms Export million dollars current	% Arms Export to Total Export	% Arms Export to GNP
1967	58	0.27	0.029
1968	98	0.39	0.044
1969	101	0.35	0.040
1970	189	0.55	0.067
1971	130	0.33	0.042
1972	320	0.68	0.112
1973	120	0.18	0.038
1974	210	0.23	0.061
1975	420	0.47	0.113
1976	700	0.69	0.170
1977	900	0.76	0.200
1978	975	0.68	0.195
1979	1200	0.70	0.212
1980	1400	0.73	0.223
1981	1400	0.80	0.203
1982	900	0.50	0.135
1983	1800	1.10	0.257
1984	2300		

Source: Extract from *ACDA* 1978 p. 131 and *ACDA* 1985 pp. 63, 105.

Table 4.4: *Percentage of Arms Exports as Part of Total Exports*

Year	France	U.K.	Italy	Switzerland	FRG
1973	2.3	2.0	0.6	0.4	0.2
1974	1.5	1.4	0.6	0.5	0.2
1975	1.3	1.2	0.7	1.2	0.5
1976	1.9	1.6	1.0	1.6	0.7
1977	1.8	1.6	0.8	1.8	0.8
1978	2.3	2.1	1.4	1.2	0.7
1979	1.5	1.4	0.9	1.3	0.7
1980	2.4	1.7	0.9	2.2	0.7
1981	4.1	2.7	1.5	1.3	0.8
1982	3.7	2.1	1.6	1.4	0.5
1983	4.5	1.7	1.4	1.3	1.1

Source: Extract from *ACDA* 85, pp. 104, 105, 109, 124, 127.

the Bundeswehr Plan, spanning 15 years, give good indicators for industrial planning and balance the uncertainties of this unusual market. Under these circumstances it should be possible to adapt capacity to domestic demand. This postulates keeping existing facilities steadily busy, which is one of the intentions of the government.[97] It is also a demand of the unions.[98] In fact, defence production is "burdened by unavoidable procurement cycles which come in patches." It is characterised by the peaks and hollows of orders:

> The manufacturing of defence products is burdened with one characteristic, namely the discontinuity of the military requirement. Periods of keeping busy and operating above capacity are followed by periods of order decline. The high-grade specialization of employees and manufacturing means that changes are only possible on a limited scale. On the other hand, the opportunities available to the governmental purchaser are limited to means of postponing replacement — and modernization terms.[99]

From the point of view of the military, harmonising the production time of weapon systems with their time in service is impossible because only short delivery times will guarantee the latest equipment. Consequently, trying to keep the industry busy with exports appears to be a worthwhile pursuit.

Germany provides the largest portion of the Alliance's land forces and over 60 percent of the main battle tanks earmarked for the defence of Central Europe. It is clear that Germany cannot abandon national tank production. Battle tanks of the Leopard series are considered to be among the best in the world. The Leopard 1 and its family of vehicles was an immense export success in several NATO countries and in Australia between 1968 and 1979, but such major military powers as the U.S., United Kingdom, and France never did become customers. Total production of the Leopard series was absorbed as follows:

Bundeswehr	2437 tanks and 745 family vehicles
Export Market	1404 tanks and 234 family vehicles
Italy (in licence)	720 tanks

Recipient countries in chronological order were: Belgium 334 tanks, Netherlands 468, Norway 78, Italy 200, Denmark 120, Australia 90, and Canada 114.[100] The unit costs undoubtedly would have been reduced because of the extension of the original order by about 57 percent, but the existence or extent of any such reduction is difficult to document. However, it seems reasonable to assume that, on average, 5000 jobs were created or secured.[101] One must question the often-heard remark that arms exports simply create over-capacity.[102] As Appendix 4.2 indicates, the peak of production was required for procurement of the Bundeswehr's needs, and exports only maintained production on a lower scale until the commencement of the new Leopard 2 series.

Cautious estimates indicate that production costs could be lowered by more than five percent and joint spare-parts supply could also result in price reductions. For the foreign customers, the deal was made sweeter by the fact that they were not required to pay a share of development costs, which reached a level of 102,000 DM per tank.[103] In addition, Krauss-Maffei offered offset business to help secure orders and allowed Italy to produce tanks under licence. (Appendix 4.4)

The Leopard 2 tank has not been able to establish the export successes of its predecessor to date, although it is rated as a top model. Since the government's decision not to give a licence for export to Saudi Arabia, no new customers have appeared. Co-production with Egypt, for example, is inconceivable for the same reason.[104] So far there have been 445 Leopard 2 sales to the Netherlands, which also receives 100-percent offsets that are guaranteed 40 percent by industry and 60 percent by government.[105] A further 35 tanks have been exported to Switzerland, which will also build 345 under licence, to keep its own defence industry busy and to obtain transfer of technology.[106] The production of the Leopard 2 will thus be completed very soon, although the Bundeswehr has purchased 250 more, for a total of 2050 tanks. The commencement of production of a new battle tank cannot be expected before 1999. An order gap of more than 10 years will result, and orders for weapons systems supplied by the four tank-builders (Krauss-Maffei, Thyssen-Henschel, Rheinmetall, and Krupp MAK) will likely decrease to a mere 15 percent of the volume attained between 1975 and 1985, according to Krauss-Maffei officials.

The attempt to sell the air-defence system, the Wildcat, which was not ordered by the Bundeswehr, failed. The future for some firms will clearly be difficult. To alleviate some of their problems, Krauss-Maffei and Diehl have developed an armoured combat-vehicle family, Puma, at their own risk and without government orders or financial aid, hoping to replace the American M113. The German state secretary responsible for armament declared, referring to this weapon system: "The industry cannot invent requirements and then push us to acquire the product under any circumstances." The head of Krauss-Maffei responded that he expected the best chances for the vehicle in export.[107] Insufficient orders forced them to limit their capacity to one production line[108] since, in the words of one Krauss-Maffei official, "the ultimate-purpose of a company is to earn money."[109] However, the decision will influence the capabilities of the German industrial base in peace and war and, therefore, government will be involved in either reducing the capacity or lifting some export restrictions.

The case of shipbuilding

The shipbuilding industry in Germany, as in other industrial countries, has been hit hard by both the decline of the world market in merchant shipbuilding and the rise of offshore capacity. The situation is complicated by the fact that the yards are located in a poor region highly dependent on shipbuilding, so employees released from shipyards further increase the already high German unemployment rate. Despite a reduction in their number and attempts to diversify, the German yards are under extreme competitive pressure, which reflects the worldwide trend that "commercial shipbuilding in general is in such critical condition that many yards are becoming more and more dependent on naval work."[110] The situation was so disastrous that the Minister of Defence decided to build six frigates of the 122 class for the Bundesmarine in five yards. He admitted that the construction of "all six frigates in one yard [would be] the most economic solution," but insisted that "it is also necessary to take into account the total economic imperatives which are given by an insufficient number of orders to the yard industry."[111] According to Maritime Defence, "Germans, among all other European shipbuilders and despite a number of closures, are probably most healthy despite being at the bottom of the subsidy table."[112] Under those conditions it is no wonder that the Chief of Staff for the Navy declared that it would be useful for the defence industrial base to protect the yard capacities of today; and the government, significantly, has been more supportive of ship exports than of tanks, taking responsibility for the provision of guarantees (called Hermes credits) for exports to Turkey, Malaysia, Oman, and Argentina.[113]

The German shipbuilding industry took its opportunities, and today more than 200 ships and boats from German yards or from German designs are in service in 23 of 150 foreign navies. It is striking that the traditional large blue-water navies are not included in this list of customers, and that from its NATO allies only Belgium, Denmark, Greece, Norway, Portugal, and Turkey have purchased ships. German boats are spread worldwide from the Eastern Mediterranean to the South Atlantic, Southeast Pacific, Caribbean, Indian and South Chinese Oceans, and the Indonesian archipelago. With the exception of Uruguay, Guayana, and Surinam, every South American coastal country is a customer, and Germany is the main supplier to Argentina (see table 4.5).

Table 4.5: *Recipient Countries of German Warships/Boats*

NATO	South America	Africa	Middle East	Asia-Pacific
Belgium	Argentina	Ghana	Bahrain	India
Denmark	Brazil	Nigeria	Kuwait	Indonesia
Greece	Chile			Korea
Norway	Colombia			Malaysia
Portugal	Ecuador			Singapore
Turkey	Peru			Thailand
	Venezuela			

Source: *Jane's Fighting Ships* 85-86 (Extract).

In contrast to army and air force equipment, naval exports are not direct reproductions of ships and boats in the Germany navy.[114]

One exceptionally successful arrangement has been the export of conventionally propelled submarines. Since 1950, more of these submarines have been built in Germany than in all other countries in the world except the Soviet Union. Altogether, 112 submarines were ordered, 34 of which were built for the German navy. Of the remaining 78 boats, an order of six from Iran was stopped by Bonn in 1979, and 16 have been built under licence by foreign yards (three at the Vickers yard for Israel); Norway, Greece, and Turkey are the only NATO partners who have received them. The boat concept and development was completed by the Ingenieur-Büro Lübeck (IKL) with 290 highly qualified employees. The Howaldt-Deutsche Werft in Kieddl and the Thyssen-Nordseewerft in Emden are constructing the boats with an employee force of 2000 constantly employed in the submarine business. The costs for a submarine are between 80 and 200 million DM and the value of total sales is approximately 10 billion DM.[115] These figures show the economic importance of submarine exports in the region, since this is the only feasible way in which the highly specialised employees could be retained. The development of this technical capability has come as a direct benefit of the construction of modern U-boats for the German navy.

The Luerssen yard, a world leader in the production of fast patrol boats, in which Germany and France have the lion's share, reports a similar pattern.[116] It has not been able to keep its work force of 1,100 busy through construction of civilian ships since 1975. In the last 10 years, therefore, the repair and civil construction portion of its business has been around 20-percent capacity, while 80 percent is engaged in naval shipbuilding, of which three-quarters is construction for foreign navies. That means that 60 percent of its total capacity is devoted to naval exports.

Germany also entered the frigate and corvette market by successfully developing a special export type called MEKO, which is built in many foreign shipyards under licence.[117]

By the end of the 1970s, the German shipbuilding industry declared officially that the average annual value of ships delivered to foreign navies was 200-400 million DM, and this figure doubled in the early 1980s. It had orders to a value of four billion DM in 1983 but that amount will doubtless decline due to lack of bigger projects. Exports to foreign navies are "to the German yard industry an indispensable part in securing its survival in the near future."[118]

It might be argued that warship-building does not improve the chances of survival of the German shipbuilding industry over a longer period, because other countries, influenced by licenced-building, will be capable of establishing their own facilities within the next 10 years. As a result, there will be greater overcapacity and fiercer competition for survival. This is possible, maybe probable, but an industry like Germany's, embedded in a free-market economy, should be able to compete, especially given its high technical standards and its reliability. Nevertheless, Bonn might have to decide which facilities should survive independently of economic considerations in order to protect the German defence industrial base. To sum up, the export of warships and boats has secured and created jobs, preserved yard capacity and sustained profits, provided the technical know-how for the Germany navy, and enhanced the defence industrial base for peace and war. However, all of this comes at the political price of making Germany one of the leading arms exporters in the world.

The Federal Republic cannot renounce a national defence industry for political reasons related to security, economics, and employment. Defence industry is integrated into civilian industry and obeys the rules of the market economy. It is profit-oriented first and foremost and seeks product turnover. Recently it has been prepared to moderate capacity, but it is in its interest to create requirements either by extending the market through exports or by pressing the government to protect its capacity for reasons of self-defence. The government must be responsive to this pressure because it is the government that makes the decision about access to the market and, as the only customer, determines the requirements for the Bundeswehr. As shown by the examples of the tank and ship-building industries, productive capacity cannot be fully utilised as long as the Bundeswehr is the only customer. There may be periods of more than a decade without production, and yet it is necessary to retain highly qualified and specialised employees. The same can be assumed for the industrial branches that depend more on arms production, such as ammunition and the aerospace industry. Turnover in the latter will be reduced through production of the European Fighter Aircraft, of which the German Air Force will buy 250 to replace its 324 Tornados.[119]

Arms export is one means of moderating fluctuations in production, thereby retaining technical skills and industrial capacity. The minimum level of capacity for political-security reasons can only be determined and then subsidised by the government. The economic demands can be regulated by the market, which is highly influenced by the licencing practices of the government. It should be noted that the government does not wish to absolve German defence producers from participating in hard competition. The industry may have to follow the route of exporting special lower-cost products manufactured, for example, by the shipbuilding industry or by the armoured vehicle division of Thyssen-Henschel. The Bundeswehr may also benefit from such production.

ARMAMENT COOPERATION IN THE ALLIANCE

The former Secretary General of NATO, Lord Carrington, called for the strengthening of arms cooperation in NATO to avoid "structural disarmament."[120] In November 1986, Chancellor Kohl expressed his country's agreement that the "continuation and intensification of armament cooperation improves the ability of our forces to cooperate in operations, promotes necessary standardisation, and not least provides a means of using budgetary money effectively"; he particularly stressed cooperation with France.[121] Indeed, the Federal Republic depends on cooperation, because it neither possesses nor aspires to autarky. It supports the European pillar first and foremost and then seeks balanced transatlantic armaments.[122] Accordingly, more than 50 percent of all cooperative projects are carried out with European partners only, and the ratio of armaments flow between the United States and the Federal Republic has been reduced from 10:1 during the 1960s and 1970s to 2:1 in 1985.

Armament cooperation is defined for this purpose as purchase, licenced production, or joint research, development, production, and logistics. We have in mind primarily cooperation based on governmental agreements, while the direct industrial cooperation favoured by the U.S. will, in the German view, only be used to supplement governmental cooperation.

Armament cooperation in NATO has to begin with the principle that it is an alliance of sovereign members, in which any contradiction between national and alliance interests can lead to conflicts at any time. A declaration by the former German Armament Director seems frank on this point: "Every partner hopes to get advantage for its benefit in this cooperation."[123] This observation indicates a desire for compromise, but it remains a caution against utopian hopes.

From a German perspective armaments cooperation is intended to maximise benefits in the political, military, economic, and technological domains.[124] In terms of *political* objectives, an even closer integration of the Alliance is useful because collaborative development and production of equipment enhances the Allies' knowledge of and confidence in each other. This aim seems unarguable, but stressing the importance of a more independent Europe versus the U.S. (or even North America) can lead to political differences and conflict within the Alliance as long as Europe has no security policy of its own.[125]

Insofar as concerns the *military* aims, combat power will be improved if cooperation increases standardisation and integration. Such standardisation did exist in the 1950s and early 1960s, when American equipment dominated the Alliance (for instance, M47 and M48 tanks, Fletcher-class destroyers, and F-84 and F-86 combat aircraft). However, the build-up of German and other European defence industries led to a lack of standardisation, as in the case of the procurement of national tanks in Germany, France, Great Britain, and, more recently, Italy. German industry will have a special importance in supplementing the combat power of the Alliance in wartime. Consideration must be given to its location, however, since a battle on national territory has the advantage of short lines of communication but the disadvantage of placing industry at risk.

The economic benefit of cooperation is clear: more effective use of national public funds for defence can be made. Economic advantages can result from sharing the cost of development and production work, larger production runs, common logistics and training. These advantages should not mean that the cheapest solution is always chosen because consideration must also be given to the requirements of national industry. Thus, the Chief of Staff of the German Air Force, Lt.-General Eberhard Eimler, stated that the GAF could have fulfilled its mission with the American F-18 instead of the European Fighter Aircraft, and that this would have achieved savings of 10 billion DM.[126] However, the decision to build the EFA is of the greatest significance to Germany's aerospace industry; one source concludes that as a result of the EFA, "penetration of the European market by the U.S. aerospace industry is blocked.... Also, survival of a highly capable European aerospace industry should be ensured for many years to come."[127] As the Federal Republic's Armament Director observed, armament cooperation demands "balanced participation"; ideally, the project should be directed according to requirement figures. Officials of the Ministry of Defence believe that rationalisation will be able to increase efficiency by about 30 percent over the next few years. On the other hand, armament State Secretary Dr. Timmermann has stated more pessimistically that because of national self-interest, possible cost advantages will be more than balanced.[128]

Finally, *technological* benefits can accrue as a result of the exchange of technical and scientific expertise. The European Fighter Aircraft project is the best current example of the perception that arms collaboration makes technological sense. Former Minister of Defence Wörner expressed this sentiment when he told the parliamentary Defence Committee that Germany would "not allow ourselves to get into the situation in the 1980s and 1990s where we are only a licenced producer for the Americans and nothing else."[129] To the Europeans, he made clear that only full technology transfer would allow German participation, saying, "we have to insist that our own national aviation industry retain its viability.... I would neither join the French prototype nor the English prototype.... Let's make a common aircraft, or we'll make our own."[130]

Thus it can be said that the above four aims of armament cooperation sometimes reinforce, but at other times conflict with each other. Germany will use cooperation in a bid to preserve its capacity, without necessarily ever determining the size of that capacity. German industry can be expected to participate in all cooperation projects to the extent the Bundeswehr requires, although in the category of defence products, some exceptions are conceivable where no national capacity now exists. In future, procurement and licenced-manufacture will be the exception and collaborative research, development, production, and logistics will be the norm. Only in that way can national self-interest and the common good of the allies be harmonised. NATO's armament cooperation, therefore, can be interpreted as a special form of offset policy in which balanced interests are decisive to success.

It should be noted that all countries handle their export licences differently and that cooperation could be imperiled if the partners are limited in their freedom of action. In particular, that is true of the cooperation of the Federal Republic with its main partners, France and the United Kingdom, both of whom are more aggressive in their export policies. The Federal Republic continues to give priority to cooperation rather than enforcing its own export restrictions. Thus German industry profits from the exports of its partners, while Bonn can disclaim any official political responsibility for those exports. For instance, German industry directly participated in the export of 72 Tornado aircraft to Saudi Arabia by the United Kingdom, as well as in the French export successes of Alpha Jet aircraft and Milan, Hot, and Roland missiles. The sales of these latter three missiles will have the effect of increasing orders to German industry by about 150 percent, while reducing the costs to the Bundeswehr by 10 to 20 percent.[131]

The advantage of armament cooperation for German industrial exports can also be seen in the French-German anti-tank-helicopter project (PAH2), where Germany is the pilot nation but the joint enterprise was established with a seat in Paris, acting under French law. On the other hand, it can be supposed that Germany is a favourite partner for cooperation because its presence is not felt in all parts of the world and it is not an aggressive competitor with a complete range of defence products.

Appendix 4.3 shows that the Federal Republic is working with France primarily with army equipment; cooperation with the United Kingdom includes equipment for all the services. The main effort with the United States is in high-technology aerospace products. According to information provided by the Ministry of Defence, the number of collaborative efforts is steadily increasing. During the last 30 years, about 55 cooperative projects (without subsystems) were completed; during the next 15 years, 44 projects are planned. The percentage of the value of military procurement based on cooperative projects will increase from 45 percent between 1985 and 1990 to 70 percent between 1985 and 2000.

To achieve that aim, Bonn is willing to go to unusual lengths as can be seen in the cases of airborne early-warning system, AWACS, and the air- defence missile system, PATRIOT, both of which are being produced with the U.S. The AWACS offset arrangement is expected to strengthen the integration of the forces in different fields. German industry is directly involved in the AWACS program; the German 120-mm smooth-bore tank gun is being built under licence by the U.S. for its tanks; and the latter purchases communication systems and commercial non-tactical wheeled vehicles for its troops in Europe.[132]

The PATRIOT offset will strengthen air defence in Central Europe:

> The decisive feature of this arrangement is that goods are being exchanged for goods plus services. The United States makes available to the Federal Republic of Germany, from U.S. stocks, Patriot systems for the air defence belt in the Federal Republic of Germany. In exchange, the Federal Republic of Germany procures for the U.S. forces Roland systems for the protection of U.S. airfields in the Federal Republic of Germany and mans and operates these systems as well as additional tactical U.S. Patriot systems until U.S. and German expenditures are balanced.[133]

In this case, three of the four cooperation aims can be achieved; it remains unclear, though, how Germany will be able to reap any of the technological gains associated with the PATRIOT system, notwithstanding former Defence Minister Wörner's rather vague claim that there will be such gains, associated with logistical support.[134]

The Federal Republic cannot renounce armament cooperation in NATO, due both to its lack of self-sufficiency and its need to achieve political, military, economic, and technological goals. Germany is protecting its own defence industrial base through cooperation, even if it cannot expect to extend that base at the expense of its allies. Real mission-and burden-sharing, which will influence the defence capacity of all NATO countries, is not yet in sight on a transatlantic basis; but more narrowly focused European cooperation is already a reality. Germany directly benefits from the export successes of its partner countries through cooperative production, while hoping it will not have to pay the political price associated with arms exports.

CONCLUSION: IN SEARCH OF POLICY COHERENCE

German arms exports and policy are currently in crisis. The Federal Republic has established itself as one of the five leading arms-exporting countries in the world, although it has officially committed itself to a very restrictive arms-export policy, one that puts Germany's credibility in doubt both at home and abroad. This is a problem even though arms exports are only 0.3 percent of total exports, making Germany less dependent on such exports than either Switzerland or Sweden, and on a par with Canada. It should also be noted that Germany's official development aid and total exports to developing countries are substantially higher than its arms exports to these same countries.[135]

A decisive aspect of the crisis stems from the difference between appearance and reality. Foreign-security and economic-political aims are often lost in a confusion of individual decisions. Postulated distinctions between deadly weapons and less lethal defence products, between dangerous and less dangerous weapons, and between offensive and defensive weapons escape logic. Declaratory policy notwithstanding, non-NATO countries and not the Allies are the main customers of German arms makers.

Economic welfare does not depend primarily on the defence industry, but security and political intentions do force the government into securing a defence industrial base. The existing form of market-economy (and therefore privately provided) defence capacity is encountering more and more difficulties, especially with large high-technology weapon systems, because neither the Bundeswehr nor cooperative projects with NATO can keep the facilities fully utilised. The military market is characterised by high development costs, small orders, and erratic demand. The profit-oriented industry must react to demand either by finding additional markets or through the reduction of defence-goods production.

This conflict can be resolved only by the federal government, because it has to suffer the political and economic costs as both the export licencer and the customer. The delivery of defence products to a foreign country implies that the country and its government are supported. The delivery, however, may have a stabilising or destabilising influence, and of necessity carries risks. The people of Germany must be made aware of the political risks that are always inherent in acting in the world.

There are two possible ways in which Bonn can restore credibility to its arms-export policy. It could limit the trade of defence products to NATO and similar countries. This would minimise the risk that German defence products could be committed to peace-disturbing actions, but at the cost of also drastically reducing Germany's own capacity. Or, it could draw up a list of countries to which it is willing to deliver defence products, and which it is willing to accept as visible partners in production and export. It is not intended that this list follow the government line as in the case of military aid, where recipients are reviewed yearly. Such a list would instead be a clear signal that the Federal Republic has assumed the responsibilities and the risks of world policy. The list would give the export policy a higher degree of credibility, but would also limit its flexibility. Germany's defence industry would be permitted to compete in a more open global market, but on the other hand there would be less of a propensity for government intervention to guarantee German capacity in defence production. Such intervention probably would not be excluded altogether because of the fierce competition in the world market.

Independently of these solutions, there remains the hope of rationalising arms exports as a part of a common security-political strategy in NATO, or in the Western European Union. Above all, there is a compelling need to adapt the "Export Principles 82" to the real world, which would *inter alia* require redefining the terms "war weapons" and "defence goods."

As an arms exporter, the Federal Republic need wear neither a hair shirt nor a halo.

Notes

[1] Manfred Timmermann, " Rüstungs kooperation - Innovation und Wettbewerb," *Truppenpraxis* 4/1985, p. 319.

[2] Manfred Wörner, "Wennman die Zweibahnstrasse ernst nimmt, heisst das auch Technologie austauschund darauf bestehen wir," *Wehrtechnik* 2/1985, p. 18.

[3] Klaus Peter Treche, "Rüstungs kapazitäten in der Bundesrepublik Deutschland," *Wehrwissenschaftliche Rundschau* 4/1981, p. 107.

[4]U.S. Arms Control and Disarmament Agency (ACDA), "World Military Expenditures and Arms Transfers 1985," Stockholm International Peace Research Institute (SIPRI), "World Armament and Disarmament Yearbook 1985." While ACDA counts all conventional "weapons of war, parts thereof, ammunition, support equipment, and other commodities designed for military use," SIPRI is only counting heavy weapons.

[5]Federal Minister of Defence, "The Situation and the Development of the Federal Armed Forces," No. 841 (White Paper 1985).

[6]Translation of the law by Joachim Krause and Gale Mattox, "From Kiel to Port Stanley: The Arms Sales Debate," *United States Naval Institute - Proceedings* (March 1984): 180.

[7]Eckehart Ehrenberg, "Die deutsche Rüstungs export," *Wehrtechnik* 4/1981, p. 16.

[8]Hagen Hartmann, "Waffen fürden Frieden? Zur Philosophie deutscher Wehrtechnik," *Criticon* 69, Januar/Februar 1982, p. 35.

[9]Michael Brzoska, "Rüstungs export politik in der Bundesrepublik," *Aus Politik und Zeitgeschichte/Beilage zur Wochenzeitung - Das Parlament* 18/1984, p. 20.

[10]Reinhard Lichtenegger,"Entwicklungstendenzen und Probleme der Rücksichtigung eines möglichen Rüstungsgeschäftes mit Saudiarabien," *Dokzent*, BW-RB1600.

[11]Presse-und Informations amt der Bundesregierung, *Stichworte zur Sicherheits politick*, Nr. 1/1987, Bonn vom Januar 1987, pp. 13, 14.

[12]See, footnote 9 and Cindy Cannizzo, *The Gun-Merchants: Politics and Policies of the Major Arms Suppliers* (New York: Pergamon Press, 1980), p. 106.

[13]See, Cannizzo, *The Gun-Merchants*, p. 107.

[14]See, Presse-und Informations amt der Bundesregierung, Nr. 11/1987, *Stichworte zur Sicherheits politik*, pp. 14, 15.

[15]Frederic S. Pearson, "Of Leopards and Cheetahs: West Germany's Role as a Mid-sized Arms Supplier," *Orbis* (Spring 1985): 17; *Dokzent* PA6116.

[16]Hagen Hartmann, "Waffen für den Frieden?," p. 35.

[17]See Pearson, "Of Leopards and Cheetahs."

[18]*Washington Post*, 12 December 1986, p. 1.

[19]Bruce E. Arlinghaus, *Arms for Africa* (Lexington, Mass.: D.C. Heath, 1983), p. 6.

[20]Brzoska, "Rüstungs export politik," p. 17.

[21]Ibid.

[22]See, Presse-und Informations amt der Bundesregierung, *Stichworte zur Sicherheits politik*, pp. 17, 18.

[23]See, Presse-und Informations amt der Bundesregierung, "*Bulletin - Politische Grundsätze der Bundesregierung für den Export von*

Kriegswaffen und soustigen Rüstungs gütern vom 28.4.1982," Nr. 38 vom 5. Mai 1982, pp. 309-11.

[24]Regina H. E. Cowen, *Defense Procurement in the Federal Republic of Germany* (Boulder, Colo.: Westview Press, 1986), pp. 269-71; also see, Cannizzo, *The Gun-Merchants*, p. 107.

[25]Joachim Krause, "Trendwende in der deutschen Rüstungs export politik," *Europa archiv*, Folge 17/1982, p. 527.

[26]Ibid.

[27]See, Presse-und Informations amt der Bundesregierung, Nr. 11/1987, p. 17.

[28]Wilhelm Dietl, *Waffen für die Welt* (München: Droemer und Knaur, 1986), p. 114.

[29]Ibid., p. 117.

[30]*Frankfurter Allgemeine Zeitung*, "Der U-Boot Ausschuss beginnt Vernehmungen," vom 12.1.87, and "U-Boote für Israel von der SPD/FDP Regierung geuehmigt," vom 3.1.87.

[31]See, Brzoska, "Rüstungs export politik," p. 24.

[32]See, Presse-und Informations amt der Bundesregierung, Nr. 11/87, p. 18.

[33]See, Krause,"Trendwende in der deutschen Rüstungs export politic?," p. 532.

[34]Brzoska, "Rüstungs export politik," p. 22.

[35]Pearson, "Of Leopards and Cheetahs," p. 167.

[36]Wolfgang Hoffmann, "Deutsches audie Front-Die Bundesrepublik demnächst Waffenschmiede der Welt," *Die Zeit*, vom 30 Januar 1981, p. 10.

[37]Wolfgang Flume and Jürgen Rohwer, "U-Bootbau in Deutschland," *Marinerundschau*, 9/1982, p. 478.

[38]Ulrich Albrecht, "The Federal Republic of Germany and Italy: New Strategies of Mid-sized Weapons Exporters?," *Journal of International Affairs* 40 (Summer 1986): 130-31.

[39]Presse-und Informations amt der Bundesregierung, *Weissbuch* 1971/1972, No. 172.

[40]Joachim Krause, "Trendwende in der deutschen Rulstungs export politik?", *Europa archiv*, Folge 17 in 1982, p. 532.

[41]*Welt am Sonntag*, vom 25.1.1987, p. 2.

[42]Krause, "Trendwende in der deutschen Rüstungs export politik?" p. 532.

[43]Franz-Josef Strauss, "Wer die Deutschen kriminalisieren will, der fälscht Geschichte," *Die Welt* vom 19.1.87.

[44]SIPRI Yearbook 1985, p. 362.

[45]Carl v. Clausewitz, *On War*, edited and translated by Michael Howard and Peter Paret (Princeton: Princeton University Press, 1976), Book 6, Chapter One, p. 357.

[46]Der Bundesminister der Vertedigung - Führungsstab des Heeres - III 6 vom 28.9.1973, *Führung im Gefecht* (TF/G) HDv 100/100-VS-NfD, No. 1036.

[47]Carnes Lord, "Taking Soviet Defenses Seriously," *Washington Quarterly* (Fall 1986): 84.

[48]Wehrpolitische Informationen 23/24 in 1982, p. 4.

[49]*Die Welt*, vom 28.11.1986, p. 2.

[50]The Federal Minister of Defence, "White Paper 1985 - The Situation and the Development of the Federal Armed Forces," No. 369.

[51]Brzoska, "Rüstungs export politik," p. 21.

[52]Cowen, "Defense Procurement in the Federal Republic of Germany," p. 260.

[53]Die Grünen - Bundesgeschäftsstelle, *Lasst die Republik er Gruunen*, für den 6.3.1983, p. 1.

[54]F.D.P. - Landesverband Baden-Württemberg, "Beschluss des 64. ordentlichen Landesparteitages vom 27.2.1982," p. 14.

[55]*Die Welt*, vom Januar 1987, "Möllemann als Bote der Saudis."

[56]Schäuble, Bundesminister "Interview," *Frankfurter Neue Presse*, vom 20.12.1986.

[57]Strauss, "Wer die Deutschen kriminalisieren will."

[58]Wolfgang Hoffmann, "Deutsches au die Front," *Die Zeit*, vom 30.1.1981.

[59]Wehrreport - Berufspolitische Information für den Verteidigungs bereich 12/1981, *Dokzent* No. AA4605.

[60]Klaus Mehrens, "Gewerkschaften und Abrüstung," *Frankfurterhefte*, 12/1980, pp. 30-35.

[61]H. Fiedler, "Zur Rolle des Militär - Industrie-Komplexes der BRD in der NATO - Hochiüstung," *Militärwesen*, 1/1981 (DDR), pp. 48-52.

[62]G. P. Melnikow, "Militärhilfe," *Sowjetische Militäreuzyklopädie* - Militärverlag (DDR) 1981, pp. 90, 91.

[63]Cowen, "Defense Procurement in the Federal Republic of Germany," p.260.

[64]*Wehrpolitische Information*, No. 32/1984, pp. 6-8.

[65]*White Paper 1970*, No. 194; *White Paper 1971/1972*, No. 173; *White Paper 1973/1974*, No. 255; *White Paper 1979*, No. 53; *White Paper 1985*, No. 835.

[66]*White Paper 1985*, No. 835.

[67]*White Paper 1971/1972*, No. 173.

[68]*White Paper 1973/1974*, No. 256.

[69]*White Paper 1985*, No. 830.

[70]*White Paper 1985*, No. 829.

[71]*White Paper 1973/1974*, No. 255.

[72]*White Paper 1970*, No. 194

[73]*White Paper 1985*, No. 828.

[74]*White Paper 1985*, No. 832.

[75]*White Paper 1985*, No. 827.

[76]*White Paper 1979*, No. 53.

[77]*White Paper 1970*, No. 194.

[78]*White Paper 1985*, No. 827.

[79]*White Paper 1973/1974*, No. 255.

[80]Dr. Manfred Wörner, "Take into account 5,000 exercises, 100,000 low-flying — really low-flying — missions, 400,000 foreign soldiers in garrisons in January. Those kinds of burdens I want taken into account when you are speaking of fair shares." *Armed Forces Journal International*, August 1985, p. 68.

[81]*White Paper 1985*, No. 827; *White Paper 1970*, No. 194.

[82]*White Paper 1983*, No. 235.

[83]Eberhard Finger, "BWB - Partner nicht nur der deutschen Streitkräfte," *Wehrtechnik* 2/1984, pp. 109, 110.

[84]Millard Barger and Benjamin F. Schemmer, "In the Era of NATO Arms Cooperation, Germany Gears Up for More Aggressive, Imaginative Sales Offensive," *Armed Forces Journal International* (August 1985): 52.

[85]Walter Gerent, "Aufbau einer Pauzerinstandsetzungskapazität in der Türkei," *Wehrtechnik* 9/1981, pp. 49-51.

[86]Deutscher Bundestag-10. Wahlperiode Drucksache, 10/2263 vom 7.11.84, p. 6.

[87]Finger, "BWB - Partner nicht nur der deutschen Streitkräfte," p. 109.

[88]Jehuda L. Wallach, "Militärhilfe als Mittel der politischen Strategie," *Wehrwissenschaftliche Rundschau* 3/1980, p. 83.

[89]Hans Peter and Wilfred Klank, "Neue Tendenzen der Herausbildung des Militär - Industrie-Komplexes in der BRD," IPW-Berichte (DDR) 3/1986, *Dokzent* No. CC0699, p. 19.

[90]*White Paper 1985*, No. 831.

[91]*White Paper 1985*, No. 359, and Albrecht, "The Federal Republic of Germany and Italy," p. 130.

[92]*White Paper 1985*, No. 244, and *ACDA 1985*, p. 63.

[93]*ACDA 1985*, p. 11.

[94]Klaus-Peter Treche, "Rüstungskapazitäten in der Bundesrepublik Deutschland; eine qualitative Analyse," *Wehrwissenschaftliche Rundschau* 4/1981, p. 107, and Cowen, "Defense Procurement in the Federal Republic of Germany," p. 214.

[95]Dr. Professor Manfred Timmermann, Staatssekretär, "Bedarfsgerechte Wehrtechnik zu wirtschaftlichen Bedingungen," *Soldat und Technik* 11/1985, p. 648.

[96]*White Paper 1985*, Nos. 827, 828.

[97]*White Paper 1985*, No. 832.

[98]Klaus Mehrens, "Gewerkschaften und Abrüstung," *Frankfurter Hefte* 12/1980, p. 34.

[99]Jo Rodejohann, *Die Rüstungsindustrie in der Bundesrepublik Deutschland auf dem Weg in die Krise*, HSFK (Hessische Stiftung Friedens-und Konfliktforschung) - Forschungs bericht 8/1985, p. 51.

[100]Oberstleutnant von Fritz Wyszecki, BWB unpublished document given to me.

[101]Hans-Peter Kaufmann, "Analyse von Wirkungen zentraler Rüstungskäufe auf die Wirtschaft der Bundesrepublik Deutschland und von Möglichkeiten einer wirtschaftspolitisch ausgerichteten Auftragsvergabe - untersucht am Beispiel des Kampfpanzer Leopard I," Hochschule der Bundeswehr München - Wirtschafts - und Organizations wissenschaften - Diplomarbeit vom 16.7.1980 (unpublished), p. 58.

[102]Rodejohann, *Die Rüstungsindustrie in der Bundesrepublik Deutschland*, p. 57.

[103]Kaufmann, "Analyse von Wirkungen zentraler Rüstungskäufe," p. 36.

[104]*Defense Weekly*, 2 March 1987, p. 7.

[105]Dr. Karl Schnell, Staatssekretär, "Rüstungskooperation in der NATO Bilanz und Ausblick," unpublished lecture to Gesellschaft für Wehrtechnik, April 1980, *Dokzent* No. 9408, p. 28.

[106]SIPRI Yearbook 84, Table 11B.

[107]*Wehrausbildung in Wort und Bild*, 5/1986, p. 316, and *Europäische Wehrkunde*, 8/1986, p. 479.

[108]*Jane's Weapon System 85-86*, p. 65.

[109]Harald Helex and Wolfgang Sadlowski Flume, "Krauss-Maffei - Just More than Tanks," *Military Technology* 9/1983, p. 59.

[110]*Maritime Defence* No. 1, January 1987, p. 3.

[111]Rodejohann, *Die Rüstungsindustrie in der Bundesrepublik Deutschland*, p. 83.

[112]*Maritime Defence* No. 1, January 1987, p. 5.

[113]*Wehrtechnik* 12/1986, p. 42.

[114]Eckhard Rohkamm, "Kriegssohiffexport - Die Sicht der Werftindustrie," *Marine forum* 3/1984, p. 54.

[115]Wolfgang Flume and Jürgen Rohwer, "U-Bootban in Deutschland," *Marine-Rundschau* 9/1982, pp. 474-84.

[116]Ugo Mazza, "The Naval Market: Trends and Prospect," *Military Technology* 4/1982, p. 84.

[117]*Martime Defence*, "The naval defence industry of the Federal Republic of Germany," September 1984, p. 318.

[118]Rohkamm, "Kriegsschiffexport," p. 120.

[119]Wolfgang Flume and Erhard Heckmann, "Neue Programme aber doch Soigen," *Wehrtechnik* 5.1984, p. 19.

[120]*Jane's Defence Weekly*, 28th February 1987, p. 32.

[121]Presse-und Informations amt der Bundesregierung "Bulletin" No. 135 vom 7.11.1986, p. 1133.

[122]*White Paper 1985*, Nos. 820, 822; and Dr. Manfred Wörner, "Interview," *Armed Forces Journal International*, August 1985, p. 56.

[123]Hans Eberhard, "Rüstungskooperation für die 90er Jahre," *Soldat und Technik* 8/1980, p. 416; and *White Paper 1985*, No. 816.

[124]*White Paper 1985*, Nos. 820, 822; and Dr. Manfred Wörner, "Interview," *Armed Forces Journal International*, August 1985, p. 56.

[125]Karl-Helmut Schnell, "Eine solide Grundlage," *Wehrtechnik* 2/1984, p. 20.

[126]Eberhard Eimler, "Unser Problem ist nicht die Verfügberkest von moderner Technologie, sondem die rechtzeitige Beschaftbarket moderner Waftensysteme in ansolichender Anzahl," *Wehrtechnik* 12/1986, p. 27.

[127]Erhard Heckmann, "EFA: A dream materialised(?)" *Military Technology* 2/1984, p. 53.

[128]Schnell, "Eine Solide Grundlage," p. 21; and Manfred Timmermann, "Rüstungskooperation - Innovation and Wettbewerb," *Truppenpraxis* 4/1985, p. 317.

[129]Wolfgang Flume and Erhard Heckmann, "Neue Programme aber doch Soigen," *Wehrtechnik* 5/1984, p. 19.

[130]Wörner, "Take into account," p. 68.

[131]Wolfgang Flume, "Rüstungskooperation mit Frankreich," *Wehrtechnik* 2/1984, p. 26.

[132]Peter Runge and Knut Schloenbach, "TransAtlantische Rüstunskooperation," 1.10.1984, unpublished manuscript.

[133]*White Paper 1985*, No. 826; and Bundesministerium der Verteidigung - Informations-und Pressetab, "Mittelungen an die Presse," vom 12.7.1984.

[134]Manfred Wörner, "Wenn man die Zweibahnstrasse ernst nimmt, heisst des auch Technologieaustansch und der auf bestehen wir," *Wehrtechnik* 2/1985, p. 18.

[135]Official figures of the German foreign office.

Appendix 4.1: MAJOR GERMAN ARMAMENTS PRODUCERS as of 1986

(Current Million DM)

Trust	Turnover Defence Products	Turnover in Total	Ranking in Defence Turnover	Percent Defence/ Total	Essential Products
Messerschmidt-Bölkow-Blohm GmbH (MBB), München	3375	5720	1	59	Aircraft, Helicopters, Laser Airspace Technology
Krauss-Maffei AG München	1550	1930	3	80	Tanks, Armoured Vehicles
Daimler-Benz AG Stuttgart	400				Trucks, Tank Development
AEG AG Frankfurt	1650	11000	2	15	Electronics, Radars, Electro-technics
MTU-Motoren-u. Turbinen GmbH München, Friedrichshafen	1208	2150	4	51	Engines, Turbines
Dornier GmbH Friedrichshafen	695	1510	8	46	Aircraft, Air Space Technology
Siemens AG München, Berlin	1145	45820	5	2	Electronics, Radars, Avionics
Rheinmetall GmbH Düsseldorf	980	2640	6	37	Guns
Krupp-MaK Maschinenbau GmbH Düsseldorf	720	1200	7	60	Tanks, Armoured Vehicles
Diehl-Gruppe Nürnberg	618	1810	9	33	Tracks, Ammo, Electronics Rockets, Small Weapons
Blohm u. Voss AG Hamburg	610	1220	10	50	Warships, Tank Parts

Source: Hans Peter and Wilfred Klank, "Neue Tendenzen der Herausbildung des Militär

Appendix 4.2: DELIVERY OF LEOPARD 1 TANKS

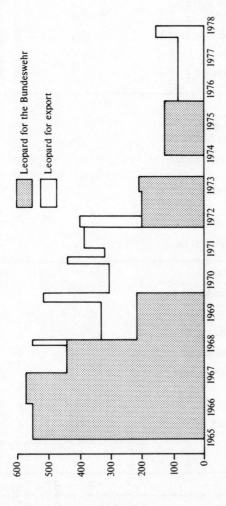

Leopard for the Bundeswehr

Leopard for export

Source: Hans-Peter Kaufman, "Analyse von Wirkungen zentaler Rüstungskaufe auf die Wirtschaft der Bundesrepublik Deutschland und von Möglichkeiten einer wirtschaftspolitisch ausgerichteten Auftragsvergabe untersucht am Beispiel des Kampfpanzer Leopard 1," p. 43.

Appendix 4.3: COLLABORATIVE COOPERATION WITH GERMAN PARTICIPATION

	Project	BE	CA	DA	FR	GR	IT
	Naval ground mine 80			x			
	Anti-invasion sea mine			x			
	Remote control for sea mines			x			
	Very short range air defence weapon system (RAM)			x			
	2nd generation anti-ship missile				x		
	Type 124 frigate		x		x		x
	Submarine class 211/ULa						
	Tornado MRCA						x
	Advanced Short Range Air-to-Air Missile (ASRAAM)						
	PATRIOT air defence missile system						
	Long-range air-to-ground guided missile						
	European Fighter Aircraft						x
	NATO identification system						
	155-1 field howitzer						x
	155-1 self-propelled howitzer						x
	CL289 reconnaissance drone		x		x		
	MARS/MLRS basic system				x		x
	PAH-2 anti-tank helicopter				x		
	Roland-2 air defence missile system				x		
	Mine laying system 85	x			x		
	3rd generation PARS				x		
ALL	Helicopter family				x		x
	TOTAL	1	2	4	9		7

Source: Extract from *Whitepaper 85* No. 824 and other documents, especially Noeske, Rolf, "Rüstungskooperation im Bünduis," *Marineforum* 10/1986, pp 343-46.

NL	NO	PO	SP	TU	UK	US	Remarks
							GE-developed
							GE-developed
	x				x		
						x	GE/US-developed
							Pilotnation FR
x			x		x	x	
	x						GE-developed, NO systems
					x		
	x				x		AMRAAM by US exchange possible
						x	US-developed and produced, offset by goods and services
					x	x	
		x			x		
					x	x	
					x		
					x		Future uncertain
					x		
							Pilotnation GE
x							
					x		
x					x		Not Started yet
3	3		2		12	5	

Appendix 4.4:
COMPENSATION COMMITMENTS OF KRAUSS-MAFFEI

(in million DM)

for: Leopard 1, Leopard 2, Gepard (anti-aircraft tank)
status: 23.2.83

Country	NL	NL	BE	DA	GR	CA	NO	AUS
Fulfilled	783	284	400	225	206	170	21	80
Overfilled	29	42.5	32	37.2	—	34	—	—
Remaining								25

Source: Harald Helex; Wolfgang Flume, Sadlowski, "Krauss-Maffei—Just more than tanks," *Military Technology* 9/83, p. 55.

5

The Swedish
Defence Industrial Base:
Implications for the Economy

Michael K. Hawes

INTRODUCTION

Sweden is a wealthy, western, industrialised nation long known for
its high standard of living, its unique brand of social democracy
(the so-called middle way), and its commitment to neutrality.
However, the "Swedish model" has come under increasing scrutiny
in recent years. Mounting public concern and confusion over the
frequent intrusions of Soviet submarines[1] off the Swedish coast,
dramatic increases in the cost of maintaining an independent
defence, the relative weakening of the Swedish economy, strains
within the Social Democratic party, and the growth of economic
interdependence have all challenged the credibility of the Swedish
model in general and Swedish neutrality in particular.[2] Yet, since
the return to power of a Social Democratic government in 1982,
Sweden has reaffirmed its long-standing commitment to disarmament and international negotiation on the one hand and the need
for a strong defence on the other.

Contemporary Swedish defence policy, then, has to be understood in terms of two critical facts. First, Sweden maintains a
policy of non-participation in alliances, thus is committed to
neutrality in the event of war. Second, for both practical and moral
reasons, Sweden has been a strong proponent of disarmament and
active peace. While these two factors are clearly interrelated, it is
the first that concerns us here. In particular, this chapter attempts
to address some of the implications of Swedish neutrality through
an analysis of Swedish defence industrial preparedness and an examination of the implications of such a policy on the economy.
While the primary task is to assess the domestic economic value
of such a policy, this chapter also hints at some of the security

implications of increasing interdependence and questions implicitlywhether the Swedish model is "exportable" elsewhere, such as to North America (where some, in Canada at least, have been known to advocate its importation).

The central thesis here is that the Swedish policy of neutrality, and the high level of defence industrial preparedness, is primarily a reflection of unique historical and geostrategic realities. I argue that defence spending, which takes place within the framework of neutrality, has (however indirectly) helped to sustain a level of industrial development and technological sophistication beyond the reasonable expectations of a small open economy. Further, I suggest that the level of integration between business and government is extremely high — such that the government's commitment to the principles of open competition does not appear to place it in conflict with the (seemingly) contradictory policy of neutrality, which requires that Sweden maintain a significant domestic capacity for defence industrial production.

The analysis begins with a brief historical review of Swedish defence policies and priorities, followed by an examination of the notion of "total defence" and an assessment of the level of defence industrial preparedness. It then proceeds to a survey of the structure of the Swedish defence industry and to an assessment of the implications of defence spending on the economy. Finally, the chapter sketches out some general conclusions about the relationship between government and industry with respect to defence, the value of military research and development to the economy, and the increasing vulnerability of smaller states in a world characterised by both economic and strategic interdependence.

THE ROOTS OF SWEDISH NEUTRALITY

Swedish neutrality is, in many ways, a unique phenomenon. In contrast to Swiss neutrality, Swedish neutrality is not guaranteed internationally. Also, unlike the Swiss who proclaimed their neutrality at the Congress of Vienna in 1815, the Swedes never formally declared themselves neutral. Nor, for that matter, is there any domestic or legal basis for their neutrality. The Austrians, by contrast, passed a neutrality law in 1955, and, in contradistinction to the Finnish, who remain neutral within the context of a special relationship with the Soviet Union[3], the Swedes are not formally tied to either of the superpowers. However, while Sweden is not a member of the North Atlantic Treaty Organization (NATO), it is undeniably a "western" country. To call Sweden non-aligned inappropriately suggests that it has no sympathies for either the east or the west. Perhaps, Sweden's situation can best be described as "alliance free" during peacetime and armed neutral in the event of war.[4] Another critical feature of Swedish neutrality is the fact that there is a solid consensus within Sweden with respect to this policy. As one Swedish government official noted "[both] the necessity and [the] virtue of neutrality is deeply ingrained at all levels of society ... it isn't an issue".[5]

While it is difficult to give a specific date for the origins of this policy, it is worth noting that Sweden successfully maintained its neutrality during both world wars and that the tradition of neutrality can be traced back to the early part of the 19th century. In fact, in January 1834, King Karl Johan wrote a confidential memorandum to the British and the Russian governments outlining a "formal explanation of my system of strict and independent neutrality."[6] The king was attempting to stay clear of war between the British and the Russians, which he believed would ensue from the Eastern Crisis of 1834. His reasons for enunciating this policy, which remain the basis for Swedish neutrality, were simple. Neutrality was a means of expressing Sweden's desire for independence while at the same time recognising its geographic and commercial vulnerability.

Karl Johan also recognised that a simple declaration of neutrality was not sufficient in itself. He understood that there must be a firm commitment to the policy and adequate means to defend it. The king received the support to build up a strong (coastal) defence and managed to stay out of European conflicts. However, after his death in 1844, the mood in Sweden shifted. Support for the Polish uprising in 1863 (carried over from the uprising of 1830) and for Denmark in its conflict with Prussia and Austria led to considerable antipathy toward Russia among liberal Swedes. Scandinavianism, which had affinities with the national unification movements in Italy and Germany at the time, gained widespread popularity from the 1850s to 1870s. On the foreign-policy front, it favoured activism over neutrality.

By the late 1800s, Scandinavianism began to fade. As Germany emerged as a key European player, it was clear that the danger of Sweden being drawn into a German-Russian conflict was quite substantial. Moreover, the dissolution of the Swedish-Norwegian union in 1905 made Sweden even more skeptical of its ability to maintain its neutrality. Given these concerns, Sweden undertook a fairly major modernisation of its defences.[7] At the same time, however, defence policy was at the heart of much of the conflict on the domestic political scene. Many critics argued that Sweden could not withstand an attack from Russia and that neutrality was a futile policy.

It was the outbreak of the First World War that really solidified Sweden's policy of neutrality. With the start of the war, a formal declaration of neutrality was issued by the government in Stockholm. There was some concern in official circles that Germany might not accept Swedish neutrality and would insist that Sweden support the German war effort. However, "Sweden's position as a neutral state was not threatened by any of the belligerents during the war."[8] There were no specific challenges to Sweden's territorial integrity and there was no real pressure brought by the German government. Partly, this reflected the widespread acceptance of the Hague Convention of 1907 on the rights and duties of neutrals and partly, it reflected the fact that drawing Sweden into the conflict did not offer significant benefits to any of the main participants. In any event, Sweden's ability successfully to pursue its policy of neutrality in the face of a major European conflict lent additional credibility to the policy both at home and abroad. Moreover, it tended to confirm Karl Johan's proposition that neutrality necessitated a strong defence.

The interwar years reflected a different collection of concerns for Sweden and, as a consequence, saw neutrality played down and international cooperation take its place as the key component of Swedish foreign policy.

> The end of the war led to a totally new strategic situation in the Baltic region. Both of the two former great Baltic powers, Germany and Russia, were defeated and weakened. At the time it would have been difficult even for the most alarmist of security experts to identify any credible threats to the Nordic area. Against this background, a policy of general disarmament seemed attractive — and morally defensible as well as realistic.[9]

However, when Sweden joined the League of Nations in 1919 there was a great deal of trepidation about the notion of collective security. In fact, one of the conditions of entry was the agreement that Sweden could return to its policy of neutrality in the event of a war.

As the 1930s unfolded, the failure of the League became clear enough. At the same time, it was growing increasingly likely that Germany would take Europe into another "great war." Once again the Swedish government was concerned about its ability to withstand the pressures of such a conflict. As Bo Huldt notes:

> To rebuild Sweden's armed strength would take time and, facing a darkening European horizon, Foreign Minister Sandler — almost entirely on his own within the Swedish cabinet — tried to pursue a **Nordic** policy in the years 1936-39. Sandler's hope was to convert the rather vague edifice of Nordic cooperation into a basis for security and possibly for the joint defence of the Nordic area. His partners, inside as well as outside of Sweden (with the notable exception of the Finns), were all reluctant.[10]

The nordic alliance failed but the Swedes perservered with their policy of neutrality, managing to survive another world war without being drawn into the fighting.

In 1948, in the immediate aftermath of the War, Prime Minister Tage Erlander attempted to resurrect the nordic alliance idea. He had no more success than had Sandler a decade earlier. Denmark, Iceland, and Norway joined NATO, leaving Sweden with the choice of following suit or maintaining its policy of armed neutrality on its own. The decision of the government of the day was, in essence, a reaffirmation of Karl Johan's prescription for Swedish security policy. Sweden had built up its military and industrial capacity during the war to the point where it was (in 1945) a respectable military power. These capabilities, combined with a firm commitment from the post-war Social Democrats, proved to be the foundation for a strong defence in the 1950s and 1960s. "The notion of a 'strong defence' upon which Sweden's neutrality rested," Huldt has written, "implied a conviction that even if diplomacy should once again fail and a new war break out, Sweden's military resources would still be adequate for deterring (or repelling) an aggressor." [11]

SWEDISH SECURITY POLICY

Sweden's experience of remaining neutral through two world wars and its decision not to join NATO in 1949 has had a very significant impact on contemporary Swedish security policy — a policy that has been rather invariant for the past four decades. Specifically, Sweden has attempted to pursue a course that would promote détente and disarmament. It has played a key role, along with Canada and Britain, in United Nations peacekeeping operations and it has acted as a mediator between east and west in various international fora, such as the recent Conference on Security and

Cooperation in Europe (CSCE).[12] Unlike its Scandinavian neighbours, Sweden is committed to the principle that Nordic security is a direct reflection of the level of superpower involvement in the area: the lower the level of superpower involvement, the higher the level of security. For this policy to be credible and effective, Sweden has had to demonstrate a strong commitment to its own territorial integrity and a strong commitment to remain outside of the major alliances.

Officially, Sweden's security policy was most recently set out in the 1982 defence decision, which was based on the report of the 1978 Parliamentary Defence Committee. According to the committee:

> Sweden's security policy, like that of other countries, aims to preserve the country's independence. The goal of our security policy is therefore decided to assure the nation's freedom of action in all situations by means we ourselves choose, in order to be able, within our borders, to preserve and develop our society in accordance with our own values in political, economic, social, cultural and all other respects and, at the same time, work for international détente and peaceful development.[13]

Not surprisingly, the twin themes of neutrality and disarmament are reflected in official policy. Their relative significance, however, is largely determined by the vagaries of the international system and by the realities of domestic politics. In the 1950s and 1960s security policy focused almost entirely on the need to meet potential military threats, in particular, the threat of conventional attack by the Soviet Union. Since the mid 1960s, more emphasis has been placed on international cooperation and the pursuit of peace. More recently, with the relative decline of the United Nations system, the death of the 1970s version of détente, and concerns over Soviet intentions in the Baltic, Sweden's attention has once again been directed toward its own protection. Renewed interest in the Nordic area by both the Warsaw Pact Treaty Organization (WTO) and NATO point to the increasing importance of northern Europe in strategic terms.

At the present time, Swedish security policy is facing a number of serious challenges.[14] These challenges include, *inter alia*: the increasing cost of modern military equipment; the relative decline of superpower influence on all matters except strictly military ones and the increasing likelihood that both East and West Europe will seize the opportunity to "decouple" in various ways; the continuing crisis of the modern welfare state, both from below via popular movements and social disintegration and from above, through the rationalisation of multinational business interests and the technological revolution; and changes in the relative economic and military status of Nordic countries. On the last point, it is instructive to note that Norway and Finland are growing faster, in both military and civilian terms, than Sweden and Denmark. Norway, for example, increased its military expenditures 27 percent between 1976 and 1983. In the same period, Swedish expenditures rose only 3 percent.[15] Norway has also taken on more importance from a strategic perspective, owing largely to its proximity to the Kola Peninsula, which is the primary base for the Soviet Navy's Northern Fleet.

SWEDISH DEFENCE POLICY

Swedish defence policy is determined primarily by decisions taken by the government and Parliament. Specifically, defence policy derives from the reports of ad hoc Parliamentary defence committees which evaluate Sweden's security policy goals in light of its overall foreign policy strategy, budget restrictions, and the like. These committees produce five-year plans that set out defence-policy priorities and establish budgetary guidelines. Sweden adheres to what is called "total defence." The implication here is that military defence is only one component of defence policy; civil defence, economic defence, and psychological defence round out the total-defence strategy. The logic of total defence "is to be so well prepared for war that it serves to maintain peace."[16]

Swedish defence policy derives mainly from the need to provide a strong defence to back up Swedish neutrality. It is organised around what Swedish policy-makers have long perceived to be the principal threats to Sweden's security. These include the threat of conventional war, the fear of escalation to nuclear war, military threats during peacetime, and protracted supply crises and other economic threats.[17] The threat of conventional attack is clearly seen as the most persistent and credible threat to Sweden's security.

In the event of a conventional European conflict, the Swedes assume that the Soviet Union would undoubtedly place a great deal of emphasis on the protection of its bases in the Kola Peninsula, as well as on ensuring the effectiveness of its strategic submarines (SSBNs) and on securing better access to airbases in Northern Europe. NATO, by contrast, would be expected to be directing its energies towards keeping Atlantic sea routes open and restricting the activities of Soviet submarines. The Swedish response to this scenario, which Ministry of Defence officials characterise as "the most plausible threat to Swedish security,"[18] is a defence policy based on a system of conscription and rapid mobilisation which involves the entire population.

MILITARY DEFENCE

Since the end of the Second World War, Sweden's military defence has been characterised by an extremely high degree of organisational efficiency and by a modern, technologically advanced armed forces. In the words of defence analyst, Steven Canby: "Sweden's three services are among the most efficient in Europe, allowing a small nation to field forces almost as large as those fielded by the great powers of Europe. Technologically, up to now, Sweden has been at the forefront, probably second only to the United States."[19]

The services are divided into the three traditional areas, Army, Navy and Air Force. Overall command is the responsibility of the Supreme Commander, Bengt Gustafsson, who reports directly to the government. Each service has its own commander-in-chief, but overall command is broken down further into six command areas. Wartime organisation, which is composed mainly of conscripts, includes as many as a million troops. Peacetime organisation, by contrast, employs roughly 45,000 people. Their job is to perform defence policy, provide a planning function, carry out training, and procure military equipment.

On the administrative side, the chief decision-making body is the Ministry of Defence (MOD). The MOD, with a staff of roughly 125, functions as a secretariat to the Minister, coordinating the interaction between the Government and the various agencies responsible for defence. Much of the administrative work is carried out by the 21 central government authorities, each of which has a defence section. The two most relevant bodies are the Defence Material Administration (FMV), whose primary responsibility is the procurement of military equipment, and the National Board of Economic Defence (OCB), whose job is to coordinate the civil-defence side. While these organisations are much larger than the MOD they are currently undergoing significant reductions in personnel. FMV, for instance, is being cut back from 3,362 to roughly 2,400 employees. Between the end of World War II and the mid 1960s, Sweden spent 4 to 4.5 percent of gross domestic product

(GDP) on defence. Since that time, defence budgets have remained static (barely keeping pace with inflation) while the economy has grown steadily. By 1986, defence spending had reached a postwar low of 2.8 percent of GDP. The reality is that Swedish defence has been systematically eroded for the past 20 years. Notes Supreme Commander Bengt Gustafsson: "Swedish defence has weakened over the past 15 years with a 50-percent reduction in aircraft and a 30-percent cut in ships."[20]

The defence budget for fiscal year 1987-88, set at 26.4 billion Swedish crowns (roughly $4 billion), was the first real increase in 20 years and promises a small but steady real increase over the 1987-92 period.[21] The main focus of these additional revenues is the improvement of the Air Force and the anti-submarine-warfare (ASW) capabilities of the Navy. It is important to note, however, that the increases themselves are not very substantial, averaging only 1.2 percent over the next five years. While most MOD officials and defence analysts view this as a step in the right direction, these increases seem particularly small in comparison to increases in other Nordic countries, which have been averaging approximately three percent a year.[22] Moreover, this level of spending will not return Sweden to the 3.5 percent level that most analysts believe is the minimum necessary to maintain Sweden's strong defence and its policy of armed neutrality.

The argument here is not that Sweden will deviate from its policy of being alliance-free in peace and armed neutral in war. Rather, as Steven Canby suggests:

> The key question is whether Sweden can continue to afford an extrovert strategy based on highly competent high-technology air and naval forces or whether she will have to shift to a putatively cheaper introvert strategy based on territorial defence. The former gives Sweden a politically visible presence and force projection capability that is a virtual prerequisite for maintaining the equilibrium of the Nordic system. The latter implies that Sweden will, at best, be able to defend her own territory, but not the Baltic and its air space. The first can affect external events and give weight to Swedish counsel; the second can not. The first makes Sweden a contributor to the larger scheme of Nordic and global stability; the second views Sweden in a strategic vacuum, with implicit drawing rights on the strength of others.[23]

The recent decision to proceed with the development of a new generation of Swedish fighter aircraft, the JAS 39 Gripen, and to purchase 30 of these (with an option on 110 more by the year 2000) suggests that the Social Democratic government is trying to reaffirm the traditional party commitment to a strong defence and an extrovert strategy.

CIVIL, ECONOMIC, AND PSYCHOLOGICAL DEFENCE

Total defence calls for the coordination of military defence with the civil, economic, and psychological components. With respect to civil defence, the primary task is to protect the population against the effects of a conventional war. Participation is mandatory for all citizens between the ages of 16 and 67, with mandatory military conscription for all males between 18 and 47. Those who would be expected to perform a military function keep their uniform, supplies, and personal weapons at home. The peacetime civil-defence organisation is run by the National Civil Defence Board, at Karlstad, whose primary responsibility is to plan responses to various potential crises and to coordinate the local civil-defence authorities. The civil-defence function is extremely well organised. All citizens have instructions about their own responsibilities in the event of war or other crises. In addition, the Civil Defence Board has built shelters that can accomodate almost six million of Sweden's eight million people.

Economic defence involves the task of ensuring that vital services, such as the provision of food, clothing, transportation, communications, and postal services, remain active and effective during a crisis. The responsibility for economic defence rests with the National Board of Economic Defence (OCB). Among other things, the OCB maintains stockpiles of strategically significant materials — materials that are either unavailable in Sweden or involve too lengthy a time period to produce. There are seven stockpile "villages" throughout Sweden, 5,400 supply depots, and several underground caverns storing crude oil. Since Sweden is almost 100 percent dependent on foreign oil a large share of these stockpiles (roughly 50 percent) is crude oil. These reserves are, however, currently being reduced. Other critical items, such as specialty pharmaceutical products, are becoming a larger proportion of stockpiled materials. The current value of the stockpiles stands at some 10 billion SEK. The OCB also plans and coordinates crisis production. Roughly 15,000 firms have all or part of their production designated as "K" production and are required by law to maintain that capability and store the necessary materials (to a specified level).[24]

The costs of this preparedness are largely born by the individual firms. Again, what is striking here is the level of organisation. The OCB has mapped out and evaluated the whole of the industrial output and encouraged (subsidised) industrial production deemed necessary to the maintenance of Sweden's self-sufficiency and the protection of its independence. However, the country is increasingly vulnerable to external economic developments and here, as elsewhere, the budget squeeze has led to a situation where commitments are outpacing capabilities. As one OCB official argued, "Swedes do not seem willing to spend [the] larger amounts of money on civil and economic defence that increasing [economic] interdependence requires."[25]

Psychological defence is directed by the National Board of Psychological Defence, which is a result of the merger, in July 1985, of the National Committee for Psychological Planning, the National Defence Committee on Public Information, and the Central Agency for Information. Its primary responsibilities are public morale and the provision of information concerning total defence, security policy, and national preparedness.

To summarise, Swedish defence policy is predicated on the notion of total defence. Its aim is to integrate completely the military, civil, economic, and psychological components of defence and to include all of the population in these efforts. The primary task is to defend the population with the least amount of disruption. A secondary, though equally important task, is to defend Swedish territorial and political integrity. The chief strength of the Swedish position is the broad consensus that exists at all levels of society. The pursuit of such a defence policy has necessitated a very close relationship between government and business and helped to foster a vigorous, competitive, and profitable defence industry in Sweden. In order to understand the implications of defence spending for the economy it is important to get a clear sense of the Swedish defence industry and the nature of defence procurement.

DEFENCE PROCUREMENT

As in most countries, the process of procurement follows four distinct stages: study and investigation, design and testing, purchase, and manufacture. The process begins with the recommendations of the Supreme Commander, whose planning operates on rolling 15-year plans.[26] In the first stage, proposals are evaluated and studies are conducted. As a matter of practice, potential suppliers are involved even in the earliest stages. However, the principal actors at this stage are the FMV and the National Defence Institute (FOA). Progress to the second stage requires a commitment from the government to support the project. At this point tenders are offered by various contractors. In fact, private industry is very much involved at this stage. Moving to the next stage, the actual decision to purchase, requires a firm commitment on the government's part to allocate funds.

The principal participants in the procurement process are the Ministry of Defence (MOD) and the Defence Material Administration (FMV). The MOD is primarily involved in the decision-making, while the FMV is formally charged with acquiring, testing, inspecting, and maintaining the equipment. In addition, the FMV coordinates the research and development function. The FMV is divided by service. Of the total defence budget, which amounts to 26,378 million SEK in FY 1987-88, roughly 30 percent is devoted to material procurement and 10 percent to research and development.[27] The remaining share is taken up by training and administration. Of the monies specifically devoted to procurement, the lion's share has traditionally gone to the Air Force. In general terms, the distribution of funds is 45 percent to the Air Force, 30 percent to the Army, and 25 percent to the Navy. As the JAS 39 Gripen program comes on stream, the Air Force is expected to take an even larger share.[28]

The government position on procurement is that a project must meet the requirements set out in both international and domestic law and that it must follow the official guidelines. With respect to the MOD requirement, the principal motives for a particular project must be in keeping with general security norms, overall war requirements, the policy of neutrality, and economic efficiency. General procurement policy is based on the following criteria: open competition, minimum life cycle costs, economic independence and domestic economic benefit (the so-called "Swedish profile"), strategic sources, and the potential for cooperation with other countries. There is no question, given these criteria, that domestic suppliers would have some advantage though they are definitely *not* directly subsidised through defence contracts.[29] Legally, defence purchases must follow the general rules established by the Procurement Ordinance. Here, the central or guiding principle is one of commerciality: "When procuring items, the agency shall take advantage of the opportunities arising from competition and shall, in other respects as well, adhere to commerciality and shall deal with tenders and tenderers objectively."[30]

The principle of non-discrimination is also embodied in the General Agreement on Tariffs and Trade (GATT), to which Sweden is a signatory. However, as Inga Thorsson has noted, "a general exception is granted for procurement which is indispensable for national security or for national defence purposes."[31] The implications of this exemption are far-reaching. Quite simply, "this means that it is possible to place contracts for the most advanced weapons systems and many other defence items with a Swedish producer even if foreign competitors can offer better conditions."[32]

In contrast to this strict commitment to the principle of commerciality (and to the logic of commerciality) is the reality that a credible policy of neutrality necessitates the domestic sourcing of critical materials or the stockpiling of significant quantities of spare parts and other strategic materials. As the 1982 Defence Committee realised: "The industrial capacity to develop, produce and maintain defence equipment domestically is of importance both for the credibility of our security policy and for the structure and utilization of our defence forces."[33] Put simply, excessive dependence on military equipment developed and produced offshore would seriously undermine the credibility of Swedish neutrality and jeopardise its effectiveness. For neutrality to work, critical weapons systems must be developed (or adapted) and supplied by domestic producers. This would account for the recent decision to proceed with the next generation of Swedish fighter aircraft (the JAS 39 Gripen), as opposed to buying a foreign plane "off the shelf."[34]

In short, while defence procurement follows the Government's official commitment to the principle of commerciality, "the Swedish armed forces are often ready to pay a surcharge when acquiring new weapons systems in order to promote security and defence policy goals."[35] An interesting paradox exists here between the official (and practical) commitment to commerciality and the reality of making procurement decisions that support the policy of neutrality.[36] The fact is, as I will discuss below, Swedish firms do have to compete in an open market for defence contracts. However, their "natural" advantages (i.e. access to key officials and advanced knowledge of defence needs) provide them with the opportunity to compete very successfully against outside suppliers. This paradox can be explained by the fact that the industry-state relationship is so well developed and the commitment to neutrality so deeply ingrained that the government simply does not view this process in terms of trade-offs.[37]

THE STRUCTURE OF THE SWEDISH DEFENCE INDUSTRY

When speaking of "the defence industry" most analysts are discussing the aggregate industrial resources that are employed to develop, manufacture, and maintain goods and services that are produced specifically for military applications and lack a corresponding civilian application. In Sweden, as in other developed market economies, official statistics group industries by sector (such as the automobile sector or the aircraft sector) as opposed to purpose. As a consequence, generalisations about relative levels of technology, export dependence, and research and development are difficult to determine. However, it is both possible and desirable to analyse specific national defence industries by exactly these criteria and to determine what impact they have on their domestic economies.

The Swedish defence industry can be summarised by the following characteristics. First, the industry is highly concentrated, with five firms and their subsidiaries accounting for more than 80 percent of all deliveries to the Swedish armed forces; in addition, the majority of the remaining 20 percent is shared by another five firms. Second, with the exception of state-owned Forenade Fabriksverken (FFV), the companies involved are large, highly diversified, private, Swedish-owned firms with significant civil divisions. Third, their level of dependence on military sales varies, but each makes a significant share of its domestic market profits through military sales. Fourth, the defence industry provides roughly 70 to 75 percent of all military equipment used by the Swedish armed forces. Finally, export sales of military equipment represent a very small share of total exports.

The five largest arms producers are Saab-Scania, Bofors, FFV, Volvo Flygmotor, and Ericsson Radio Systems. The next group includes: Hägglund and Soner (armoured vehicles), Kockums (submarines), Karlskronavaret (missile ships and patrol boats), Philips Elektronikindustrier, and SATT Electronics (both producing communications systems and radar).

Svenska Aeroplanaktiebolaget (Saab) was the result of a merger between the two largest aircraft producers in Sweden in the 1930s;

with the support of the government, by 1939 Saab had a virtual monopoly on the production of aircraft. Roughly 90 percent of the aircraft produced in the postwar years have been for the Swedish Air Force. Since 1968, when Saab acquired Scania- Vabis, military production has dropped to roughly 10 percent of total sales. However, while the company produces cars, buses, and various electronic components, "the technical core of the group is the production of aircraft."[38] Moreover, while the aerospace division at Linkoping accounts for only 10 percent of total sales, it involves more than 30 percent of the company's research and development facilities and earns roughly 30 percent of total profits.[39] In addition, the Swedish government has traditionally absorbed 100 percent of development costs for aircraft production and has been willing to guarantee minimum profits to the producers.[40] While this is changing somewhat, with the IG JAS consortium led by Saab investing more of their own capital in the JAS 39 Gripen project, the potential for greater profits and more spin-offs is greater than with the Viggen program.

Another major participant in the Swedish aircraft industry is Volvo Flygmotor (VFA), a division of the powerful Volvo group. Volvo Flygmotor, whose principal customer is the Swedish military, accounts for approximately three percent of Volvo sales. However, like Saab aerospace, it is generally more profitable than the larger automobile and bus divisions. In contrast to Saab aerospace, VFA's adaptation and production (under licence) of the GE F404 engine for the JAS 39 Gripen is less advantageous than its production of the RM8 engine for the Viggen. Volvo also sells cars, trucks and rocket engines to the Swedish military.

The third major participant in the aircraft industry, and in the JAS 39 Gripen consortium, is Ericsson Radio Systems (ERA). ERA develops and produces radar and other electronic systems for aircraft and missiles. Like Volvo, Ericsson is a large multinational enterprise whose commitments to the Swedish military are only a small portion of its overall sales. However, the research and development associated with the ERA division and with military contracts has undoubtedly played a key role in establishing the technological sophistication of the company.

Bofors, the largest defence industry employer in Sweden, specialises in the production of artillery, ammunition, and missiles. Bofors is very dependent on sales to the Swedish military. In 1970, approximately a third of total sales were defence-related. By 1983, more than half of all sales were through the Ordnance and Nobel divisions, both of which produce almost exclusively for military customers.[41] Moreover, as is apparent from Table 5.1, profitability in the defence-related divisions has been both steady and healthy; indeed, it is not unreasonable to conclude that the strong performance of the Ordnance and Nobel divisions is all that has kept the company out of serious financial difficulties. The performance of the Steel and Nohab divisions has been particularly weak. Bofors is the only Swedish arms producer that (at the present time) has significant export contracts for defence materials. However, its success here has been tainted by charges that company officials have offered bribes to Indian government officials and that Bofors has channelled arms sales through Singapore in a direct attempt to sidestep Sweden's restrictions on arms exports.[42]

The last, and smallest, of the big five is state-owned Forenade Fabriksverken (FFV). Like Bofors, FFV produces mainly arms and ammunition. Unlike Bofors, who are increasingly focusing on the missile industry and on improving export markets, FFV is playing a larger and larger role in the maintenance of defence equipment. FFV is almost completely dependent on military sales, with more than three-quarters of all sales going to the Swedish military.[43] However, during FFV's recent expansion drive it has reduced its dependence on military contracts through the acquisition of civil-sector firms

Table 5.1: *Bofors: Profit Margins According to Division, 1973-1983*

	1973	74	75	76	77	78	79	80	81	82	83
Ordnance	8	10	7	11	9	9	10	11	9	6	5
Nobel	6	10	2	4	8	7	6	4	6	7	6
Plastics									- 8	1	0
Kilsta								- 3	-12	-11	-11
Steel	- 3	7	8	- 2	- 9	- 6	- 2	2	0	2	
Electronics	-43	0	6	- 5	3	11	6	0	14	7	0
Nohab	3	3	3	2	- 5	- 11	- 2	-10	- 7	-14	
UVA	2	10	3	- 7	- 43	2	-5	- 20	- 4		
TOTAL	3	7	6	3	2	3	5	5	4	4	2

Source: Bofors, *Annual Reports*, 1973-1983.

Note: The Plastics Division was part of the Nobel Division until 1980. The Steel Division was reorganised in 1980 at which time those parts remaining in the company were divided among the Kilsta and the Industry

Divisions. The companies now constituting the Electronics Division were included in the Industry Division in the years 1980-1982, as has been Nohab since 1980. UVA was also included in the Industry Division in 1980-81; thereafter the company was closed down.
Profit margins have been calculated as operating income after planned depreciation as a percentage of invoiced sales.

Sweden's defence industry is very much directed at and by the needs of the Swedish military. There are a number of explanations for this, two of which are particularly compelling. The first is that because Sweden is not a member of a collective-defence arrangement, sales to developed market economies are restricted. The second is that Swedish law prohibits the sale of arms to countries that are involved in an armed conflict, that are likely to enter an international conflict, that are experiencing civil war, or that would be likely to use those materials for the suppression of human rights. According to Swedish law:

> the export of war materiel is forbidden unless the approval of the government is obtained. The reason for this restriction lies primarily in Sweden's foreign policy. The unrestricted export of war materiel would contradict Sweden's policy of promoting international disarmament agreements and peaceful solutions to international conflicts. It is not in Sweden's interest to export weapons to countries involved in war, to unstable countries or to countries whose governments violate human rights.[44]

Given the language of the weapons-export law, the government has clearly opted for a position that allows it the most flexibility. It can choose, within limits, on an individual basis the export sales that seem appropriate. The impact of these regulations, which have been in place since the 1930s, is that Swedish defence materials can only be exported easily to other Nordic countries or to neutral and non-aligned countries in Europe.[45] Or, to put it in the words of one frustrated FMV official, "the Swedish defence industry can only export to those customers who can clearly demonstrate that they do not need the weapons and that they will not use them."[46]

The feeling in official circles in Stockholm is that the government is prepared to ease up on these restrictions.[47] However, the scandal associated with Bofors' record 8.4 billion SEK contract to supply the Indian Army with howitzers may have significant negative impact, especially since Bofors has openly admitted to circumventing Swedish law by "laundering" its export sales through Singapore. Reactions to the Bofors scandal include proposals to tighten the existing export restrictions, the imposition of additional restrictions that would cover the marketing of arms in foreign markets, and a proposal (by Energy Minister Brigitta Dahl) to nationalise Bofors.[48]

DEFENCE SPENDING: IMPLICATIONS FOR THE ECONOMY

Generally speaking, military officials at the FMV do not view the potential for industrial spin-offs or the possibilities for generating employment when making decisions about weapons acquisition. Their decisions tend to reflect concerns about such matters as effectiveness, compatibility with existing hardware, and the adaptability to Swedish needs. They are concerned, however, with the long-term viability of the Swedish arms industry and its relationship to overall defence capabilities. The government (including the MOD) tends to think in broader terms. In addition to the concerns of the military, it must factor in the implications for foreign policy (in particular the policy of neutrality) as well as for the economy.

There are many direct and indirect benefits that result from the purchase of defence materials from domestic suppliers. In general terms, these include: a higher level of research and development than might otherwise be the case; the possibility of civil-sector spin-offs; larger and more competitive firms; the opportunity to generate employment; and the possibility of using high-technology Swedish defence products (such as the Viggen) to showcase Swedish technology. There are also some significant costs. These are mostly social costs, or costs that reflect the alternate value of production.

Since most of the potential benefits derive from a single source, public spending on defence research and development (R&D), it is critical at this point to examine whether military spending is more R&D intensive than civil-sector spending, whether military R&D encourages additional civil-sector production, and whether military R&D offers technological leadership to the rest of the economy.

Table 5.2: *R&D as a Percentage of Value Added: Defence Sector, Civilian Sector and Total Industry, 1967-81.*

Year	Defence Sector Companies			Civil Sector Companies	Total Industries
	Military	Civil	Total		
1969	15.7	8.1	11.7	4.8	3.2
1971	20.5	10.9	15.5	5.5	3.8
1973	25.4	9.7	16.2	6.7	4.1
1975	26.3	8.5	14.8	8.4	4.4
1977	24.4	9.0	15.2	9.2	5.5
1979	21.7	10.7	14.9	11.4	5.7
1981	29.3	11.8	18.4	15.4	7.1

Source: Inga Thorsson, *In Pursuit of Disarmament: Conversion from Military to Civilian Production in Sweden*, Special Report to the Swedish Government (Stockholm: Liber Allmanna Forlaget, 1984), p. 128.

Conventional wisdom suggests that the defence industry is more R&D-intensive than other industrial activities. For Sweden, at least, this appears to be the case. Most estimates put defence-related R&D at between 20 and 25 percent of all R&D carried out in Sweden and most suggest that defence-related R&D is significantly higher than comparable civilian R&D.[49] Unfortunately, the bulk of these studies do not distinguish between defence and civilian R&D within defence-industry companies, and most do not compare these companies (most of which are very large enterprises) with comparable firms. These difficulties were overcome in a study prepared for Inga Thorsson's report to the Parliamentary Defence Committee in 1984 — a report that came to some very interesting conclusions. First, the military divisions of defence-industry companies did spend more money (as a percentage of value-added) than all other groups. Second, the R&D intensity for the military divisions of defence-industry companies almost doubled during the period.[50] Third, there was a narrowing of the discrepancy between the spending of civil-sector companies and the spending of the military divisions of defence industry companies. In fact, the civil-sector companies actually increased their spending on R&D by a factor of three. Finally, the discrepancy widened between the civil divisions of defence-industry companies and the military divisions of those companies. The implications here are quite clear. The development of defence materials is still considerably more R&D-intensive than comparable civil-sector production (though the difference is narrowing), and the defence-industry companies are devoting an increasingly larger share of their R&D to defence production. It is important at this stage to remember that there are critical differences between the various types of defence producers. In general terms, military electronics and aircraft design are considerably more R&D-intensive than other defence production.

While the total budget allocated for defence did not change significantly between the mid 1960s and the mid 1980s, the same cannot be said for defence-related R&D. As Table 3 suggests, there were sharp increases in R&D expenditures in FY 1981-82 and FY 1982-83. These figures can, however, be somewhat misleading as the government (and the suppliers) do not clearly distinguish between development and actual procurement. "Surges" in R&D expenditures may simply reflect the different stages of large capital projects. In this case, the big increases in the early 1980s reflect the advance payments made to the aircraft industry for development work on the JAS 39 Gripen. Since that point, defence-related R&D financed through the budget has levelled off at approximately 2.5 billion SEK.

Table 5.3: *FMV-Financed R&D Payments to the Swedish Defence Industry 1978/79-82/83*

(million SEK)

Company	1978/79	1979/80	1980/81	1981/82	1982/83
Bofors	36	61	30	58	59
ERA	84	94	93	82	110
EFV	43	33	42	48	58
HB Utveckling	8	8	18	15	20
Hägglunds	10	1	0	1	1
IG JAS					505
Karlskronavarvet	2	0	6	7	2
Kockums	22	23	22	28	22
PEAB	4	2	5	5	9
Saab-Scania	185	215	113	136	62
SATT	2	3	7	7	8
SBMC			4	11	9
Volvo Flygmotor	10	15	21	61	16
TOTAL	406	455	361	459	881

Source: Defence Materiel Administration (FMV)

The question now is whether this level of R&D intensity has, either directly or indirectly, provided significant benefit to the economy. Various arguments have been put forward but few concrete studies have been carried out. This is largely due to the lack of appropriate data and the inability to demonstrate that turnover in the volume of military orders or growth in civilian R&D (the two most popular indicators of the impact of R&D) is directly linked to defence-related R&D. In a recent study of the aircraft industry, G. Regardh concluded that the industry increased its turnover by 60 to 65 percent of the value of FMV orders. In a similar study, 300 million SEK spent on aircraft research was reported to have produced as much as 200 million SEK in civilian-sector research.[51] Neither of these studies manages to overcome serious methodological difficulties inherent in the undertaking, and both seem to exaggerate the indirect benefits of defence-related R&D.

That being said, there is ample evidence to support the claim that defence-industry companies are more profitable in their military divisions than their civilian divisions and that R&D carried out on the military side "spills over" onto the civilian side. Partly, this is a reflection of the fact that when it comes to basic technology there is no appreciable difference between civil and military technology. There are, perhaps, military applications with no evident directly corresponding civilian application. Missiles might come to mind. However, if one thinks of a missile as a bundle of technologies it is easy to see how even these could have important civilian spin-offs. This is especially true in the area of electronics. There is also sufficient evidence to support the claim that defence spending has relatively significant employment implications, both in terms of highly trained technicians (mostly engineers) and in terms of the general population. Finally, there is (an admittedly weaker) case to be made for the argument that defence-related R&D provides technological leadership to the civil sector. A senior MOD official argued that "the need to maintain industrial capacity for security reasons has been taken as a national challenge for Swedish industry." By the same token, he conceded "the basis for Ericsson's success has to do with spin-offs from defence contracts."[52]

There are, however, costs associated with the level of defence-industrial preparedness that Sweden maintains. To begin with, there is a loss in GDP growth as a reflection of defence expenditures. There are also considerable costs involved in the extensive training program for conscripts and in the stockpiling required for civil and economic defence. It is difficult to measure the value of these costs since they can only really be understood in relative terms and there is not an appropriate sector with which to compare defence. In addition, it has been the practice of Social Democratic governments to "recover" some of these social costs. In particular, they have used the conscript system as an instrument of employment policy.

All in all, assessing the relationship between defence spending and economic well-being is an extremely difficult task. The Swedish economic "miracle" is a reflection of many factors, including: the unique relationship between capitalist production, social equality, and economic well-being that the Swedes call the "middle way"; the opportunity and the willingness to innovate; effective employment policies; and a government committed to public spending on R&D. There is little question that the significant defence industrial capacity and defence-related R&D have played a positive role in this equation.

CONCLUSION

The foregoing analysis has suggested a number of things. To begin with, both the content and the direction of Swedish defence policy has changed very little over the past four decades. What has changed, beginning in the mid 1960s, is that political and financial restrictions have effectively frozen defence budgets, while the costs of maintaining a strong defence have risen considerably; and to quote Holmstrom and Olsson, "the problem has been to balance ideological demands against economic and political requirements."[53] The Swedish consensus on the value of neutrality has not disappeared. On the contrary, it remains the key to Swedish foreign and defence policies. However, there is some concern over whether Sweden can exercise the kind of "extrovert" policy that it traditionally has without the necessary budget support. The decision to proceed with the production of a new generation of Swedish fighter aircraft (as opposed to purchasing a foreign aircraft) and the real increase in the defence budget for FY 1987-88 indicates that the Social Democratic government under Ingvar Carlsson remains committed to the notion of a strong defence. As long as there is not a significant downturn in the economy, this seems to be the direction of government thinking.

This chapter has also suggested that there is an extremely high degree of integration between the state and the defence industry. While the state seems committed to the principle of commerciality (as laid out in the national Procurement Ordinance) the reality is that domestic suppliers have much greater access to defence contracts than do their foreign counterparts. The need to maintain industrial capacity seems to go well beyond calculations of national security. Independence, for Sweden, as measured by industrial capacity and advanced technology, is a source of both national pride and economic well-being.

With respect to the implications of defence spending on the economy, "the greatest value to the Swedish economy seems to be in terms of developing R&D capacity."[54] There appear to be significant civil sector benefits accruing from a healthy and technologically sophisticated defence industry.

The increasingly troublesome discrepancy between financial limitations and the desire to maintain a strong defence industry may (even with the Bofors scandal) militate against existing restrictions on the export of arms. One obvious way to get more value for the defence dollar is to reduce the dependence of the Swedish defence industry on sales to the Swedish military. Increased export sales could help to reduce the burden on the public purse. It may be, however, that this simply cannot be reconciled with the moral position that Sweden takes with respect to disarmament.

In this regard, however, it is important to note that a recent report by a government-appointed panel has castigated the governmental policy on arms exports for not addressing the core problem of Sweden's arms dilemma. This panel, the five-member Citizens' Commission on Arms Exports, was set up to investigate the country's export practices, in the wake of the Bofors and FFV scandals. Prime Minister Carlsson's warning that arms exports might face abolition drew the wrath of the commission chairman, Ambassador Olof Rydeeck, who has accused a succession of Swedish governments, especially those headed by Social Democrats, of failing to confront the fundamental reality that Sweden's security interests are critically dependent upon the country's maintaining a viable defence industrial base. The Commission recommended that arms exports be continued "when it is deemed necessary to ensure a requisite supply of equipment to the Swedish defence forces and when it is compatible with the principles and aims of Sweden's foreign policy."[55]

Notes

Much of the material in this chapter derives from confidential interviews conducted with officials at the Swedish Ministry of Defence (MOD), the Swedish Ministry of Foreign Affairs, the Defence Materiel Administration (FMV), and the National Board of Economic Defence (OCB) in August

1985 and May 1987. I am also indebted to Dr. Bo Huldt, Deputy Director of the Swedish Institute of International Affairs (UI), and Dr. Ingemar Dorfer of the National Defence Institute (FOA), for their helpful advice and insightful comments.

[1] The Swedish government has only been able to verify two intrusions of Soviet submarines (Karlskrona in 1981 and Harsfjarden in 1982). Officially, these are the only two that are claimed to be of Soviet origin. Unofficially, however, the assumption is that all the citings are of Soviet submarines.

[2] While this paper is directed specifically at the challenges to Swedish defence policy, a broader critique of the so-called "middle way" is presented in Marquis Childs, *Sweden: The Middle Way on Trial* (New Haven: Yale University Press, 1980); Francis Castels, *The Social Democratic Image of Society* (London: Routledge and Kegan Paul, 1978); and *Limits of the Welfare State*, ed. John Fry (Hampshire: Gower Publishing, 1980).

[3] This arrangement is laid out in the Treaty of Friendship, Cooperation and Mutual Assistance (the FCMA Treaty) between the Government of Finland and the Government of the Soviet Union. The FCMA Treaty, which was concluded in 1948 and renewed without alteration in 1955, 1970, and 1983, involves the security policies of the two countries while recognising Finland's desire to avoid participation in any conflict between the major powers.

[4] I am indebted to Clive Archer of the Centre for Defence Studies at the University of Aberdeen who suggested the term "alliance free" and helped clarify Sweden's unique brand of neutrality.

[5] Interview, Swedish Ministry of Defence, Stockholm, May 1987.

[6] Krister Wahlback, *The Roots of Swedish Neutrality* (Stockholm: The Swedish Institute, 1986) p. 8.

[7] Modernisation took place largely under the auspices of the defence law of 1901.

[8] Wahlback, *Roots of Swedish Neutrality*, p. 23.

[9] Bo K. A. Huldt, "Swedish Disarmament and Security Policy from the 1920s to the 1980s", *International Review of Military History*, special issue, Neutrality and Defence: The Swedish Experience, 57 (1984): 38.

[10] Ibid., p. 44.

[11] Ibid., p. 45.

[12] Sweden's foreign-policy initiatives in this area are very much like those of Canada, especially during the so-called "golden age" of Canadian foreign policy. Sweden's alliance-free status has, however, lent significant additional credibility to its efforts on this front.

[13] Sweden, Ministry of Defence, *Our Security Policy*, Swedish Official Report Series, no. 42, (Stockholm, 1979), p. 19. Swedish defence policy is directed by a series of five-year and 15-year plans. The last five-year plan dealt with the period between 1982 and 1987. The most recent plan, for

1987-1992, was released in June 1987. Not only do these plans dictate the direction of defence policy, they establish relatively firm budgets.

[14]For a thorough and insightful discussion of these and other challenges to Swedish security policy see Jan Oberg, "Towards Understanding Common Nordic Security Alternatives," *Current Research on Peace and Violence* 1/2 (1986): 74-93.

[15]Ibid., p. 82.

[16]"The Swedish Defence System," *Fact Sheets on Sweden* (Stockholm: The Swedish Institute, 1985), p. 1.

[17]For a thorough discussion of the Government's perception of these threats see Sweden, Ministry of Defence, *Sweden's Security Policy: Entering the 90s*, Report of the 1984 Defence Committee, Swedish Official Report Series, no. 23 (Stockholm, 1985), pp. 56-64.

[18]Interview, Swedish Ministry of Defence, May 1987.

[19]Steven L. Canby, "Swedish Defence," *Survival* 23 (May/June 1981): 117

[20]Sara Webb, "Defence: Dismay at the Budget Rise," *Financial Times*, 22 May 1987, p. 3.

[21]Sweden, Ministry of Finance *The Swedish Budget 1987-88* (Stockholm, 1987), p. 70.

[22]Webb, "Dismay at Budget Rise," p. 3.

[23]Canby, "Swedish Defence," p. 117.

[24]The Swedish words for crisis and for war both begin with the letter K, hence the designation K production.

[25]Interview, National Board of Economic Defence, Stockholm, May 1987.

[26]The current 15-year plan, which is coincident with the Government's five-year defence plan, lays out defence priorities into the 21st century.

[27]Interview, Defence Material Administration, Stockholm, May 1987.

[28]Figures are estimates provided by the FMV. Actual figures beyond 1984-85 are unavailable. On the matter of the Air Force's share increasing, a senior FMV official characterised the current 15-year plan from the Supreme Commander as "the Air Force's turn." Interview, FMV, Stockholm, May 1987.

[29]Interview, MOD, Stockholm, May 1987.

[30]Government of Sweden, "Regulations Governing Public Procurement" (Stockholm: Liber Forlag, 1983), p. 4.

[31]Inga Thorsson, *In Pursuit of Disarmament: Conversion from Military to Civil Production in Sweden*, Special Report to the Swedish Government (Stockholm: Liber Allmanna Forlaget, 1984), p. 93.

[32]Ibid, p. 93.

[33]Quoted in ibid., p. 94.

[34]This is not to say that the Swedish MOD did not undertake a lengthy exercise in "comparison shopping." The principal alternatives, American and French, were either too expensive or too advanced for the specific requirements of the Swedish Air Force. Interview, MOD, Stockholm, May 1987.

[35]Thorsson, *In Pursuit of Disarmament*, p. 93.

[36]The commitment to commerciality cannot be explained away as a case where Government policy is inconsistent with reality. MOD officials do appear to be committed to the logic of open competition.

[37]I am indebted to Professor Bengt Sundelius of the University of Stockholm for this point.

[38]Per Holmstrom and Ulf Olsson, "Sweden," in *The Structure of the Defence Industry*, ed. Nicole Ball and Milton Leitenberg (London: Croom Helm, 1983), pp. 150-51.

[39]Ibid., pp. 151-54. In the 1970s, when Viggens were being delivered, as much as 50 percent of Saab-Scania profits derived from the aerospace division.

[40]Interview, FMV, Stockholm, May 1987. In the 1970s the government guaranteed a minimum 10-percent profit for Saab aerospace in the production of fighter aircraft. The norm now is to guarantee "reasonable profits."

[41]Thorsson, *In Pursuit of Disarmament*, p. 117.

[42]See Dilip Awasthi, "Defence Deals: Bofors and After," *India Today*, 15 May 1987, pp. 12-30; and Sara Webb, "Arms Industry: Dilemma over Exports," *Financial Times*, 22 May 1987, p. 4.

[43]Thorsson, *In Pursuit of Disarmament*, p. 115.

[44]Ibid., p. 112.

[45]Holmstrom and Olsson, "Sweden," p. 149.

[46]Interview, FMV, Stockholm, May 1987.

[47]Interview, MOD, Stockholm, May 1987.

[48]Webb, "Dilemma over Exports."

[49]Holmstrom and Olsson, "Sweden," p.174. While estimates vary, virtually all figures are around the 20 percent mark.

[50]FMV figures for the years 1982 to 1985 suggest that the R&D commitment of this group has levelled out at just above 30 percent of value-added.

[51]Reported in Holmstrom and Olsson, "Sweden," p. 177.

[52]Interview, MOD, Stockholm, May 1987.

[53]Holmstrom and Olsson, "Sweden," p. 177.

[54]Ibid, p. 178.

[55]Jack Burton,"Panel: Arms Exports Essential to Sweden," *Defense News*, 23 May 1988, pp. 1, 36.

6

Israel and the Lavi Fighter-Aircraft: The Lion Falls to Earth

Galen Roger Perras

INTRODUCTION

On 30 August 1987, the Israeli Cabinet voted 12 to 11 (with one abstention) to cancel production of the Lavi (Hebrew for lion) multi-role combat aircraft (MRCA). [1] The decision, which followed months of ministerial and military infighting, ended an ambitious program that some had hoped would catapult Israeli industry into the twenty-first century. Instead, thousands of workers face unemployment and the aircraft promises to remain a divisive political issue for some time to come.

In many ways, the Lavi program is a classic example of what can go wrong in the process of designing and producing a complex weapon system. Originally envisioned as a small, cheap ground-support aircraft, the Lavi was transformed into a large and very expensive multi-role aircraft, forcing Israel to look to the United States for most of the financial backing. The rise in cost destroyed the broad support for the program in Israeli and American governmental and military circles. The Reagan Administration, originally a supporter of the aircraft, reversed its position and brought to bear severe financial and political pressure upon Israel to scrap the Lavi. Within Israel itself, the project faced opposition from a wide spectrum of organisations and individuals, including the Ministry of Finance, the Army, the Navy, the Chief of Staff of the Israeli Defence Force (IDF), most of the senior members of the Labour party, and even the Israeli Air Force (IAF). Proponents of the Lavi included its main contractor, Israel Aircraft Industry (IAI), and the majority of the members of the right-wing Herut party and the Likud bloc.

While considerations of cost remained the prime factor behind the struggle over the aircraft, the debate acquired a distinctive Israeli flavour. For the Likud, the Lavi became entangled within and identified with the right-wing notion of a large, secure, and powerful "Greater" Israel. Some even likened the program to the American effort to put a man on the moon.[2] The Labour party, in contrast, took a far more pragmatic approach to the problem, preferring to oppose the Lavi almost solely in terms of the heavy financial burden it represented. The situation was further complicated by the fact that since the autumn of 1984, Labour and the Likud have ruled together in a coalition or "National Unity" government. By early 1987, the result of this effort was governmental paralysis with the Lavi becoming yet another bludgeon in the battle for pre-election supremacy. Now that the Lavi has been cancelled, the political struggle continues and the issue promises to raise its head in the next general election.

This chapter will focus on the entire span of the Lavi program from its origins in the 1973 Yom Kippur War to its death in the late summer of 1987. But to do so requires also that attention be paid to the growth of a modern defence industrial base in Israel, of which the Lavi program was a logical if ill-fated step.

THE ORIGINS OF THE ISRAELI DEFENCE INDUSTRIAL BASE

The origins of the Israeli aviation sector date back to 1951 when Prime Minister David Ben-Gurion gave orders that an aircraft company be organised.[3] Two years later the Bedek Aviation Company, the forerunner of the state-owned Israel Aircraft Industries (IAI), was formed around a core of American aviation engineers who had moved to Israel. The company's mandate was to maintain and repair military aircraft, but according to Shimon Peres, Director-General and later Deputy Minister of the Israeli Ministry of Defence from 1953 to 1965, "among the initial aims was nothing less than the eventual construction of jets."[4] By 1955, Bedek was repairing and upgrading aircraft for the IAF and servicing jet engines previously shipped to France.[5]

With the outbreak of war in Algeria in 1954 and the subsequent crisis in Franco-Arab relations, the French proved willing to provide Israel with weaponry, including aircraft. The ties between France and Israel were cemented when the Israelis joined in the

Anglo-French campaign against Egypt in 1956. Not content only to acquire French arms, Israel also wanted licences to produce French-designed weapons, particularly aircraft. On 24 July 1957, IAI and the French company Air Fouga signed an agreement permitting the Israeli firm to build Fouga Magister CM-170 close-support fighters and trainers in Israel using domestically manufactured parts. The first aircraft left the assembly line in June 1960, and 48 were produced by June 1967.[6] With the end of the war in Algeria in 1962 and French attempts to re-establish good relations with oil-producing Arab states, Franco-Israeli relations deteriorated. Prior to the outbreak of the Six Day War in June 1967, France blocked the delivery of 50 Mirage-5 fighter-bombers, already paid for, to Israel. In January 1969, France imposed a total embargo on arms sales to Israel.[7]

The embargo placed Israel in a very unpleasant situation. Most of its high-performance aircraft were of aging French designs, and no foreign supplier seemed very eager to take France's place. Left to their own devices, the Israelis upgraded 75 Mirage-3CJ fighter-aircraft with American General Electric engines and, in 1969, introduced the Nesher fighter-bomber, a hybrid of the Mirage-3 and Mirage-5 powered by a French engine.[8] The Nesher was succeeded by the Kfir fighter-bomber, an updated Nesher with more advanced avionics and a General Electric engine. Development of the Kfir was initiated by IAI in 1970 and the first copy was delivered to the IAF in early 1973. A second model, the Kfir C2, went into production in 1976.[9]

These aircraft were only the most visible products of an expanding and confident Israeli arms industry. The various embargoes against Israel in the 1950s and 1960s had led many Israelis to assert that indigenous arms production had political and strategic value. Such efforts had the prospect of liberating Israel from the judgement of other nations — judgements that could prove damaging if accompanied by arms embargoes. Moreover, many Israelis held the view that a nation's military strength was measured not only by the type and quantity of weapons in its possession but also by the capacity to produce arms in times of need.[10]

A number of political and economic steps were taken after the Six Day War to reach the goal of military self-sufficiency. The Ministry of Defence set up the Procurement and Production Administration to encourage local and civilian manufacture. A joint committee of the Ministries of Defence and Commerce and Industry was formed in 1969, its goal being to facilitate the doubling of output of the electronics, metals, and machine industries in five to seven years, with a concentration on the production of currently imported defence products. A comprehensive set of benefits and subsidies, including suspension of taxes, subsidies for employee training, and substantial Israeli government grants for initial start-up (up to 70 percent),[11] was instituted to attract private and particularly foreign investment to Israeli industry.

Budgetary allotments reflected this new priority. Six to seven percent of the 1968 defence budget was allocated to research, a figure equal to the amount available for all areas of civilian research combined. By 1982, 46 percent of all Israeli government expenditures in research and development were earmarked for military projects as compared with two percent in Japan, three percent in the Netherlands and eight percent in Canada.[12]

The investment in the defence industry and industrial infrastructure produced dramatic results. Output in the metal products, machinery, and electrical and electronic equipment industries, the three major groups in which defence production is concentrated, showed a sharp rise. From 1965 to 1977 their share in the total value of industry (excluding diamonds) increased from 18.9 percent to 29.8 percent. During the same period industrial production multiplied by a factor of 2.48. Defence-related output accounted for 80 percent of production in the metal and electronics industry. The average annual rate of growth for the metals and electronics sectors between 1967 and 1973 was 13 percent; the rate for electronics alone was 30 percent, a consequence of these industries having absorbed about one-third of all industrial investment between 1968 and 1974. In 1966, Israeli military production totalled $80 million. Seven years later that figure exceeded $400 million.[13]

Given the amount of money being pumped into arms production, it is not surprising that the number of people directly employed in the defence industry increased by 20,000 between 1968 and 1972. At the same time the labour force working in other industrial sectors expanded by 35,000 workers. The proportion of defence-related salaries among total wages in the economy climbed from five percent in 1966 to 10 percent in 1980 with the proportion of defence-sector employees to all wage earners increasing from 10 percent to 25 percent between 1967 and 1980. By the early 1980s it was estimated that some 60,000 Israelis or 18 to 20 percent of the entire non-Arab industrial workforce were employed in defence industries, and that perhaps 300,000 Israeli workers depended directly and indirectly on defence production for their livelihood. By comparison, only five percent of the workforce in the United States is employed in the defence sector.[14]

The three largest defence firms (all state-owned), IAI, Israel Military Industry (IMI or TAAS) and Rafael (the National Weapons Development Authority), experienced rapid expansion. Between 1967 and 1972, production expanded six-fold for IMI and doubled for IAI with increases in personnel of 200 and 300 percent respectively. Rafael boosted its manpower complement by 250 percent. By the early 1980s, IAI, the largest firm in Israel, consisting of five divisions and 15 subsidiaries, and employing some 22,000 scientists, engineers, managers, and production workers, produced 400 military and civilian products. The company alone accounts for 39 percent of Israeli industrial exports, with a fiscal year 1985-86 turnover of approximately $945 million. IAI, as mentioned above, was the main contractor for the Lavi. The increased investment in the defence industry soon produced results. In May 1970, the first major weapons system to be developed entirely in Israel, the Gabriel ship-to-ship missile (SSM), was introduced. With the introduction of the Nesher aircraft and then the Kfir fighter-bomber, Israel became the seventh country to develop and build an advanced supersonic combat aircraft.[15]

THE GENESIS OF THE LAVI

It was during this period of unbridled optimism concerning Israel's military and industrial future that the Lavi had its origins. Given the success of the newly introduced Kfir, it seemed logical to do more in the aviation field. In early 1973, the IDF Chief of Staff, David Elazar, proposed that in the future all IAF aircraft be manufactured in Israel. Elazar had the support of the Deputy Minister of Defence (and former Chief of Staff), Zvi Zur. But Moshe Dayan, the Minister of Defence, was not as enthusiastic, insisting that Israel should build only some of the aircraft and that the rest could be purchased from the United States.[16] The period of buoyancy was soon to end with the arrival of yet another war between Israel and its Arab neighbours in October 1973. The war imposed a heavy cost on Israel, and shook Israeli confidence. Some 2,500 Israelis died, and material losses totalled over 800 tanks and 114 aircraft, all but 20 of the jets falling prey to Arab anti-aircraft defences — and this, in less than three weeks of fighting.[17]

The effectiveness of the Arab missile defences came as a surprise to the Israelis who had become accustomed to operating against poor ground defences. As a result, the IAF began viewing air-ground attack as the most demanding of tasks for multi-mission aircraft. Most impressed by the heavy wartime losses was IAI, the builder of the Kfir. IAI saw the war as being a turning point in aircraft design. The increasingly dangerous environment in which aircraft had to operate seemed to stress three basic design criteria: survivability, mission effectiveness, and affordability.[18] The problem was to come up with a design that would incorporate these attributes and thus convince the Israeli government to put up the money.

In December 1974 IAI presented Shimon Peres, the Minister of Defence, with a plan to replace Israel's aging fleet of American A-4 Skyhawks and the Kfirs with a second-generation aircraft. The company argued that because of the Kfir project, research and development teams and equipment were already in place and should therefore be utilised. Peres raised the issue with the Cabinet but no decision was taken. The air force was more interested in acquiring American-made F-16 fighter-aircraft and Israel's Labour government was attempting to strike a deal to co-produce F-16s in Israel, a proposition that the United States Secretary of Defense, James Schlesinger, vetoed.[19]

The idea of producing a new aircraft had not died. When former IAF commander, Ezer Weizman, became Minister of Defence in 1977 in a Likud government, he asked IAI to give him plans for a new generation of fighter-aircraft. He was presented with two options, one for the Ariyeh, a two-engined aircraft, the other a one-engined airplane. Again, however, the air force was more interested in F-16s and a new American fighter-aircraft, the F-15. In 1977, Israel tried to obtain co-production rights for the F-15, a product of the McDonnell Douglas Corporation. The company refused to negotiate co-production but proved willing to give out subcontracts to Israeli firms for $20 million worth of F-15 parts in 1979.[20]

In 1979 the IAF also began considering its options for the 1990s and into the twenty-first century. Three alternatives came to mind: the production of an Israeli-designed aircraft, co-design and production of an American aircraft, and purchase of an off-the-shelf, foreign-built aircraft. A joint U.S.-Israeli team was also set up to consider co-production. Weizman had other ideas. He cancelled the Ariyeh option, claiming it was simply too expensive. In its place he suggested upgrading Israel's F-4 Phantoms and buying F-18s from the United States.

Weizman was not finished, however. He returned to IAI's proposal for a one-engined aircraft, and in February 1980, approved Lay-Out 33, the plan advocating such an aircraft. As the Minister described it in a Cabinet meeting, the aircraft, known as the Lavi, would be small, compact, and low-cost "with low-level penetration capabilities. Not an interceptor, but a second line aircraft, designed to replace Israel's aging Skyhawks and Kfirs." Tentative government approval to go ahead with the project was given in February 1980, with 450 aircraft to be produced to serve as a second line of defence spearheaded by 100 American-supplied fighter-bombers.[21]

Weizman resigned shortly afterwards and was replaced in his portfolio by Prime Minister Menachem Begin. In 1981, the IAF re-examined the operational requirements of Lay-Out 33 and found flaws. IAI had designed a small aircraft equipped with a General Electric F404 engine for the simple reason that it believed smaller equalled cheaper. The air force, led by its commander, Major-General David Ivri, claimed that the small aircraft did not fit its requirements. Instead, the IAF pressed for substantial alterations in the original blueprints, demanding a multi-purpose aircraft with a longer range and a greater complement of armaments. The air force and IAI, with the approval of Begin, apparently bypassed the Cabinet and the Ministry of Defence and changed the specifications. The General Electric F404 engine was rejected as underpowered and composite materials and state-of-the-art avionics were added to produce an aircraft equivalent to the F-16. Along with the changes came a dramatic rise in cost. In 1979, development costs for the Lavi were estimated at $750 million with a unit fly-away price of $7 million (a figure that did not include the cost of development). The changes forced up development costs to $1.5 billion with a unit fly-away price of $10.8 million.[22]

There was little opposition to the project in its early stages. The Knesset's Foreign Affairs and Defence Committee gave its approval to the Lavi in 1980, with only two of its 25 members voting against it, one of whom was a former IDF Chief-of-Staff, Yitzhak Rabin.[23] There was, however, some criticism of the way IAI had handled the matter. The Israeli State Comptroller, in his 1981 report, criticised the company for investing millions of dollars in the Lavi without authorisation. The result, in his opinion, was the presentation of a *fait accompli* to the government.[24]

THE PROJECT IS RESHAPED

The increased cost of the Lavi, however, led IAI and the Defence Ministry to restructure the project. A three-pronged approach was adopted. The number of aircraft to be procured was reduced from 450 to 300. It was also decided to lobby the United States to divert military assistance money to the Lavi. Lastly, attempts were to be made to contract for scientific data packages with American companies, a move that required approval of the United States Department of Defense (DOD).[25]

The desire to involve the United States stemmed from two basic considerations: money and technology. Initially the Israelis had planned to produce many of the components of the aircraft, including the all-important engine, domestically. However, the notion of developing an Israeli engine was soon dropped after studies indicated that a minimum of $2 billion was needed to do the job.[26] IAI then looked to Europe as a European power plant would avoid the problem of a third-party veto on export sales, something the Israelis would face if the Lavi was powered by an American engine. Weizman insisted that Israel wanted a guarantee of "no strings attached" if a European engine was selected. However, no European country or company wanted to work with Israel and risk losing sales in the Arab world. The United States Department of Defense was approached in 1980 and permission was given to Israel to co-produce the General Electric F404 engine.[27]

Faced with the prospect that Israel would have difficulty, financially and technologically, building the Lavi, the project managers chose to outline a strategy to obtain the needed components. Three categories of items were selected for external procurement. The first included equipment for which the technology did not exist in Israel. Only the engine fell into this area. In the second, were components that could be made in Israel but which were critical if the first aircraft was to be delivered in 1990, with an initial operational capability in 1992. The wings and most of the elements of the flight control system were in this group. The last category included those items for which domestic production was not justified — gearboxes, pumps, and other standard items. Retained for domestic development were all the aerodynamic-associated elements (except the wing), any items where new technical solutions were likely, and all avionics except the head-up display. Advancing the state-of-the-art was the aim for all design aspects and equipment directly related to the primary goal.[28]

Moreover, as IAI President Gabriel Gidor stated in 1979, the Israelis believed they were more advanced than the United States in the field of avionics; in his words, Israel was "one class ahead of the F-16 in avionics."[29]

Attempts to find foreign firms willing to work with IAI met with mixed results. Practically no European firms were interested. The Israelis proved to be more successful in finding an American company to provide an engine. In June 1981 the Pratt and Whitney PW 1120 powerplant was selected as suitable for the Lavi and a contract was signed in February 1982. One month later, the United States Department of Defense authorised Israel to use FMS credits to produce the engine in the United States. American-based Grumman Aerospace was permitted also to begin designing composite wing and tail sections for the Lavi. Within a year, IAI awarded Grumman a $120 million contract to manufacture the wing and tail assemblies for the prototype Lavi and for 20 shipsets for the initial batch of production aircraft. [30]

The funding of the project, however, had still to be resolved. In late 1980, Weizman had met with his American counterpart, Secretary of Defense Harold Brown, in an unsuccessful attempt to acquire FMS credits for the Lavi to be spent in Israel and the United States. With the election of Ronald Reagan in 1980, however, things began to look up for the Lavi. The United States, as noted previously, allowed FMS credits to be used to acquire the PW 1120 engine. Encouraged by this, Israel mounted a spirited campaign with both the Congress and the Executive to obtain American funding for the Lavi, stressing three reasons why the Lavi deserved American support: the United States had begun selling advanced aircraft to Arab states, thus threatening to erode Israel's qualitative edge; by building the Lavi, Israel could maintain its technological edge and the United States would not be under pressure to sell Israel's most advanced fighter to the Arabs since it was not American-made; and Israel would have an advanced aircraft industry that would provide considerable local employment and possible export monies.[31]

The proposal met stiff resistance. The Chairman of the Northrop Corporation, Tom Jones, vehemently attacked the notion of funding the Lavi with American money, particularly since his own firm was developing its aircraft, the F-20, without United States government backing. Jones cited a 1980 presidential directive, endorsed by Reagan, that established a need for a new fighter but stipulated that "aircraft companies will assume all financial and market risks." By funding the Lavi, the United States was changing the market risks and exporting American jobs.[32] Jones received support from Lyman Joseph, the Vice-President of General Dynamics, who complained "why should the U.S. spend money to set them [the Israelis] up to compete against us?"[33]

The American firms received backing from Secretary of Defense Caspar Weinberger and the Pentagon. In testimony before the House of Representatives' Foreign Affairs Committee in February 1983, Weinberger advocated withholding financial assistance for the Lavi on political and commercial grounds. First, Israel had no need to develop a new-generation aircraft since the F-15s and F-16s already in the Israeli inventory were superior to the Lavi; second, the real reason Israel was so anxious to build the aircraft was to promote its own exports and compete against American aircraft in foreign markets. Moreover, the Pentagon was reluctant to allow Israel access to advanced composite technology and the American Joint Chiefs of Staff saw no reason for the Lavi, judging the IAF to be of more than sufficient size and quality to meet expected threats. Within the Reagan Administration, only Secretary of State George Shultz was in favour of funding the aircraft (against the wishes of the Department of State) while President Reagan tried to maintain some distance from the matter.[34]

The Israelis had better luck with Congress. Strong lobbying resulted in the introduction of an amendment to the FY 1984 Continuing Budget Resolution in November 1983 calling for $550 million for the Lavi, $300 million to be spent in the United States, the rest in Israel. Approval was given within four days with little floor debate and without committee hearings. The Department of Defense delayed the release of the funds claiming the portion earmarked for use in Israel was for production, not research and development, but this obstacle was soon removed. Reagan signed the bill into law in late November 1983.[35] Congress appropriated another $400 million for the Lavi in FY 1985 ($150 million to be spent in the United States, $250 million in Israel) with relatively little debate. In 1985, Congress appropriated a further $800 million for FY 1986 and FY 1987, entitling Israel to spend "not less than" $250 million per fiscal year domestically, bringing total American support for the Lavi to $1.75 billion through FY 1987.[36]

The Israelis were also successful in gaining the release of American technology. Licences for 25 items including fabrication technologies for wing and tail structures and a computerised flight system were released by Secretary Shultz in May 1983 over the objections of the Departments of Defense and State. Approval for the transfer of composite wing technology to IAI was given late the following year.[37]

SOME PROBLEMS START TO EMERGE

With the financial and technological requirements falling into place, IAI was able to put the project into high gear. However, even as the Lavi began to take shape, concern mounted that the program's cost was rising too quickly. Prior to obtaining American funding, Israel had spent $198 million on the aircraft in FY 1982 and a further $210 million in FY 1983. Moreover, the estimated cost of development had risen from $750 million in 1979 to $1.5 billion in 1983. Production of 300 aircraft was estimated to cost $3.27 billion, and the total for the program, including spares, fuel and land maintenance expenses, was estimated to be in the range of $10.96 billion over a 15-year period.[38]

The news of the escalating price of the Lavi program could not have come at a worse time, for Israel, in the early 1980s, was suffering through a severe economic crisis. The invasion of Lebanon, which had started in June 1982, had absorbed anywhere from $1.2 billion to $2.5 billion from the Israeli treasury by late 1983. Inflation in 1984 had reached a staggering height of 450 percent and Israel's external debt was $25 billion, the largest per capita in the world.[39] Servicing that debt in 1982 had cost the Israeli government over $800 million, soaking up a full 32 percent of that year's export earnings. Furthermore, Israeli industry was in a serious slump in the early 1980s. From October 1982 to June 1983, industrial exports fell by 25 percent, the metals and electronics sectors declining 35.7 percent in one year. Government economists and industrialists blamed the poor trade performance on one cause — a sharp reduction in arms sales brought about by unfulfilled aircraft sales to Argentina after the Falklands conflict and the diversion of production to the Israeli military as a result of the war in Lebanon. With defence expenditures and servicing the debt accounting for 57 percent of the Israeli budget in FY 1982, all aspects of defence, including the Lavi, came under review.[40]

Defence spending fell in 1985 by $300 million (a 10-percent cut) following a smaller decline in 1984. Some 2,000 officers and civilians were discharged in 1984-85, the first time the IDF had ever let go employees and servicemen. Rumours began circulating in the press that the air force wished to see the Lavi cancelled, prompted by Hebrew University professor Dan Horowitz's comment that the IAF wanted "a first-class plane at the best possible price and the Lavi is a second-stringer and too costly."[41] In late 1985, a review of the entire Lavi program was ordered, the second time such a review had been undertaken. The first took place in 1982 when Ariel Sharon assumed the post of Minister of Defence. Then the project had been frozen for a few months while Sharon acquainted himself with the details. This second review involved the entire Israeli Inner Cabinet which met three times to discuss the aircraft. The original backer of the Lavi, Ezer Weizman, argued for cancellation, claiming the expensive Lavi was not the plane he had approved. His was the only voice of opposition, however, and the program was renewed with funding intact for FY 1986. The Inner Cabinet, acknowledging that the treasury was not bottomless, instituted an annual spending cap of $550 million. Shortly afterwards Defence Minister Rabin, one of the original opponents of the Lavi, approved a production schedule of 24-30 aircraft a year beginning in 1990.[42]

Neither the review nor the spending cap did much to silence the growing domestic opposition to the Lavi, and they accomplished even less with the project's foes in the United States. Weinberger and the Department of Defense continued to oppose funding for the aircraft. A DOD team, led by Dr. Dov S. Zakheim, United States Deputy Under Secretary for Defence Planning and Resources, was appointed by the Pentagon in 1985 to study the Lavi. Their report, delivered in February 1986, claimed Israeli price estimates for the project were 30-35 percent too low and could cost the United States $16 billion above current military aid levels over the next 15 years. Unit fly-away costs were deemed to be $20.7 million in FY 1983 dollars, not $14.7 million as the Israelis claimed.[43]

The report drew an immediate Israeli counterattack. IAI claimed that its labour rates were $24 an hour, not $45 to $49 as Zakheim had stated, the discrepancy amounting to $2 million per aircraft. Citing 65 percent commonality between Pratt and Whitney's PW 1120 and F100 engines, the Israelis asserted that they could produce the engines at $3 million a copy, not $4.5 million. Finally, the American team was accused of overpricing the cost of materials to be purchased by $2 million per aircraft.[44] The development cost, somewhere between $2.2 and $2.6 billion was not a source of major disagreement. The Israelis, however, declined to provide the United States with any specifics concerning the Lavi spending cap

— whether it was in constant or current dollars and if it applied to production as well as development of the aircraft.[45]

Concerned by Israeli intransigence, both Weinberger and Shultz asked Israel in July 1986 to participate "fully, immediately, and completely" in an American study of possible Lavi alternatives. Weinberger warned Israel that the United States felt itself under "no obligation" to continue funding the aircraft once the study was completed. To ensure that the message was received, the Pentagon blocked the release of $67 million already appropriated for the Lavi. At a press conference in Israel on July 20, one day before the prototype Lavi was to be unveiled, Defence Minister Rabin countered by refusing even to consider alternatives until the money was released. The funds were unfrozen in mid-August but the Pentagon refused to back down from the new study, appointing Zakheim to lead the DOD team.[46]

While Zakheim went about his work, the Reagan Administration tried to convince Israel to cancel the Lavi. Rabin visited Washington in late September 1986 and met with Weinberger and a delegation from General Dynamics, the builder of the F-16. The company, which had already agreed in August 1983 to purchase $300 million worth of Israeli-made components for 75 F-16s sold to Israel, made a significant offer. If the Lavi was cancelled, Israel would be allowed to build 300 updated F-16s under licence with the United States government making a considerable contribution in setting up the needed industrial infrastructure. Rabin turned the proposal down, arguing that the termination of the Lavi project would cost Israel more than $500 million in compensatory damage payments to American firms.[47]

The carrot was accompanied by a stick. In late September 1985 in a lecture at Georgetown University, John Lehman, the United States Secretary of the Navy, attacked not only the Lavi, but also France's Rafale fighter and Britain's Experimental Aircraft Project (EAP). Labelling the aircraft as "nationalist projects," Lehman stated that they were all attempts "to reinvent the F-16" done "at the expense of the deployable force structure within...the alliance." This marked the first time a Pentagon official had publicly criticised American allies about their combat aircraft programs.[48] The Pentagon was not finished. In November, it declared that it would cost Israel $13 to $15 billion to produce 300 aircraft, at a fly-away cost of $22.1 million.[49]

The Pentagon did not have to work very hard to convince some Israelis that the Lavi was too expensive and should be scrapped.

Indeed, some Israelis had reached that opinion quite independently of American pressure. Ezer Weizman, for instance, continued to be vocal in his opposition to the aircraft, claiming that "we set out to build an Austin Mini, and we have ended up with a Cadillac."[50] Perhaps the most damaging domestic opposition to the Lavi emanated from within the Israeli military. Senior officers were concerned that the rising cost of the aircraft, in tandem with shrinking budgetary allotments for defence and American reluctance to increase aid to Israel, threatened the IDF's capability to defend successfully Israeli security. A work plan issued by the General Staff in early 1986 indicated that at least $100 million had to be excised from the military budget in 1986. Two years of defence cuts, however, had left little fat in the budget other than major programs such as the Lavi. Fearing that the aircraft project could cut seriously into funds available for other programs, the staff made reference to the need to "re-evaluate" the Lavi.[51]

Some of the other criticisms from within the military were less circumspect than the General Staff's report. Major-General Dan Shomron, in his capacity as IDF Deputy Chief of Staff (he was promoted to Chief of Staff in 1987), attacked the Lavi as too ambitious and too expensive for a country with Israel's resources. Shomron was joined in his criticism by his superior, Lt. General Moshe Levy, the IDF Chief of Staff, and both men, in July 1986, were ordered to refrain from attacking the Lavi. Levy did not stop. In testimony before the Knesset's Foreign Affairs and Defence Committee in January 1987, he claimed that if he had been Chief of Staff when the project first came up for discussion, he would have voted against it. Even the air force commander, Amos Lapidot, added his voice to the debate in a speech before the Tel Aviv Chamber of Commerce in early 1986 when he commented that the Lavi was "not the only solution for the IAF future requirements."[52]

Cost was not the only problem plaguing the Lavi. Reports surfaced in 1986 that there were problems with the integration of the aircraft's electronic-warfare systems. The difficulties were said to be serious enough to prompt officials to consider reducing the number of internal electronic-warfare systems, perhaps substituting remotely piloted vehicles and helicopters to operate in a standoff-jamming role. The result was substantial delays in the program's timetable. Initially it had been hoped that the prototype would make its first flight in 1985. The first flight, however, did not take place until 31 December 1986, with the second on 8

January 1987.[53] In spite of these problems, General Menachem Eini, the Lavi Program Director, continued to insist that the first delivery of aircraft would take place in 1990 with a production run of 24 a year and the possibility of increasing that figure to 36 without any additional investment. Senior IAF officials were less optimistic, however, stating in 1986 that they expected no aircraft before 1995 or 1997, and only 210 by the year 2000.[54]

The second Zakheim Report and its aftermath

The controversy over the Lavi heated up considerably when Zakheim arrived in Israel in January 1987 with his long-awaited study of possible alternatives. At a press conference on 8 January, Zakheim made it clear that he thought the Lavi program should be cancelled. He acknowledged, on paper at least, that the Lavi appeared to be superior in many respects to American aircraft. However, he reminded his audience that the plane was still an "unproven aircraft" and that if the Lavi turned out as planned, it would be "nothing short of a miracle." Furthermore, he estimated that the annual cost of the project would soon amount to at least $1 billion and not the $550 million as the Israelis claimed. Zakheim also made it clear that Israel could not expect the United States to increase aid. The American-imposed ceiling of $1.8 billion in military aid was "hard and fast," and should Israeli cost estimates for the Lavi prove too low, other programs would suffer. Zakheim also attacked the rumour that the United States would be willing to buy the Lavi at some later date. Not only did the United States have "absolutely no interest" in adding the Israeli aircraft to its inventory, it retained the option to veto sales to other nations as at least 40 percent of the Lavi was being produced in the United States.[55]

The report itself, directed by Zakheim, was a joint production of the Departments of State and Defense, the National Security Council, the Office of Management and Budget, the United States Air Force and several private defence firms. The companies were asked to suggest alternatives to the Lavi, keeping in mind, among other things, the need to budget a production run of 300 aircraft with a 20-year life cycle that maximised indigenous Israeli manufacturing of components and subsystems as well as possible airframe production and co-production opportunities. Some 19 options were put forward, with the five most important being discussed in an unclassified "Executive Summary" (the report itself remains classified). None of the choices provided the 96 million man-hours of employment that the Lavi was estimated to bring.

McDonnell Douglas offered 300 AV-8B Harriers incorporating maximum Israeli content including co-development of a new avionics system involving 39 million man-hours of work. Per unit fly-away cost was put at $21.4 million for a total program price of $7,428.3 million. A second McDonnell Douglas option, involving 40 million man-hours, included 250 Harriers and 50 deep-attack variants of the F-15 at a unit cost of $21.4 million for the Harrier and $27.6 million for the F-15, for a total cost of $8,194 million. A third alternative, the licenced production in Israel of 300 F-16s, was put forward by General Dynamics. Fly-away unit costs were put at $14.6 million, or $4,671.8 million for the entire program, and some 43-55 million hours of employment would be provided. Licenced production of F-16s with Lavi avionics was also suggested. This option provided the most hours of employment for Israeli industry, 68 to 80 million with a reasonable price; a unit cost of $16.9 million and a program total of $5,842 million for 300 aircraft. The last alternative involved 300 McDonnell Douglas F-18 Hornets, providing 31 million hours, but costing $27.1 million per plane, or $9,494.6 million in total.[56]

The Lavi was dealt another quick blow within a month after Zakheim presented his report to Israel. In February, the U.S. General Accounting Office (GAO), the investigative arm of Congress, painted a bleak financial picture for the aircraft project. The GAO estimated fly-away costs at $17.8 million per aircraft and predicted the Lavi would cost Israel $1 billion a year by 1990 and $1.4 billion by 1994.[57]

Supporters of the Lavi were quick to counterattack. The project leader, Menachem Eini, rejected the alternatives as too expensive and unrealistic, claiming that 3,000 to 4,000 workers would have to be fired if the Lavi was scrapped. Moshe Keret, Director-General of IAI, argued that there was no point in discussing Zakheim's proposal as "the Lavi was and will be the best alternative as long as we are talking about producing a plane locally..." IAI declared the unit fly-away cost for the Lavi to be $14.5 million. Even if initial development and engineering expenses were factored in, IAI maintained that the per-copy price would not exceed $24 million. The debate turned personal when Eini publicly attacked Zakheim, an Orthodox Jew, asserting that Zakheim, who "claims to be motivated by love of Israel is in fact causing tremendous damage to Israel." Under pressure from Defence Minister Rabin, Eini retracted his statement the next day, saying his comments were "out of place" and should not have been made.[58]

The attacks on Zakheim's plan could not obscure the fact that support for the Lavi among senior civilian and military officials was starting to disintegrate. Reports on Israeli television in late December 1986 had cast doubts on the reliability of IAI cost estimates when it was revealed that wage increases and currency fluctuations had increased the cost of one man-hour on the Lavi project to $37, not $24 as IAI had been claiming.[59] During a press conference in early February 1987, Yitzhak Rabin declared that both the Lavi and Zakheim's alternatives could exceed Israel's financial capabilities. Moreover, the Defence Minister found it "extremely difficult to envision...completing the Lavi's development and production" within the existing budgetary framework. He noted that if he was facing a new situation, without the investment of $1.25 billion, he doubted whether he would vote for the Lavi.[60]

Within a matter of weeks, two serious blows were delivered to the Lavi program by the IDF General Staff and the Israeli State Comptroller. On 3 March, Israel's senior military men recommended the Lavi be scrapped, proposing instead the acquisition of 75 to 100 General Dynamic F-16s, equipped, possibly, with Israeli avionic systems. This move, it was hoped, would save enough money to reactivate the development of so-called "force-multiplying" weapon-systems cancelled in 1986 because of defence budget cuts. Before March ended, a secret report on the Lavi written by the Israeli State Comptroller was leaked to the press. Singled out for criticism was the General Staff and particularly IAF commander, General Amos Lapidot. According to the report, development costs for the Lavi had risen 148 percent between 1980 and 1985, while the unit cost per aircraft rose by 108 percent. The Staff and Lapidot were accused of not considering the adverse effect of the project on other IDF programs or the needs of the air force in general. Given financial constraints, the Comptroller claimed only 210 Lavis could be built, further inflating unit costs. Purchasing F-16s instead would result in a saving of 33 percent and the Comptroller insisted that cancellation of the Lavi would not seriously damage Israeli industry or cause unemployment.[61]

The result of all this conflicting information was virtual paralysis in the decision-making process. When Zakheim had presented his study to the Israeli government in January 1987, he was assured that a decision would be made within six weeks. This did not happen. Instead the Defence Ministry and the Cabinet preferred to continue studying Zakheim's alternatives as well as the General Staff's recommendation to scrap the Lavi. In the interim, flight testing of the prototypes continued while the Ministry of Defence scheduled orders concerning the Lavi for six months rather than a year in case the Cabinet chose to scrap the program.[62]

The Lavi was struck yet another blow when Dan Shomron succeeded Moshe Levy as the IDF's Chief of the General Staff in April 1987. Well-known for his opposition to the Lavi, Shomron's promotion to Chief of Staff only fueled speculation that the Lavi's days were numbered. The change at the top of the IDF came hard on the heels of a rumour that Defense Secretary Weinberger was planning to freeze funds earmarked for the Lavi. In an attempt to restore some confidence, IAI agreed to contribute $57 million of its own money to the Lavi project. Whatever IAI hoped to accomplish was soon undone. Defence Minister Rabin held a series of meetings with the Defence Ministry and IDF officials in April to discuss the Lavi, and the information they brought to him was not encouraging. If research and development was included, the project would cost $13.8 billion between 1987 and 2004, fully $4.4 billion more than the budgetary ceiling set by the government. In 1981, a Lavi was estimated to cost five percent more than an F-16; by 1987 a Lavi would cost 57 percent more.[63]

More dismal projections emerged when the Defence Ministry's Lavi project management committee met on 2 May. The committee estimated that the Lavi would cost $593 million in 1989, $637 million in 1990, $817 million in 1994, $928 million in 1997, and $995 million in 1999. Faced with such gloomy statistics, the project leaders concluded that the purchase of 150 F-16s would be 46 to 50 percent cheaper than the manufacture of 150 Lavis.[64]

When the senior officers of the IDF met with the Cabinet in a special session held on 20 May, the military made it clear that something had to be done quickly. Major General Avihu Ben-Nun argued that the Lavi be cancelled and Israel purchase 75 F-16s. Air force commander, Major General Lapidot, was more circumspect. In his view, the Lavi and the F-16 had similar operational capabilities and each offered certain advantages. However, each Lavi could end up costing nearly twice as much as an F-16. Whatever the Cabinet chose to do, Lapidot stressed the need to reach a quick decision. Even if the Lavi was retained, a certain price would be paid elsewhere. If $550 million was allocated annually to the aircraft (the minimum figure being discussed), a badly needed program to modernise the navy, including the acquisition of five patrol boats and four submarines, would have to be scrapped. [65]

IAI objected to the pessimistic projections issued by the IDF and the Defence Ministry, claiming that the program was "on time, on cost and performing better than expected." Moreover, Moshe Keret, IAI's Director-General, warned that should the Lavi be cancelled, his firm would have to fire 4,500 skilled employees, adding that it might be years before the Israeli economy could absorb such a large number of workers. The company also denigrated the F-16, stating that "to the best of our knowledge the Lavi is superior to the F-16 in air-to-ground missions, and more or less has the same capabilities in the air-to-air role."[66]

Other Israeli companies were less than enthused about the Lavi. During a meeting of the Manufacturer's Association on May 25, the various members could not agree on a common policy concerning the plane's future, and consequently resolved not to take a position during discussions of its fate. Most disgruntled by the massive infusions of money into the Lavi program were the managements of IMI, Rafael, and Tadiran, who complained that research and development activities had come to a halt because of the Lavi. Rafael's management also disputed the claim that cancellation of the project would cause massive unemployment, arguing that the projects revived after the end of the Lavi would require more workers than those working on the aircraft.[67]

To the disgruntlement of nearly all involved, the Cabinet did not come to a quick or final decision. Three of Zakheim's options, the Harriers, the combination of Harriers and F-15s, and the F-18s, were rejected; two others, the co-production of F-16s and the manufacture of F-16s with Israeli avionics, would remain under consideration. In the interim, funding for the Lavi was approved until April 1988. Rabin made it clear that if the Israeli government wanted the Lavi to continue beyond that date, funding for it would have to come from outside the defence budget. By mid 1987, development costs were being estimated at $2.8 billion, of which some $1.4 billion had already been spent. With a 1987 defence budget of $2.6 billion, Rabin declared his Ministry could no longer support the project financially.[68]

One of Rabin's Cabinet colleagues, Vice-Premier Shimon Peres (Premier from September 1984 to October 1986), was not as pessimistic concerning the funding problem. The founder of IAI, Peres was impressed by the technological achievement the Lavi represented, and he promised to find the money required to see the aircraft through to fruition. In order to get the project out of its moribund state, Peres suggested that 75 and not 100 Lavis be constructed in the first stage, although he admitted he did not know how much this would cost. The proposal was rejected by the military on the grounds that the cost of such a short production run would be prohibitive.[69]

The badly battered Lavi program achieved a much-needed success in early June when its second prototype broke the sound barrier for the first time. During July, however, the Lavi came under harsh scrutiny. In a public address, the Israeli naval commander, Major General Avraham Ben-Shushan, remarked that as long as the Israeli government debated the Lavi, his service would remain in limbo. If the navy could not acquire new missile boats and submarines, it would mean the "physical extermination of the Israeli Navy."[70] The harshest public attack against the Lavi to date was delivered by Michael Bruno, the Governor of the Bank of Israel. Speaking before the annual meeting of the Israel Management Institute, Bruno asserted that there was no justification whatsoever for continuing the program. The money saved by cancelling the project could be used to enlarge Israel's capital stock by 10 percent, the increase being used to make exportable products and provide more income.[71]

Further woes: the Maltz Report

Bruno's attack on the Lavi paled in comparison to the content of a report issued by Ya'arov Maltz, Israel's State Comptroller. Maltz asserted that the Lavi had been rammed through the political and defence establishment without any serious discussion of its economic viability or contribution to Israel's security needs. He noted that no investigation was made of the Lavi's projected costs, development risks, projected capabilities, production timeframe, or the effect the project would have on technology, exports, and employment. Moreover, an alternative plan suggested by the IDF Chief of Staff and the IAF commander, the upgrading of the Kfir, had been ignored by Weizman during his tenure as Defence Minister. A team appointed by the United States to work with Israeli experts in framing the program had been ignored, the Israelis refusing to allow the Americans to see the plans for the Lavi. In effect, Maltz charged, Weizman and the Ministerial Defence Committee made a "decision in principle" when approving the Lavi, the decision makers having no idea of the plane's cost, size, and purpose or its role in the battlefields of the future. As well, in at least one case, the Committee was given misleading data to make the aircraft seem more attractive.

The most damaging criticism directed against the Lavi concerned the aircraft's technological contributions and production schedule. Proponents of the Lavi had always been quick to point out that the program would bring much-needed expertise in the handling of modern technologies and materials. However, in the Comptroller's opinion, these things were important "only if there is a reasonable chance that they will be used," and that depended on whether Israel would or could build a successor to the Lavi. This was unlikely, in his opinion, as the costs of such an undertaking were prohibitive and would require additional expertise that would put the successor aircraft in direct competition with the best technology in the East and West. As it was, Maltz pointed out, half of the Lavi was being produced in the United States and most of the funding was American.[72]

In terms of the production schedule, it was likely that the initial aircraft would not be delivered until at least 1992, although some officials claimed it could be 1995 or 1997 before the air force saw the first operational Lavi squadron. The aircraft produced by 1992, however, would not be equipped with the specially designed avionics systems scheduled to be completed in 1995. If any further delays ensued, the IAF risked being stuck with outdated aircraft or too few replacements as older jets went out of service. Maltz also labelled the scheduled cost of production per aircraft as misleading. When the Ministerial Defence Committee reviewed the program in 1985, the cost of unit production had been calculated on the basis of a run of 300 aircraft, even though the schedule called for only 210 Lavis to be built. A shorter run, the State Comptroller asserted, would have obvious "effects on the average cost of each plane."[73]

Not surprisingly, the Israeli government struck back at Maltz, offering a point-by-point rebuttal of many of the Comptroller's allegations. The government contended that had it made its decisions with the Defence Minister on the basis of accurate and updated information, arguing that in a program as complex as the Lavi, some risks could not be accurately quantified. The government also rejected another claim made by Maltz, that it had too quickly refused General Dynamic's 1982 offer to have the F-16 co-produced in Israel. The American firm's insistence on building the nose scuttled the project, it was insisted, as that section of the aircraft was filled with the type of avionics that IAI wanted to produce. Moreover, the F-16 could not accommodate all the equipment IAI wanted to put into it.[74]

The Israeli government's attempts to control the damage inflicted by the Comptroller's findings were undermined when word leaked out of a visit by Rabin to Washington at the end of June. The Israeli Defence Minister had met with Weinberger and Shultz to discuss the future of the Lavi. The Americans asked Rabin to scrap the plane in favour of 75 to 100 F-16s at a cost of $2.4 billion, with deliveries to begin in 1991. The Defense Department agreed to help pay the costs of terminating program contracts, estimated to be as high as $400 million. Rabin, in turn, had two requests. He wanted the United States to increase the amount of FMS credits that could be spent annually in Israel from $300 million to $400 million. In addition, the Americans were requested to continue directed offsets valued at $150 million per year for another two years rather than letting them lapse at the end of the fiscal year. Directed offsets required American firms selling military items in Israel to buy specified amounts of equipment from Israeli companies. The United States agreed to negotiate increased levels of FMS credits but were reluctant to continue the offset program. While Rabin was most interested in buying off-the-shelf aircraft, the Americans made it clear that they were willing to negotiate co-production or licenced production agreements on the F-16s. [75]

Rabin returned to Israel with the new promises, engendering yet another round of inconclusive Cabinet meetings. The Defence Minister added to the paralysis by refusing to give an absolutely clear verdict either for or against the Lavi. Indeed, rumours abounded that while in Washington, Rabin had met with an American aircraft manufacturer (thought to be Grumman), offering a share in Israeli technology in return for development funds. Press reports indicated that the Cabinet was virtually deadlocked over the issue, with both Prime Minister Shamir and Vice-Premier Peres trying to salvage not only the Lavi, but their fragile three year-old National Unity government. One major Cabinet minister was not so eager to see the Lavi saved. At a joint meeting of the Knesset's Foreign Affairs and Defence Committee and the Finance Committee, Minister of Finance Moshe Nissim called for an immediate halt to the project. Nissim stated that the money earmarked for the aircraft should be used to finance other vital weapons projects and he went on record in opposing any attempts to use compulsory or volunteer loans to raise money for the Lavi. He also reported that development costs were now estimated to be $3.5 billion, $1.5 billion of which had already been spent.[76]

After the hectic events of June and early July, a lull in activity concerning the Lavi ensued amid rumours of a Cabinet split down the middle on the issue. The pause ended quickly, however, in mid August when two Knesset committees voted 22 to 6 in favour of continuing the program. The vote drew an immediate response from the United States. On 11 August, Charles Redman, a spokesman for the United States State Department, called openly for Israel to terminate the Lavi project, an action that would be in the "best interest" of Israel and the United States. If the Lavi continued, Redman stated, it would "crowd out other important projects" in Israel currently funded by the United States. The following day, George Shultz sent his own message to the Israeli Cabinet urging an end to the project. The Secretary of State stressed that the continuation of the Lavi ran counter to Israeli interests given the availability of cheaper options and he reaffirmed American willingness to help Israel with the alternatives.[77]

DECIDING THE LAVI'S FATE

Hopes were high that a decision would finally be made when the Cabinet met to discuss the Lavi on 16 August. Rabin came down against continuation, telling his colleagues that it would take five years and a further $4 billion (on top of the $1.5 billion already spent) to get 90 Lavis operational, almost twice the cost of an equivalent number of F-16s. Rabin was supported by Finance Minister Nissim and Economics Minister Gad Ya'acobi who reported that if the Lavi were to continue, $200 million a year would have to be added to the defence budget for the next decade. In addition, IAI had admitted that its previous estimate of $14.5 million per aircraft had been in error, the firm now accepting the GAO figure of $17.8 million as more accurate. The Cabinet, however, also could not have been ignorant of a public opinion poll published two days previously in which only 27.6 percent of those polled favoured cancelling the aircraft. Some 43.5 percent supported continuing the Lavi at full scale with 19.6 percent favouring development on a reduced scale. After six hours of debate, however, Shamir and Peres agreed to delay the vote for a week or two in order to investigate ways of cutting program costs. After the meeting, several ministers intimated that the real reason for putting off the vote was that a majority had been in favour of scrapping the Lavi.[78]

The anti-Lavi faction received a boost when the Governor of the Bank of Israel, Michael Bruno, re-entered the fray. In a document released by the Bank, Bruno admitted Israel had much to gain from the development and production of avionic systems, but that the country could not realistically afford the luxury of producing fighter-aircraft. Only the manufacture of a large number of aircraft could make development costs economically viable, and Israel could not afford to do this. The money could be put to better use elsewhere in industry to increase exports. If allowed to continue, Bruno concluded, the Lavi would cause uncertainty, harm economic growth, and push up long-range interest rates.[79]

When the Cabinet reconvened on 21 August, a vigorous defence of the Lavi was put forward by Yitzhak Modai, a Minister Without Portfolio. Asked by Shamir to look into alternative methods of financing the Lavi, Modai disputed the Treasury's assertion that there was not enough money to continue the aircraft program. In fact, he declared that tax revenue had been larger than expected in the last few months and there was, in his opinion, enough to cover the amount needed for the Lavi and other IDF projects. As before, it was agreed to postpone a Cabinet vote on the Lavi for another week.[80]

Shimon Peres used the respite to try to salvage something of the project. Hoping to avoid a confrontation with his fellow Labour ministers, almost all of whom opposed the Lavi, and wishing to minimise damage to IAI, the Vice-Premier suggested an alternative to IAI's top management. In a meeting at his home on 24 August, he proposed that the Lavi be cancelled and that in its place IAI be given $100 million a year to develop an advanced, twin-engined fighter for the twenty-first century. In addition, he suggested that negotiations begin with General Dynamics to allow the manufacture of F-16 parts in Israel. IAI, however, was not impressed with the plan, rejecting it as "not serious," and an attempt by Peres to extricate himself from a political trap.[81]

Peres had more success though with Rabin and Nissim, but only after changes were made in the proposal. In its original form, the document suggested that only production of the Lavi would be stopped. At Nissim's insistence, Peres re-wrote that section to read that both development and production of the aircraft would be stopped. The Finance Minister also convinced Peres and Rabin that the $100 million to be added to IAI's budget had to come from the Defence Minister's existing budget and that no extra funds would be allocated for that purpose. All three men agreed that Israel should ask the United States to allow her to participate in the Advanced Tactical Fighter (ATF) project, the American "jetfighter of the future."[82]

On the eve of the 30 August Cabinet meeting, U.S. Ambassador Thomas Pickering presented Shamir, Peres, and Rabin a letter from the Reagan Administration strongly urging the cancellation of the Lavi. In return, the United States was willing to do a number of things. An offer to improve Israel's research and development infrastructure was made, as was a pledge to help Israel finance test flights of the Lavi prototypes to develop avionic systems. The Americans also agreed to Rabin's proposal that Israel receive an increase in the amount of American aid that could be spent in Israel (from $300 million to $400 million a year). Moreover, some of the credits could be used to cover costs incurred through the cancellation of Lavi program contracts. General Dynamics, according to the letter, was ready to negotiate joint production on a "variety of current models, although the United States refused to give an unequivocal commitment for Israeli participation in the development of an advanced F-16, known as the Agile Falcon."[83]

When the Cabinet met the next day, Shamir decided to force the issue to a vote, apparently at the last minute, surmising that there would be a tie, ensuring the Lavi's continued development. To the surprise of Shamir and his colleagues in the Likud bloc, when the votes were tallied, the Lavi went down to defeat. The Cabinet rejected continuation of the project by a margin of 12-to-11, with one abstention, choosing instead to adopt the alternative proposal put forward by Peres. The margin of victory for the anti-Lavi faction was made possible when a supporter of the aircraft, Health Minister and Labour party member, Soshana Arbeli-Almosline, succumbed to party pressure and abstained. With the exception of the Health Minister, all of the Labour ministers voted against the aircraft. Within the Likud bloc, only Finance Minister Nissim broke rank and cast his ballot against the Lavi. Within minutes of the end of the meeting, Minister Without Portfolio Moshe Arens, a former Defence Minister and one-time Vice-President of IAI, offered his resignation, saying he refused to accept responsibility for the decision.[84]

DISMANTLING THE PROJECT

The cancellation of the Lavi came as a shock to the employees of IAI. Just a few weeks before, the company and workers had signed an agreement to dock one day's pay a month in order to cut costs, a move that would have saved $12 million in 1987. However, with the end of the program, between 3,000 and 4,000 engineers and technicians, some 20 percent of IAI's workforce, faced the loss of their jobs. The same fate awaited at least 2,000 and possibly 4,000 employees at various subcontracting firms. The day after the crucial vote, thousands of IAI employees blocked the main roads around IAI's main facility near Tel Aviv and forced a closure of the Tel Aviv-to-Jerusalem highway. The demonstrations lasted for three days, ending only when police warned that they would take firm action to stop the protests.[85]

On 31 August, Prime Minister Shamir met with industry leaders and promised to check the possibility of holding a new vote on the issue. Privately, Shamir was said to have stated that he would not bring the issue up for a second vote unless he was assured that at least two opponents in the Cabinet were willing to change their minds. He also refused to listen to Moshe Aren's demand that party discipline be imposed on Nissim to make him alter his vote, the Prime Minister regarding the Finance Minister as a strong electoral asset. Ariel Sharon, the Industry Minister, met with Rabin and suggested that instead of scrapping the Lavi, the project should be frozen for three months to allow an independent non-partisan committee of experts to study new funding ideas or alternatives to the Lavi. During the freeze, no IAI employees would be fired but "no new parts for the Lavi would be ordered." Rabin and Peres rejected the idea and Shamir did not present the proposal or attempt to force another vote at the 6 September Cabinet meeting. Sources within the Labour party reported that under no circumstances would they agree to a new vote, and that if the Prime Minister refused to refer the matter to the Inner Cabinet, where Lavi opponents were in the majority, the government would fall.[86]

As frustration set in, the attacks on the anti-Lavi forces became more bitter and personal. At a speech on the West Bank, Shamir called the IDF's participation in the public debate over the Lavi a "mistake" and an "intolerable deviation," remarks he later claimed had been "misinterpreted." His intent, he explained, had been to warn the military to stay away from disputes "in the future." Rabin jumped to the defence of the IDF, stating that the officers had the right and duty to express opinions in such matters, declaring that he had given them permission to present their views "in face of attacks and attempts to harm their professional credibility." Herut party leaders (the Herut party being the largest grouping within the

Likud bloc) lambasted the Labour party for its role in the Lavi's demise, claiming Labour "lacked faith" in Israel's strength and wanted to "whittle Israel down to size." Labour responded by saying that words would "not cover up the disasters which the Likud has brought upon us, such as inflation, the war in Lebanon and the embroilment of the Israel Aircraft Industries."[87]

All work on the Lavi stopped immediately after 30 August. Within the next two weeks Rabin ordered IAI to implement plans for developing new weapons in place of the aircraft, and to fire 3,000 to 5,000 Lavi workers. IAI responded by ordering the dismissal of 150 to 200 workers employed by Lavi subcontractors and some 200 foreign workers. Rabin later ordered a freeze on dismissals as it became obvious that the powerful Histadrut Labour Federation would do all it could to prevent or drastically slow the dismissal of permanent employees. A group of IAI's top managers, designers and engineers put forward a proposal to transfer one of the prototype Lavis to the United States for the United States Air Force (USAF) to study as a basis for that service's planned close-air-support aircraft while a second prototype continued flight testing in Israel. The group hoped that the Americans would accept the Lavi as the replacement for the aging A-10 aircraft. However, IAI refused officially to comment on the plan and the Israeli Cabinet showed no interest in the idea.[88]

Within two weeks of leading the charge against the Lavi, Rabin held out hope that the project might be saved. The Defence Minister confirmed that his government was trying to find a foreign partner or partners to take over as the aircraft's prime developer. The United States government and a number of American and European aerospace companies had been approached with one American firm (unnamed) showing interest, provided a customer other than Israel could be found. To date, no one had shown any such interest, but Rabin maintained that if a partner could be found within the next 30 to 60 days, Israel could still continue with the Lavi. In the expectation that no partner would be found, the Israeli Defence Ministry proposed that a two-year transitional period be instituted in which the United States would allocate production work to IAI, cushioning the anticipated 3,000 to 4,000 layoffs caused by the Lavi's cancellation. In the short term, Israel would purchase off-the-shelf weapons using FMS credits. Rabin also announced that Israel would purchase 90 General Dynamics F-16C aircraft over the next decade to replace the cancelled Lavi.[89]

Finance Minister Nissim flew to the United States for two days of meetings with Secretary of State George Shultz and Secretary of the Treasury James Baker centering on the Lavi and Israel's economy. Shultz promised that aid to Israel would be maintained at its present level for the next two years and that his government would do all it could within budget constraints to help Israel deal with problems caused by the end of the Lavi program. The Secretary also pledged to maintain the level of offsetting funds at $150 million per annum for the last two fiscal years of the Reagan Administration. Nissim was pleased and declared that the offset deal would assure employment for "3,000 Israeli workers."[90]

Despite attempts by IAI and members of Likud to reverse the 30 August verdict, the Lavi project continues to be dismantled. Israeli and American officials have begun the complex and time-consuming process of breaking all the Lavi program contracts, at a cost estimated by Rabin at around $400 million. Compensation negotiations between Pratt and Whitney, the builder of the PW 1120 engine, and the Israeli government have begun, a company spokesman denying that his firm had filed suit against the Israelis. The company is asking for a settlement of $300 million. Grumman, the contractor for the wings and tail section, claimed that it would not be severely affected by the collapse of the Lavi program since it did not have a production contract. The company predicted that it would face no layoffs although there would be a loss of potential jobs.[91]

In late September, the Israeli Cabinet allocated $25 million to complete the third Lavi prototype and install a core avionics package in it. The money, however, is not enough to fund the required flight testing, although it is expected that additional funds will be found for flight-test work in 1988. The decision will allow IAI and some subcontracting firms to retain 600 employees in total until March 1988. The prototypes are to be used as flying test beds to evaluate avionics systems designed for the Lavi with an eye towards possible export sales. A payment of $40 million was also advanced to IAI to help finance the task of eliminating as many as 3,000 to 4,000 employees from its work force, a task the Defence Ministry wants completed by the end of March 1988.[92]

The cancellation of the Lavi, in the short term at least, has meant the IDF will have an additional $200 million to $250 million a year for the next decade to spend on other projects. During its existence, the Lavi monopolised 15 percent of the defence budget and almost all of the available research and development resources, this at a time when allocations to defence were shrinking. American military aid had remained at $1.8 billion a year since 1979, and between 1982 and 1987, the IDF experienced a 20-percent cut in its domestic defence budget, from $3.2 billion to $2.6 billion. The result of this fiscal austerity was reductions in training, stockpiling, and the discharge of some 5,000 personnel. The navy, badly in need of modernisation, saw Cabinet-approved plans to buy new missile-boats and submarines delayed for eight years because of a shortage of funds. The air force was forced to shut down several squadrons and ground 15 percent of its aircraft. Since the end of the Lavi, Rabin has given the navy approval to acquire four "Saar 5" frigates and three diesel submarines, valued at $1.3 billion over ten years. Some 60 to 70 percent of the new projects will benefit the IAF, including the purchase of the F-16s, more pilotless drones, and improved helicopters. High on the list of army priorities are more Merkava MK 3 tanks and new artillery pieces and ammunition.[93]

THE FUTURE WITHOUT LAVI

The prognosis for Israel Aircraft Industries does not seem to be as good. The company has lost what may well have been a very lucrative product and now faces the difficult task of retrenchment, not to mention the dismissal of perhaps 4,000 highly skilled engineers, designers and technicians. An IAI spokesman has complained that the decision to scrap the Lavi will "prejudice the ability of the company ever again to manage and develop a combat aircraft program." Not all Israelis, however, are unhappy to see IAI take a fall. The President of the Israeli electronics firm Tadiran, Yigal Neeman, welcomed the cancellation of the aircraft project for the reason that it would release resources that will benefit the Israeli electronics industry as a whole. His company, like many others in Israel's defence sector that were not involved with the Lavi, had suffered through a recession as the IDF cut back in order to keep funds available for the aircraft. For many, it is now IAI's turn to bear the consequences of Israel's faltering economy.[94]

IAI's troubles may extend beyond the loss of the Lavi and its attendant jobs. In early June 1987, Rabin had remarked that Israel's defence industries had become too large and had to be reduced. Civilian products had to be emphasised in the Defence Minister's opinion, and he singled out IAI as one firm that had done little to change its ways. It would seem that the Defence Ministry will now step in and force IAI to reform. A state-owned company, IAI has always been run like a private company and the government does not subsidise its range of commercial products. The firm is run by a 13-man board of directors, each of whom serves a three-year term. The board includes businessmen, government officials, and ministerial representatives. In addition, there are two permanent members, the President of IAI and the air force commander. Plans are being made to break the company into four separate corporations, each operating independently within its own delineated field. Each corporation would have its own management and balance sheet and be made to show a profit and prove efficiency on a revenue-to-manpower ratio.[95]

While the cancellation of the Lavi was a crushing economic blow to IAI, the political fall-out of the decision has yet to be fully measured. By 1987, the broad bi-partisan support for the Lavi had evaporated and was replaced by a bitter, partisan squabble involving Israel's two major political groups, the Labour party on the left and the Likud bloc on the right. Irrespective of the merits or faults of the aircraft itself, the Lavi found itself stuck in the swamp of Israeli coalition politics. Coalition governments have been the rule in Israel, the result of a complex electoral system guaranteeing proportional representation for small political parties. However, even by Israeli standards, the government that has ruled since September 1984 is unusual. Labour and the Likud, neither of whom could form a majority even with their allies, chose to form a government of "National Unity." A power-sharing system was devised so that the Labour leader, Shimon Peres, held the premiership until October 1986, handing it over then to Yitzhak Shamir, leader of the Likud bloc.

By 1987, the cooperation between the two groups left much to be desired, and practically every issue, large or small, became a battle for advantage. The result was government paralysis as both parties geared up for the next national election, which can be held no later than November 1988. Within this political context, the Lavi became a chance for the parties to demonstrate their respective differences to the voters. The Herut party, the major grouping with the Likud bloc, "adopted" the Lavi at its national convention in 1986, pledging to see the aircraft through to fruition. For the Likud, the airplane became part of its "romantic" image of a strong and powerful "Greater" Israel. For the Labour ministers, the issue came down to a matter of cold hard sums, and having found the project too expensive, they voted against it. Party discipline was imposed, forcing the Labour Health Minister to abstain, and when the Likud Finance Minister sided with the Labour ministers, the Lavi's fate was sealed.[96]

The end of the Lavi may yet effect the Labour party. The aircraft was genuinely popular in Israel, and thousands of IAI employees and their dependents could choose to punish Labour in the next election. The Likud will certainly try to play up its defence of the Lavi, maintaining the battle was lost because of U.S. government pressure and Labour treachery. Relations between the Likud bloc and the military will probably be strained over the IDF's attack on the Lavi. Moreover, many of the military leaders, including Chief of Staff Shomron and his deputy, General Ehud Borak, are Kibbutzniks, traditionally a source of Labour party support. The three IDF regional commanders are openly sympathetic to Labour policies. Thus the alliance between Labour and the IDF in the fight against the Lavi may help the party to regain its reputation as the custodian of national security and to consider the military as a source of leadership recruits.[97]

Left unresolved in the wake of the demise of the Lavi is a consideration of the role that the defence industry plays or should play in Israel's political and economic life. In the halcyon days of the late 1960s and early 1970s, few Israelis questioned the wisdom of building a large defence industry. It provided jobs, brought in revenue from export sales, and put dependable and sophisticated weapons in the hands of Israeli servicemen. Given Israel's enduring security problems, the development of a successful and profitable arms sector was seen by many as making a virtue out of a necessity. However, the Israelis, with the Lavi project, discovered one of the major perils of building a major weapon system such as an advanced aircraft, that of reconciling the military rationale for such a weapon with the economic and technological ramifications its manufacture brings.

In the beginning of the Lavi project, reconciliation seemed easy enough. The IAF needed new ground-support aircraft and IAI, fresh from the success of producing the Kfir, was willing to meet that demand. The design staff and facilities were in place, the company told the government, but not for long unless put to use. Designs were drawn up and altered by the air force, which had its own notions of what was needed. The result was a larger, more complex and infinitely more expensive aircraft than originally anticipated, but it was a system that would be able to operate in a number of roles.

Certainly the prospect of an Israeli-built aircraft had much appeal for the Israeli government. Continually subjected to arms boycotts or delivery suspensions by its arms suppliers, the production of an Israeli fighter-aircraft would increase the latitude of Israel's military policy. No more would Israel have to answer to the United States if that country, objecting to some Israeli action, cut off delivery of F-16s or F-15s. General Ehud Borak, as Chief of Planning for the IDF General Staff, enunciated the Israeli position on this issue in an interview in December 1982: Israel had to be self-sufficient in arms, "not only to achieve technological freedom of action" but in particular because of the "urgent and critical need" to lessen "our reliance upon American money" with the grave consequences it has "for our political independence, but also for the national pride and values of Israeli society as a whole."[98]

The Israelis discovered, however, that it can be an extremely expensive and difficult proposition to design and build a combat aircraft. Considerations of time and cost dictated that two things be done: first, foreign technology had to be incorporated into the Lavi; and second, more funding had to be found for the project. In the first case, American technology in the form of aviation engines, composite wing technologies and other items were contracted for so that 40 percent of the money expended on the Lavi's development was being spent in the United States. This would mean that, despite Borak's brave words, now the United States government would have to be convinced of the merit of the aircraft, not only in a strictly military sense, but in terms of what it meant to the overall Israeli economy.

There was no shortage of advocates willing to praise the Lavi's potential contributions to Israel's industrial health. An IDF spokesman in 1986 referred to the aircraft as a "high-tech challenge, a national project, not a defense project, combining efforts of many companies. Each generation needs a challenge." Its most vociferous defender, Moshe Arens, called the aircraft "the most important program in Israel today, both in terms of defense as well as in terms of Israel's economy." It was hoped that the aircraft would spearhead the development of a series of robust high-technology industries, for as the Deputy General Manager of Engineering at IAI put it, Israel "can't just look for ways to make a better refrigerator." Even Rabin, during his period of support for the Lavi, declared that the entire issue boiled down to "a question of what sort of country we will have in the future, a country based on textile industry technology or one based on high-tech industries."[99]

In the process of producing the Lavi, the Israelis hoped to acquire expertise in the areas of structure, electronics, aerodynamics, and materials with a particular emphasis on the extensive use of computer-aided design/computer-aided manufacture (CAD/CAM). Without the Lavi and the expertise it would bring, it was predicted that Israel would not be able to establish the technological infrastructure needed to attract foreign companies and investment. It was this same desire for technological advancement and skilled jobs that led Israel to be the third nation to sign up for the United States' Strategic Defense Initiative in May 1986.[100]

If the Lavi had gone through to production, would it have generated spin-off industries and boosted Israel's technological standing? Given the fact that the Lavi is a dead issue, the only possible answer is "maybe." Its proponents claimed that it would, and compared the aircraft to the subsidised electronics industry of the 1960s and 1970s, which later performed spectacularly and more than returned its investment. However, times have changed and spin-offs are a chancy business. Electronics was a relatively new and open field at that time. Aviation is not; it is a difficult and competitive business. Furthermore, ten and twenty years ago, Israel had more room to manoeuvre in its defence budget; today, given Israeli and American financial constraints, Israel's margin for risk-taking is very low. And if an aircraft program can be defined in one word, it is "risk." Such projects are expensive with no guarantee of success, technically or economically, for even experienced aviation manufacturers. Clearly, Israel possesses no special economic advantage in building high-performance aircraft, and simply because Israel was technically capable of building it was no reason to divert great resources to do so.

CONCLUSION

In many ways, the Lavi is an excellent example of the difficulties faced by smaller powers in the field of high technology. Countries such as Israel can gradually increase their economic and technological capabilities to the level where they can produce an aircraft equal to the F-15. Having reached that point, however, they find that there has been a parallel growth of sophistication in state-of-the-art technology at such a dizzying pace that in spite of their greater production capabilities, they are even more dependent on imported technology. Thus, by the time their product achieves operational readiness, it is already obsolete; particularly is this the case in weapons system such as an aircraft, which have an estimated life span of less than ten years. Thus, countries like Israel have really only three options if they wish to field top-of-the-line aircraft: arrange collaborative partnerships with countries who have similar requirements; take up licenced production of an existing foreign system; or take an existing design and upgrade it to their requirements.[101]

The Israelis simply realised this too late. In many ways, it can be said that Israel learned too well the lesson of self-reliance taught by the various arms embargoes it faced over the years. The government sought to encourage the development of a powerful military-industrial complex that "expressed itself primarily in a constantly increasing influence upon determining national priorities and upon the societal decision-making process."[102] The result was that IAI, believing it had the resources to build an advanced aircraft, decided to build one, and called on its allies in government and the military to support its bid.

One potential conclusion that can be drawn from the Lavi case is that the power of the Israeli "military-industrial complex" is waning. The Lavi debate proved that this complex is not a monolithic grouping of individuals, all speaking with one voice. Many industrialists opposed the project (some, of course, out of self-interest, as their firms were not involved). Most interesting was the fact that some Israeli politicians, particularly Rabin, Peres, and Nissim put what they took to be the interests of the country ahead of those of the Lavi program, despite the political risks involved.

The collapse of the Lavi program may have also permanently altered the relationship between Israel and the United States. One of the original reasons many Israelis found the Lavi so attractive was that it offered the promise of avoiding American arms boycotts when the United States disagreed with Israeli policy, as had occurred with the freeze on deliveries of F-16s in the early 1980s to protest Israel's occupation of southern Lebanon. Given American pressure exerted against the Lavi, it can hardly be concluded that Israel has lessened its dependence on its superpower patron.

Much of the blame for the Lavi debacle must also rest with the United States. With little debate, the Congress approved billions of dollars for the project with apparently little thought to the consequences. The protests of American aerospace companies were dismissed as the cries of the privileged fighting to keep their economic fiefs intact. Although in part true, not all the opposition stemmed from purely selfish motives of profit or preservation of markets. Some Americans warned that it was simply imprudent to dilute the potential leverage of American military aid by encouraging Israel to build the Lavi without linking that assistance to American foreign policy goals such as a possible Arab-Israeli peace settlement. It was also claimed that by assisting with the Lavi, the United States was encouraging Israel to assume a larger burden than its economy could bear. Despite the fact that the United States was bearing a large share of the development costs, Israel would still have to carry heavy direct charges during the production phase — charges that would prove staggering unless a foreign buyer could be found. The increasing sophistication of the aircraft meant that if exported, the Lavi would have to compete against the best the Western powers and the Soviet Union could produce, "and that is not Israel's league."[103]

The United States certainly indicated that it would oppose exports of the Lavi. In July 1983, Weinberger insisted that Israel had to produce 700 aircraft, not 300, to cover development costs, the conclusion being that the other 400 would have to be sold overseas. Israel denied needing to produce 700 Lavis, claiming that exports could be contemplated only after the aircraft was fully operational and after the IAF needs had been met. Less than a year later, Moshe Arens told the *Wall Street Journal* that exports were not only possible but that a potential customer was the United States itself! Even as late as the summer of 1987, IAI expected that the Lavi "would be able to speak for itself" in export markets by the mid-to-late 1990s and thought there was a reasonable chance of selling the aircraft to the USAF, possibly in cooperation with an American firm, as a close-support aircraft or advanced trainer.[104]

However, the prospects for that never seemed other than dim. As noted above, Zakheim explained to the Israelis that not only was his country not interested in purchasing the Lavi, it also would probably exercise its veto on sales to third countries. Under the Arms Export Control Act of 1976, the United States retained the right to block the sale of American defence articles, services, or defence items with American components to third parties unless prior approval had been given. The United States has not been shy about blocking Israeli sales, having vetoed the shipment of 24 Kfirs to Ecuador in 1977 (a ban that was not lifted until November 1981). The Lavi, with its American engine, wings, tail section and flight systems, would have been subject to the export control act, because at least 40 percent of the aircraft was being produced in the United States.[105]

It is not surprising that the United States would oppose exports of the Lavi. In the past few years, the United States has lost its competitive edge in a number of fields including that of aerospace. The prospect of yet another competitor, one that ironically would have fielded an aircraft subsidised with American funds, would not have been welcome. Weinberger dismissed the Lavi as inferior to the F-16, but his opinion was not shared by everyone in the U.S. defence community. Even Zakheim, who had claimed that the Lavi was "unproven," admitted that it appeared to have superior capability and range in the air-to-ground role. With a top speed of Mach 1.8, the Lavi was slower than the F-16 (Mach 2.0 or more), but was designed to have double the combat radius. Had Israel been able to produce the Lavi at a reasonable price, it might have proved to be a formidable competitor on the export market, particularly in markets where for various reasons, political or otherwise, American sales are difficult or impossible.[106]

Could Israel have afforded the luxury of the Lavi? The answer must be a qualified no. Certainly if Israel was willing to see the project through at all costs, it probably could have done so. However, the result might have been serious and possibly irreparable damage done to the IDF's force structure as well as to the economy. Although inflation fell from three-digit levels to 19.7 percent in 1986, the Israeli economy remains insecure, and the country faces a massive debt of $25 billion, the highest per capita in the world. Debt repayments to the United States, totaling $887 million in FY 1983, are projected to rise to $1.1 billion in 1992; this despite a move in 1984 by the United States to convert loans, both for military and economic assistance, to grants in order to help reduce Israel's financial obligations.[107]

By the mid 1980s, as the United States began to confront its own debt crisis, its aid to Israel started to level off. From 1948 to 1984, Israel had received $28 billion in assistance from the United States, 67.6 percent in military aid, the rest in economic assistance (Economic Support Funds or ESF). Aid reached a level of $2.6 billion in FY 1985 and escalated to $4.5 billion in FY 1986, with all ESF money since FY 1981 and all military aid since FY 1985 being in the form of non-repayable grants. However, with the budgetary problems in the United States and the introduction of the Gramm-Rudman-Hollings deficit-reduction law, Israel watched this level of assistance diminish. The new law required a cut of 4.3 percent in the FY 1986 aid package, and Israel was forced to return $125 million.[108]

The Israelis knew that they could ill afford to lose further American aid. In the 1970s and early 1980s, between nine and 30 percent of American military assistance had been diverted to non-defence purposes, while some 40 percent of the ESF money was being allocated to defence. One third of Israel's defence budget had been funded by the United States between 1977 and 1981; this share increased to 37 percent in 1982-83. The Israeli government managed to reach a tentative agreement for 1987 so that American military aid could remain at $1.8 billion, with economic assistance levelling off at $1.2 billion.[109] Zakheim made it clear that the United States would not surpass the current aid level when he presented his alternatives study, and this reluctance to put any more money into Israel doubtless had much to do with the decision to cancel the Lavi.

Israel will survive the collapse of the Lavi program both militarily and economically, although there will likely be some problems and dislocations, particularly concerning IAI. Less easily quantified is the damage the end of the Lavi will mean in terms of prestige and Israeli self-esteem. At one time, Moshe Arens claimed that the project was "just too deeply embedded in the Israeli economy, in Israeli society" to be scrapped, declaring he did not "know of a single case where an aircraft had been developed that is one of the best in the world and wasn't put into production."[110] Arens obviously must not have heard of Canada's ill-fated AVRO Arrow fighter-aircraft, cancelled in 1959 under similar circumstances of costs escalating and export markets failing to materialise.

Notes

[1]Hugh Schofield, "Israel Scraps Production of High-Tech Fighter Plane," *Globe and Mail* (Toronto), 31 August 1987, p. A8.

[2]Michael Ganley, "Israel Appears Committed to Lavi Despite US Pressure to Kill Fighter," *Armed Forces Journal International* 124 (September 1986): 30.

[3]Aaron S. Klieman, *Israel's Global Reach: Arms Sales as Diplomacy* (McLean, Virginia: Pergamon-Brassey's, 1985), p. 17.

[4]Gerald M. Steinberg, "Israel," in *The Structure of the Defence Industry*, ed. Nicole Ball and Milton Leitenberg (London: Croom Helm, 1983), p. 280.

[5]Carol Evans, "Reappraising Third World Arms Production," *Survival* 28 (March/April 1986): 110

[6]Sylvia K. Crosbie, *A Tacit Alliance: France and Israel from Suez to the Six Day War* (Princeton: Princeton University Press, 1974), p. 112.

[7]Edward N. Luttwak and Daniel Horowitz, *The Israeli Army, 1948-1973* (Cambridge: Abt Books, 1975), p. 328.

[8]Edward H. Kolcum, "Israel Pushes Design of Strike Fighter,"*Aviation Week and Space Technology*, 16 August 1976, p. 18; Ed Duyker, "The Evolution of Israel's Defence Industries," *Defence Force Journal* 38 (January-February 1983): 51-52.

[9]Gerald M. Steinberg, "Israel: High Technology Roulette," in *Arms Production in the Third World*, ed. Michael Brzoska and Thomas Ohlson (London: SIPRI, 1986), p. 168; Gerald M. Steinberg, "Indigenous Arms Industries and Dependence: The Case of Israel," *Defense Analysis* 2 (1986): 303; Kolcum, "Israel Pushes Design of Strike Fighter," p. 18.

[10]Shimon Peres, *David's Sling* (London: Weidenfeld and Nicolson, 1970), pp. 110-11.

[11]Alex Mintz, "The Military-Industrial Complex: The Israeli Case," *Journal of Strategic Studies* 6 (September 1983): 116-17; Eliyahu Kanovsky, *The Economic Impact of the Six Day War* (New York: Praeger, 1970), p. 120; Esther Howard, "Israel: The Sorcerer's Apprentice," *The Arms Race in the Middle East*, MERIP Reports no. 112 (February 1983), p. 19.

[12]Kanovsky, *The Economic Impact*, p. 52; Mintz, "The Military-Industrial Complex: The Israeli Case," p. 112.

[13]Eitan Berglas, *Defence and the Economy: The Israeli Experience* (Jerusalem: The Maurice Falk Institute for Economic Research in Israel, 1983), p. 33; Evans, "Reappraising Third World Arms Production," p. 110; Naftali Blumental, "The Influence of Defense Industry Investment on Israel's Economy," in *Israeli Security Planning in the 1980s: Its Politics and Economics*, ed. Zvi Lanir (New York: Praeger, 1984), p. 169; Howard, "Israel: The Sorcerer's Apprentice," p. 19.

[14]Blumental, "Influence of Defense Industry Investment," p. 173; Mintz, "Military-Industrial Complex: The Israeli Case," p. 111; Steinberg, "Israel," p. 290; Howard, "Israel: The Sorcerer's Apprentice," p. 17; Alex Mintz, "The Military-Industrial Complex, American Concepts of Israeli Realities," *Journal of Conflict Resolution* 29 (December 1985): 628.

[15]Mintz, "Military-Industrial Complex: The Israeli Case," p. 117; Steinberg, "Israel," p. 284; David Nordell, "Israel Aircraft Industries," *Israel Economist* 37 (June 1981): 54; Signe Landgren-Backstrom and Wolfgang Mallman, "World-Wide Trade in Major Weapons during the 1970s," *World Armaments and Disarmament: SIPRI Yearbook 1980* (London: SIPRI, 1980): 86; Joel Bainerman, "Israel: Defense Technology," *Israel Economist* 42 (February 1986): 18; Crosbie, *Tacit Alliance*, pp. 204-5; Frank Barnaby, "The Scale of World Military Expenditure," *Disarmament and World Development*, ed. Richard Jolly (Oxford: Pergamon Press, 1978), p. 12.

[16]Yoram Peri, *Between Battles and Ballots: Israeli Military in Politics* (Cambridge: Cambridge University Press, 1983), pp. 163-64.

[17]Nadav Safran, *Israel: The Embattled Ally* (Cambridge: Belknap Press, 1978), p. 311.

[18]Graham Clark, "Lavi Bares Its Teeth," *Military Technology* 10 (October 1986): 140.

[19]Tony Banks, "What Future For Lavi?" *Jane's Defence Weekly*, 28 March 1987, p. 557; Daniel Marcus and Jeff Abramowitz, "The Lavi, An IDF Journal Report," *IDF Journal* 3 (Fall 1986): 44-45; Howard, "Israel: The Sorcerer's Apprentice," p. 20.

[20]Marcus and Abramowitz, "The Lavi," pp. 44-5; Howard, "Israel: The Sorcerer's Apprentice," p. 21.

[21]Marcus and Abramowitz, "The Lavi," p. 45; Aaron Klieman, "Lavi: The Lion Has Yet to Soar," *Journal of Defense and Diplomacy* 4 (August 1986): 23.

[22]Clark, "LAVI Bares Its Teeth," p. 140; Steinberg, "Israel: High Technology Roulette," p. 174; Comptroller General of the United States, *U.S. Assistance to the State of Israel: Report by the Comptroller General of the United States* (Washington: General Accounting Office of the United States, 1983), p. 56.

[23]Yossi Melman, "Lavi Project Divides Israeli Cabinet," *Jane's Defence Weekly*, 2 February 1985, p. 177.

[24]Martin van Creveld, "The Making of Israel's Security," in *Defense Planning in Less-Industrialized States: The Middle East and South Asia*, ed. Stephanie G. Neuman (Lexington, Mass.: Lexington Books, 1984), p. 125; Baruch Kimmerling, "Making Conflict a Routine: Cumulative Effects of the Arab-Jewish Conflict upon Jewish Society," in *Israeli Society and Its Defence Establishment*, ed. Moshe Lissak (London: Frank Cass, 1984), p. 32.

[25]Klieman, "Lavi the Lion," p. 25.

[26]Bonner H. Day, "Israel's Quest for Military Independence,"*NATO's Fifteen Nations* 23 (December 1978/January 1979): 54.

[27]Michael Moodie, "Defense Industries in the Third World," in *Arms Transfers in the Modern World*, ed. Stephanie G. Neuman and Robert E. Harkavy (New York: Praeger, 1979), p. 301; Comptroller General of the United States, *U.S. Assistance to the State of Israel*, p. 57.

[28]Brian Wanstall, "Lavi Advanced Fighter and Industrial Springboard," *Interavia* 41 (January 1986): 74, 79.

[29]Benjamin F. Schemmer, "IAI Goal: $100 Million in Sales to DOD Next Year, Ease Technology Transfer," *Armed Forces Journal International* 116 (August 1979): 14.

[30]Hirsh Goodman, "Lavi: A New Israeli Multirole Combat Aircraft," Special Advertising Section, *Aviation Week and Space Technology*, 1 June 1987, p. 50; William Mark Kehrer, "U.S. Funding for the Israeli Lavi Project: An Examination and Analysis," *Middle East Insight* 3 (Novem-

ber/December 1984): 12; Clarence A. Robinson, Jr., "U.S. Offers Israel 15% in Military Offsets," *Aviation Week and Space Technology*, 5 December 1983, p. 26.

[31] Kehrer, "U.S. Funding for the Israeli Lavi Project," p. 12; Comptroller General of the United States, *U.S. Assistance to the State of Israel*, p. 56.

[32] Donald Neff, "Goodbye to the Tigershark," *Middle East International* 308 (12 September 1987): 7.

[33] Evans, "Reappraising Third World Arms Production," p. 113.

[34] Aaron Klieman, "Israeli Arms Sales: Perspectives and Prospects," *Jaffe Center for Strategic Studies*, Paper no. 24 (Jerusalem, February 1983), p. 46; Duncan L. Clarke and Alan S. Cohen, "The United States, Israel and the Lavi Fighter," *Middle East Journal* 40 (Winter 1986): 24-30.

[35] "Reagan Approves Credits to Israel for Lavi," *Aviation Week and Space Technology*, 28 November 1983, p. 27.

[36] "Funding For Israeli Fighter Triggers Debate in House," ibid., 21 May 1984, p. 24; Wolf Blitzer, "The High Cost of Backing Out," *Jerusalem Post International Edition*, 15 February 1986, p. 13; Clarke and Cohen, "The United States, Israel and the Lavi Fighter," p. 30.

[37] "U.S. Approves Technology Transfer to Israel For Lavi," *Aviation Week and Space Technology*, 5 November 1984, p. 20.

[38] "U.S. Nears Lavi Transfer Approval," ibid., 10 January 1983, p. 21; "IAI Bases Lavi Fighter Project on 300 Aircraft Procurement," ibid., 18 July 1983, p. 23.

[39] Elisabeth Skons and Rita Tullberg, "World Military Expenditure," *World Armaments and Disarmament: SIPRI Yearbook 1984* (London: SIPRI, 1984), p. 105; Clarke and Cohen, "The United States, Israel and the Lavi Fighter," p. 24.

[40] Klieman, *Israel's Global Reach*, pp. 54, 205-6; Comptroller General of the United States, *U.S. Assistance to the State of Israel*, p. 34.

[41] "Israel: Increasing Simulation Saves Funds," *Defense and Foreign Affairs* 13 (January 1985): 2; Yossi Melman, "Israel's New Enemy Complacency," *Jane's Defence Weekly*, 8 November 1986, p. 1119; Philip Ross, "Requiem for a Fighter," *Israel Economist* 40 (December 1984): 33.

[42] "Lavi Will Continue," *Jane's Defence Weekly*, 7 September 1985, p. 433; "Israel Backs Lavi Despite Opposition," *Aviation Week and Space Technology*, 17 February 1986, p. 33; Walter Andrews, "Israeli Silence on Cost of Jet Fighter Upsets Weinberger," *Washington Times*, 11 June 1986, p. 3.

[43] James K. Gordon, "U.S. Defense Dept. Claims Israelis Underestimated Lavi Fighter Costs," *Aviation Week and Space Technology*, 10 February 1986, p. 32.

[44] "Israel Calls U.S. Defense Estimate of Lavi Cost Too High," ibid., 24 February 1986, p. 19.

[45] Michael Dunn, "C'est Lavi," *Defense and Foreign Affairs* 14 (August/September 1986): 24; Andrews, "Israeli Silence on Cost," p. 3.

[46]"Gloves Off," *Military Technology* 10 (October 1986): 45; "Pentagon Go-ahead on Lavi," *Jerusalem Post International Edition*, 16 August 1986, p. 2.

[47]Klieman, *Israel's Global Reach*, p. 180; Hirsh Goodman, "U.S. Urges Israel to Make F-16, Not Lavi," *Jerusalem Post International Edition*, 4 October 1986, p. 5; Yossi Melman, "U.S. Administration Wants Israel to Cancel Lavi," *Jane's Defence Weekly*, 4 October 1986, p. 717.

[48]Amy Bodnar, "Allies are Wasting Money on Rafale, EAP, Lavi: Re-inventing the F-16, Says Sec. Nav.," *Armed Forces Journal International* 124 (November 1986): 29.

[49]Michael Widlanski, "To U.S. Chagrin, Israel Touts Lavi as Top Jet Fighter," *Dayton Daily News*, 9 November 1986, p. 12; "Controversial Israeli Jet Inferior to U.S. Aircraft, Weinberger Says," *Los Angeles Times*, 19 February 1987, p. 9.

[50]March Nichols, William Lowther, and David Bernstein, "Declawing a Military Lion," *Macleans* 99 (18 August 1986): 35.

[51]"Israel Considers Slowdown in Lavi Program," *Aviation Week and Space Technology*, 10 February 1986, p. 32.

[52]"Israel May Scratch Its Plans to Build Lavi Jet Fighter," *Washington Times*, 4 February 1986, p. 4D; Martin Sieff, "U.S. Bids Anew to Get Israel to Kill Lavi Jet," ibid., 1 January 1987, p. 5; Glenn Frankel, "Israel Studies U.S. Plea to Scrap Costly Lavi Jet Fighter Project," *Washington Post*, 8 January 1987, p. 38; "Concern Over Lavi's Cost," *Jane's Defence Weekly*, 29 March 1986, p. 547.

[53]"Lavi Faces Cuts in EW Systems Production," *Defence Electronics* 18 (June 86): 22; Clarence A. Robinson, Jr., "U.S. Companies Oppose Lavi Aid," *Aviation Week and Space Technology*, 14 February 1983, p. 18; "Lavi Multirole Combat Aircraft Begins Flight Testing in Israel," ibid., 19 January 1987, p. 19.

[54]Germain Chambost, "Israel's Lavi a Technological Target," *International Defense Review* 19 (July 1986): 891-92; Reuven Pedatzur, "What Price, the Lavi," *Israel Economist* 42 (April 1986): 15.

[55]Joshua Brilliant, "Lavi Still Unproven," *Jerusalem Post International Edition*, 17 January 1987, p. 2; Frankel, "Israel Studies U.S. Plea," p. 38; Ganley, "Israel Appears Committed," p. 26.

[56]"Executive Summary," *Lavi Alternatives Study*, Government of the United States (Washington, January 1987).

[57]Hugh Lucas and Yossi Melman, "Lavi Still Too Expensive Despite Reduced Estimate," *Jane's Defence Weekly*, 7 March 1987, p. 364.

[58]"Zakheim Wrong About Lavi," *Jerusalem Post International Edition*, 24 January 1987, p. 5; Joshua Brilliant, "Lavi Will Not Be Grounded," ibid., 17 January 1987, p. 1; John D. Morrocco, "GAO Report on Lavi Indicates Spending Will Exceed Cap," *Aviation Week and Space Technology*, 2 March 1987, p. 20; Dunn, "C'est Lavi," pp. 24-5; Martin Sieff, "Tempers Fly Faster, Higher than the Lavi," *Washington Times*, 10 March 1987, p. 6.

[59]Sieff, "U.S. Bids Anew," p. 5.

[60]"Israel's Dilemma Over Costly Lavi Programme," *Jane's Defence Weekly*, 14 February 1987, p. 212.

[61]Ari Egozi, "Israel General Staff Rejects Lavi," *Flight International* 131 (14 March 1987): 9; Reuven Pedatzur, "Lapidot Criticised Over Handling of Lavi Project," *Jane's Defence Weekly*, 4 April 1987, p. 576.

[62]James Bernstein, "Pentagon Report Urges Israel to Buy American, Drop Lavi," *Long Island Newsday*, 14 January 1987, p. S1; Joshua Brilliant, "Thousands to Lose Jobs," *Jerusalem Post International Edition*, 11 April 1987, p. 3.

[63]Reuven Pedatzur, "Shomron Steps Into the Fray as New IDF Chief," *Jane's Defence Weekly*, 2 May 1987, p. 813; "Israel's Defence Minister Turns against Lavi," *Defence* 18 (May 1987): 226.

[64]Reuven Pedatzur, "F-16s Would Cost Israel Half the Price of Lavi," *Jane's Defence Weekly*, 9 May 1987, p. 865.

[65]Reuven Pedatzur, "Israeli Navy Will Lose Out If Lavi Goes Ahead," ibid., 30 May 1987, p. 1039.

[66]Eric Beech, "Lavi: Lion or Albatross?" *Flight International* 131 (20 June 1987): 58; Donald E. Fink, "Israel Renews Debate on Lavi Development," *Aviation Week and Space Technology*, 1 June 1987, p. 18; Ari Egozi, "Lavi on Trial," *Flight International* 131 (6 June 1987): 9.

[67]Beech, "Lavi," p. 58; Egozi, "Lavi On Trial," p. 9.

[68]Geoffrey Manners, "Father of Lavi to Oppose Production," *Jane's Defence Weekly*, 6 June 1987, p. 1099; Avi Hoffman, "Defence Budget Cannot Fund the Lavi," *Jerusalem Post International Edition*, 20 June 1987, p. 2.

[69]Joshua Brilliant, "Ministers Still Discussing Lavi," ibid., 6 June 1987, p. 4.

[70]Reuven Pedatzur, "Israeli, Navy in Limbo until Lavi Debate Resolved," *Jane's Defence Weekly*, 4 July 1987, p. 1423.

[71]"Cabinet Still Undecided on Future of the Lavi," *Jerusalem Post International Edition*, 4 July 1987, p. 2.

[72]Joshua Brilliant, "Aircraft that Shouldn't Have Been," ibid., 11 July 1987, p. 7.

[73]David Rosenberg, "State Comptroller Lambasts Lavi Fighter Plane Project," ibid., 11 July 1987, p. 7; Brilliant, "Aircraft that Shouldn't Have Been," p. 7.

[74]Rosenberg, "State Comptroller Lambasts," p. 7.

[75]"Israel Wins U.S. Financial Concessions to Cover Possible Cancellation of Lavi," *Aviation Week and Space Technology*, 13 July 1987, p. 25.

[76]Peretz Kidron, "Lavi in the Balance," *Middle East International* 304 (11 July 1987): 10; Joshua Brilliant, "The Lavi Debate: Now a Search for Compromise," *Jerusalem Post International Edition*, 11 July 1987, p. 1; Asher Wallfish, "Nissim Wants Lavi Project Stopped Now," ibid., 25 July

1987, p. 3; Joshua Brilliant and Avi Temkin, "The Lavi Project's Fading Roar," ibid., 18 July 1987, p. 2.

⁷⁷Michael Mecham, "U.S. Increases Pressure on Israel to Abandon Lavi," *Aviation Week and Space Technology*, 17 August 1987, p. 21; "Cabinet Defers Its Decision on Lavi Project," *Jerusalem Post International Edition*, 22 August 1987, p. 2.

⁷⁸Peretz Kidron, "The Lavi Grounded," *Middle East International* 308 (12 September 1987): 7; Thomas L. Friedman, "Israel Puts Off a Decision on New Jet," *New York Times*, 17 August 1987, p. A-3.

⁷⁹"Cabinet Defers Its Decision on Lavi Project," pp. 1-2.

⁸⁰Avi Temkin, Joshua Brilliant, and Asher Wallfish, "Lavi Supporters Search for Way to Keep It Flying," *Jerusalem Post International Edition*, 29 August 1987, pp. 1-2; "Shamir, Peres Delay Decision on Lavi Project," *Globe and Mail*, 22 August 1987, p. A6.

⁸¹"Peres Suggests Lavi 2000," *Flight International* 132 (5 September 1987): 9.

⁸²Avi Temkin and Pinhas Landau, "Fighting Fit," *Jerusalem Post International Edition*, 12 September 1987, p. 5; "Lavi Grounded but Research Will Continue," ibid., 5 September 1987, p. 1.

⁸³"Lavi Grounded," pp. 1-2.

⁸⁴Schofield, "Israel Scraps Production," p. A-8.

⁸⁵"Lavi Workers Sacrifice Pay," *Jerusalem Post International Edition*, 15 August 1987, p. 3; Eric Bech, "Life after Lavi," *Flight International* 132 (26 September 1987): 51; "Israelis Cancel Lavi," ibid., 132 (12 September 1987): 8.

⁸⁶"Israeli Aircraft Workers Protest Lavi Fighter Vote," *Christian Science Monitor*, 1 September 1987, p. 2; Asher Wallfish and Menachem Shalev, "Political Squabbles Follow Lavi Death Sentence," *Jerusalem Post International Edition*, 12 September 1987, pp. 1-2.

⁸⁷Menachem Shalev and Joshua Brilliant, "Row over Army Rule in Lavi's Demise," ibid., 19 September 1987, pp. 1-2.

⁸⁸"Workers Plan to Save Lavi," *Flight International* 132 (19 September 1987): 11.

⁸⁹"International Partners Sought to Complete Lavi," *Aviation Week and Space Technology*, 14 September 1987, p. 23; "Israeli Air Force to Replace Lavi With F-16C," ibid.

⁹⁰David Makovsky, "U.S. Pledge to Help Soften Lavi Blow," *Jerusalem Post International Edition*, 19 September 1987, p. 2.

⁹¹Reuven Pedatzur and Len Famiglietti, "P&W in Friendly Talks Over Cancelled Lavi Costs," *Jane's Defence Weekly*, 7 November 1987, p. 1081; "Lavi Cancellation Sets Back Pratt's PW 1120 Engine Program," *Aviation Week and Space Technology*, 7 September 1987, p. 25.

⁹²"Israel Plans to Complete Third Lavi Prototype," ibid., 26 September 1987, p. 27; Reuven Pedatzur, "Rabin Spells Out Defence Force Cuts,"

Jane's Defence Weekly, 3 October 1987, p. 725; Pedatzur and Famiglietti, "P&W in 'Friendly' Talks," p. 1081.

[93] Shlomo Maoz, "Dividing the Spoils," *Jerusalem Post International Edition*, 12 September 1987, p. 3; Tim Guest, "C'etait Lavi," *Military Technology* (October 1987): 144; Ariel Levite, "Real Impact of IDF Budget Cuts Revealed," *Armed Forces Journal International* 125 (November 1987): 26; Reuven Pedatzur and Tony Banks, "Sunset on Lavi," *Jane's Defence Weekly*, 12 September 1987, p. 542; Joshua Brilliant, "How the Army Will Benefit," *Jerusalem Post International Edition*, 12 September 1987, p. 2.

[94] "What Follows Israel's Lavi?" *Interavia* 10 (October 1987): 1008; Harold Hirsh, Michael J. Gething, and Dexter Jerome Smith, "Sun Sets On the Lavi," *Defence* 18 (October 1987): 604.

[95] Geoffrey Manners, "Rabin Warns of Defence Industry Cuts," *Jane's Defence Weekly*, 13 June 1987, p. 1166; Michael Dunn, "Israel Aircraft Industries Shows Its Corporate Maturity and Reach," *Defense and Foreign Affairs* 12 (January 1984): 34; Asher Wallfish, "Rabin Warns IAI Workers the Firm Could Go Under," *Jerusalem Post International Edition*, 17 October 1987, p. 2.

[96] Mary Curtius, "Israelis Blast Cabinet for Dragging Feet," *Christian Science Monitor*, 18 August 1987, p. 8; "Barbarians at the Gate," *Jerusalem Post International Edition*, 14 September 1987, p. 24.

[97] Hirsh, Gething, and Smith, "Sun Sets on the Lavi," p. 604; "Israel's Angry Young Men of War," *Economist* 304 (19 September 1987): 54.

[98] Klieman, "Israeli Arms Sales," p. 18.

[99] Michael Collins Dunn, "Israel Tightens the Belt," *Defense and Foreign Affairs* 14 (February 1986): 9; "Moshe Arens on the Lavi," ibid., 14 (February 1986): 12; Widlanski, "To U.S. Chagrin," p. 12; David A. Brown, "Israel Demands U.S. Funds Prior to Talks on Lavi Alternatives," *Aviation Week and Space Technology*, 28 July 1986, p. 20.

[100] Ya'akov Sheinin, "High Technology ? Economic Growth," *Israel Economist* 14 (December 1985): 36; Aron Moss, "Israel's Participation in the SDI Program," *IDF Journal* 3 (Summer 1986): 6-7.

[101] Robert E. Harkavy and Stephanie G. Neuman, "Israel," *Arms Production in Developing Countries*, ed. James Everett Katz (Lexington, Mass.: Lexington Books, 1984), p. 193; Steinberg, "Indigenous Arms Industries," p. 296; "Home-Grown Fighters," *Flight International* 132 (12 September 1987): 1.

[102] Kimmerling, "Making Conflict a Routine," p. 32.

[103] Clarke and Cohen, "The United States, Israel and the Lavi Fighter," pp. 19-25.

[104] Klieman, *Israel's Global Reach*, p. 186; Fialka, "Israel Bucks Big Leagues," p. 40; David A. Brown, "Israelis Review Decisions that Led to Lavi Cancellation," *Aviation Week and Space Technology*, 14 September 1987, p. 23.

[105]Clarke and Cohen, "The United States, Israel and the Lavi Fighter," p. 21; David Pollock, *The Politics of Pressure: American Arms and Israeli Policy Since the Six Day War* (Westport: Greenwood Press, 1982), p. 234; Howard, "Israel: The Sorcerer's Apprentice," p. 22; Frankel, "Israel Studies U.S. Plea," p. 38.

[106]"Controversial Israeli Jet Inferior to U.S. Aircraft, Weinberger Says," p. 9; "Executive Summary," p. ES-7; Michael J. Gething, "Lavi The Aircraft," *Defence* 18 (February 1987): 68. The Lavi technical data is as follows:

Type:	Light Multi-Mission Fighter		
Missions:	Air-to-Air, Air-to-Ground, Advanced Operational Training		
Crew:	1 (2 in training versions)		
Dimensions:	Wing Span	8.78	m
	Length	14.57	m
	Height	4.78	m_2
	Wing Area	33.05	m^2
	Wing Sweepback	54.0	degrees
	Basic Take-Off Weight	9,990.0	Kg
Performance:	Combat Radius, Air-to-Air	1,850.0	Km
	Combat Radius, Air-to-Ground:		
	High-Lo-High	2,130.0	Km
	Lo-Lo-Lo	1,110.0	Km
	Maximum Speed	800.0	KCAS (Mach 1.8)
	Combat Load Factor	9.0	G
	Combat Thrust Weight	1.07:	1

Cited in Clark, "Lavi Bares Its Teeth," p. 144.

[107]Avi Temkin, "Last Year's Inflation almost 20 Percent," *Jerusalem Post International Edition*, 24 January 1987, p. 5; Clarke and Cohen, "The United States, Israel and the Lavi Fighter," p. 24; Comptroller General of the United States, *U.S. Assistance to the State of Israel*, p. iv; "Israel's Economic Crisis: What Israel Must Do," *Commentary* 79 (April 1985): 16.

[108]Amy Bodnar, "Israel's Lavi Rolls out This Month; But Will It be Cancelled Next Month," *Armed Forces Journal International* 123 (July 1986): 32; Yossi Melman, "Doubts Grow about Lavi Fighter Project," *Jane's Defence Weekly*, 14 June 1986, p. 1089.

[109]Martin C. McGuire, "U.S. Assistance, Israeli Allocation and the Arms Race in the Middle East," *Journal of Conflict Resolution* 26 (June 1982): 225-26; Skons and Tullberg,"World Military Expenditure," p. 105; John M. Goshka, "Israel to Return $51 Million U.S. Aid," *Washington Post*, 22 January 1986, p. 14.

[110]Quoted in Nichols et al., "Declawing a Military Lion," p. 87.

7

"Techno-Nationalism" and the Contemporary Debate over the American Defence Industrial Base

David G. Haglund, with Marc L. Busch

INTRODUCTION

During the spring and summer of 1987 two ostensibly unrelated developments, each possessed of economic, technological, and security implications, attracted the attention of defence analysts in the United States. One, by far the more well-publicised event, involved the diversion of sophisticated military technology to the Soviet Union on the part of two of America's allies; the other concerned the sale of an American manufacturer of semiconductors (ironically, itself a subsidiary of a foreign firm) to a second domestic manufacturer of this same electronic product. Although different in several ways, the two episodes had one aspect in common: they each bore testimony to the increased salience of high-technology trade for the security interests of the United States.

The less well-publicised incident involved National Semiconductor's purchase of a French-owned American electronics enterprise, Fairchild Semiconductor, based in Cupertino, California. Ordinarily, a transaction such as this would not have attracted much attention, were it not for the fact that the year before the French parent corporation, Schlumberger Ltd., had been prevented from selling 80 percent of its ailing subsidiary to Japan's Fujitsu Ltd. The opposition to the earlier sale had been predicated on frank national-security grounds: it was the view of both the Secretary of Defense, Caspar Weinberger, and the Secretary of Commerce, Malcolm Baldrige, that should Fujitsu acquire one of the few remaining domestic semiconductor producers, the effect upon the American defence industrial base could be profound.[1] As we shall relate below, this anxiety was propelled by a combination of the recent travails of the domestic electronics sector and the increased prominence of electronics in modern weapons manufacturing. In a

234

word, it was feared that should the U.S. allow its domestic semi-conductor capability to erode further, it would be rendering itself highly vulnerable to the security consequences of economic interdependence.

The more celebrated event was the Toshiba/Kongsberg affair, in which a Japanese and a Norwegian company were discovered to have provided the Soviet Union with sophisticated milling and computing equipment that enabled it to construct better propellers for its nuclear attack submarines (SSNs), thereby allowing those boats to be operated much more quietly; this, in turn, rendered them more difficult to track by U.S. and other allied acoustic-detection methods. The transactions in question had taken place over a period of time dating from the early 1980s, but it was not until late March 1987 that the U.S. Congress and public learned, through reports from the Central Intelligence Agency and the Pentagon, of the illicit technology transfer.[2] Initially buried on the back pages of major newspapers, the affair would soon achieve national media prominence, as Congressional and administration voices alike were raised in shrill denunciation of what was termed a blatant betrayal of U.S. and Western security interests. Although opposition to the technology diversion was widespread across the U.S. political spectrum, it was from conservatives that the sharpest condemnation of the Japanese and Norwegian action came.

For instance, Republican Senator Jesse Helms of North Carolina, in words that resonated among the right-wing policy community, said from the floor of the Senate that the affair represented nothing less than a "pattern of betrayal of the free world.... Toshiba and Kongsberg have put every Japanese citizen, every American citizen, and every other free world citizen at peril."[3] Even more dramatic was a piece of theatre from the other Congressional chamber, where on 1 July, nine conservative members of the House of Representatives convoked a press conference and vividly demonstrated their anger by taking a sledgehammer to a Toshiba radio-cassette recorder.[4] Such histrionics could be said to represent a fair approximation of the mood (if not the taste) of the Congress as it pondered this latest episode in East-West trade; for the Senate, by a margin of 92 to 5, passed an amendment to the omnibus trade bill then before it calling for a two- to five-year ban on all non-military imports of Toshiba and Kongsberg products. For its part, the House voted, by a 415-to-1 margin, to seek damages from both Japan and Norway — damages that were in the view of some Congressmen likely to run to $30 billion (or the cost, generously estimated, of 30 *Los Angeles*-class SSNs).[5]

In their own ways, the two episodes are symptomatic of a contemporary problem in American defence policy, the health of the country's defence industrial base. Worry about the security implications of trade is not a new feature of American strategic consciousness; indeed, as we shall argue in the next section, one can trace a concern for the security consequences of imports to the early days of the Republic. What has changed, and what we explore in subsequent parts of this chapter, is the degree to which high-technology products, and the skills subsumed in their creation, have become critically important both for the maintenance of current American (and Allied) force levels, and for the sustainability of those forces in the event they were ever involved in large-scale protracted conflict of a conventional nature. If it can be said that the past two decades, in America, have witnessed the decline of what was once a defence industrial base of formidable self-sufficiency, it can be said *a fortiori* that this loss of self-sufficiency has been having its most recent and, to some, alarming consequences in the high-technology precincts of that base. One effect of this, but by no means either the only or an inevitable effect, has been the clamor for a set of policies, subsumed under the label "techno-nationalism," that might be capable of reversing the loss of self-sufficiency.

As we shall argue, both the import side of the techno-nationalism question (as exemplified by the semiconductor issue) and the export side (so vividly highlighted by the Toshiba/Kongsberg affair) are inextricably linked with the defence-industrial base theme. No doubt the conceptual affinity is more self-evident in the former instance than in the latter; but even the Toshiba/Kongsberg affair attests to the perceived importance of safeguarding the integrity of the domestic industrial base. This is so, notwithstanding that the technology-diversion case seemed, at least superficially, to have little to do with the *U.S.* defence industrial base *per se*, involving as it did technology and equipment that belonged not to American, but to Japanese and Norwegian, producers.

236

THE CURRENT DEBATE OVER THE AMERICAN DEFENCE INDUSTRIAL BASE: ITS MERCANTILIST ORIGINS

The current debate over techno-nationalism triggers a powerful sense of *déjà vu*. To be sure, the terminology is new enough: techno-nationalism can be considered to reflect a propensity to restrict the dissemination of a good (technology) so that the benefits flowing from its creation can be differentially distributed in favour of its producers.[6] Terminology aside, however, there is a lot about this phenomenon that is familiar. Techno-nationalism, in its concern both for the security implications of interdependence and its stress on economic statecraft as a means of achieving non-economic goals resembles nothing so much as mercantilism, and mercantilist principles and logic have been a part of American defence-industrial thinking since the inception of the country's industrialisation.[7] At the same time, there has been, particularly in the post-World War II decades, an abiding American concern with fostering international economic collaboration, for reasons related to security as well as to other considerations. Significantly, even in such historically sensitive areas as strategic raw-material supply, American policy makers have opted in most instances for globalism and interdependence over autarky.[8]

Thus there has been a continuing tension, felt perhaps more acutely in the United States than in other countries whose economies have been exposed to international competitive pressure for a lengthier time, between a fear of too much interdependence (and the eventual erosion of self-sufficient capabilities in critical sectors) and too little. The tension was less of a problem in an era when American economic competitiveness was more robust; it is a greater dilemma today, all the more so as one officially mooted cure for defence-industrial-base ills, state interventionism, may in fact end up killing, not restoring, the patient. For in an era such as ours of high-technology warfare, the race for security is likely to be won by the swiftest, and interventionism by itself has rarely been an inducement either to speed or efficiency. It may be that compared with the costs in an earlier era of mercantilism — at least, a mercantilism that emphasised *export* restrictionism — the costs in an era of high technology could well be prohibitive; this, at least, is the view of some U.S. semiconductor manufacturers, who argue that security-driven attempts to make U.S. export policy more restrictive could, ironically, weaken national security by making the domestic industry less able to compete — or even survive.[9]

Contrasted with this, however, is the view that interdependence, whatever may be its merits in an economic sense, can and does imply significant political and security costs, in the event the normal channels of trade are disrupted, for whatever reason. Not only this, but interdependence, which if it means anything should mean mutual dependence, must lead to the cession of a certain degree of autonomy on the part of states — a cession that, in turn, can entail high security risks in certain circumstances.[10] The dilemma of current U.S. policy regarding the defence industrial base is put in its starkest form, perhaps, in the high-technology sectors, especially those associated with microelectronics. For in these sectors it is clear not only that the U.S. has lost rapidly much of the competitive prowess it developed just a few short years ago, but that its dependence upon foreign sources of supply is growing at precisely the same time as the essentiality of microelectronics for military purposes is itself escalating.

Because we shall be returning, in a subsequent section, to the issue of growing U.S. dependence upon foreign military (and commercial) technology, it is useful at this juncture to analyse more thoroughly the manner in which interdependence might be said to have security implications. If the term implies a loss of state autonomy and concomitant increase in vulnerability, then it is perhaps easy to see why the process of interdependence has generated lively debate, especially in the hitherto relatively *non*-dependent United States, about the ultimate policy and normative implications, both for individual countries and the system itself, of a world in which the fate of one becomes ever more bound up in the actions of others. Put most simply, much of the recent U.S. angst over the eroding defence industrial base is attributable to the decreased insulation of the American economy from global competitive pressures. While few would dispute the contention that the U.S. economy has become more penetrated by foreign market forces, there is no consensus on whether this must, ultimately, be good or bad, either for the United States or for the world.

Some analysts, let us call them the optimists of interdependence, stress the irenic properties of interdependence, to say nothing of its prosperity-inducing effects. More than a few political scientists, for instance, have indicated their belief that emerging transnational actors and processes have been reshaping, and for the better, the very nature of international politics. To those who would temper if

not displace the premises maintained in the general body of literature on *Machtpolitik* (power politics), interdependence has
emerged as a major force for peace — a system-wide phenomenon
that enhances the propensity of states to achieve mutual goals
through economic and political cooperation and policy coordination. Thus, interdependence has meant, within much of this contemporary analysis, a transcendence of traditional security
concerns and a conviction that with growing international
economic cooperation must come both increases in global welfare
and improved relations between states.[11]

For other analysts, however, the very number and nature of con-
tacts and transactions between "interdependent" states raises serious questions about their national-security consequences. To many
who subscribe, explicitly or otherwise, to what we term "neo-
mercantilist" precepts, it is all too easy to perceive that core values
of states might become adversely affected by foreign trade.[12]
Those who share this perspective regard interdependence as being
conducive not to peace, and perhaps not even to prosperity; instead,
they are wont to stress, in the words of Robert Gilpin, that "disruption of the society's traditional values and increased vulnerability
to external influences are frequently among the costs of increasing
market interdependence among national economies."[13] Even
more: for many advocates of techno-nationalism in the U.S., the
ultimate cost of interdependence could be national extinction.

In contrast to the optimists of interdependence, the neo-
mercantilists regard the specialisation prompted by liberalised
trade to be detrimental to national industrial and resource bases,
and thus to security. The detriment may not be apparent at any
given moment, but it will assuredly, in their view, materialise in
times of national emergency or war. It is for this reason that, as one
writer has put it, "the most powerful, and least answerable, argument that a state's authorities can mobilise in defence of protective
tariffs is that of defending an economic capability that is, in some
way, essential to the country's security."[14] However, not all neo-
mercantilists would interpret the security imperative in the same
way; for some mercantilistic policies (including, but not restricted
to, protective tariffs) are of an unquestionably defensive inspira-
tion. Others, however, have construed the imperative in the
broadest possible manner, and have used it to justify policies that,
for all intents and purposes, can only be classified as imperialistic.
Robert Gilpin offers a useful distinction between these two varie-
ties of neo-mercantilism. On the one hand are those analysts and

policy makers whose economic nationalism is inspired by considerations of defensive security; these he calls "benign" mercantilists. On the other hand are those whose nationalism compels them to regard the international economy as a stage upon which to strut their aggrandising tendencies; these he considers to be "malevolent" mercantilists.[15] It is really the "benign" form of mercantilism that will concern us in this chapter, as it is our view (which some no doubt would reject) that the contemporary advocacy for techno-nationalism in the United States reflects a predominantly security-driven mercantilism.

In this sense, Alexander Hamilton may be considered the first in a lengthy line of "benign" American mercantilists. Although in his day the term defence industrial base had yet to be coined, it is clear that Hamilton's protectionism was at least as much oriented toward safeguarding national security as it was toward increasing national wealth. In his famous "Report on Manufactures" of 1791, Hamilton observed, in words that, *mutatis mutandis*, would not be out of context today, that a country's manufacturing base was of crucial significance to its economic-developmental and national-security objectives. Fearful that the fledgling American government might leave U.S. industry exposed to the full force of foreign (chiefly British) industrial penetration, the Secretary of the Treasury argued not only that America's infant industries warranted protection, but that British and other foreign producers were in any case already battening upon lavish governmental subsidisation (which he referred to as "gratuities and remunerations"). Thus we see enunciated two of the central themes of today's neo-mercantilists, above all the techno-nationalists: that dependence upon foreign source of supply is dangerous; and that foreign suppliers are stealing a march, through such "unfair trade" practices as subsidisation, on indigenous manufacturers, or would-be manufacturers. In words that would be familiar to anyone following the contemporary American debate, Hamilton reminded his Congressional audience that recent wartime supply shortages would be more than just a historical memory if policies were not put in place to create and defend an industrial infrastructure: "To effect this change, as fast as shall be prudent, merits all the attention and all the zeal of our public councils: 'tis the next great work to be accomplished"[16]

Despite some occasional setbacks along the way, the United States was able, throughout the 19th and into the 20th century, to avoid many of the security perils sketched by Hamilton. It did create an industrial base that surpassed any reasonable expectation of Hamilton or his contemporaries — a base that not only achieved self-sufficiency in numerous important sectors, but also was capable of generating exports, even in the natural-resource sector. By any reckoning, America attained global power status at a time when other great powers, in particular Germany, were singularly bereft of a comprehensive industrial self-sufficiency. Ironically, in light of the U.S. relative abundance of raw materials, it was in Washington during the interwar years that the concept of "strategic" raw material was first developed.[17] Less ironically, it was in the area of raw-material supply, during the post-World War II years, that America first began to grapple seriously with the security implications of interdependence.[18] To a significant degree, that grappling continues today, even though the policy of Washington has been, with some exceptions (e.g. stockpiling), to rely on international trade to secure American raw-material supply.

By the early 1980s, Americans were discovering that not only was their mineral supply in large measure sourced from abroad (and thus was, in some sense, "vulnerable" to being disrupted); so too were they becoming vulnerable in a variety of other "downstream" industrial sectors, which in time of national emergency or war might no longer be able — because they had disappeared or had greatly shrunk in productive capacity — to generate the "surge" capability that American industry had demonstrated during the Second World War and the Korean conflict.[19] To a growing number of analysts, the origin of the problem was clear: it was linked to the swelling tide of economic interdependence. Wrote one such analyst, during the early part of this decade: "The necessity for a U.S. industrial policy arises not from domestic economic considerations — however large these may currently loom — but rather from strategic-military concerns. As the only genuine guarantor of security for both itself and the Free World as a whole, the United States simply cannot afford to allow its industrial base to wither away."[20]

At the time Paul Seabury was issuing this warning, Americans could at least derive comfort from the fact that their high-technology industries, such as semiconductors with their obvious and many military implications, were continuing to dominate world markets. This situation, however, was quickly to change, and with it would come an additional security challenge to American benign mercantilism, the spectre of technological dependence and all it implied for U.S. security in an age of high-tech warfare.

241

THE RISE OF TECHNO-NATIONALISM

The roots of the problem of techno-nationalism can be found in the broader dilemma of American industrial performance in the late 20th century. Advocates of techno-nationalism have had a varied agenda, but uppermost among their concerns have been those related to declining U.S. productivity and its accompaniments of lagging competitiveness and burgeoning technological dependence. When economists have sought to isolate the factors responsible for the substandard record of American productivity since the early 1970s, they have focused upon a variety of considerations, including such phenomena as higher energy prices, the effect of the baby boom on the labour force, the lack of incentives for innovation and capital formation, high levels of military spending, and the shift in comparative advantage from developed market economies (DMEs) to newly industrialising countries (NICs).[21] We examine some of these developments below.

Low levels of investment and saving have plagued the American economy since at least the late 1960s. Lack of investment poses a particular difficulty in that less equipment can be purchased for the work force, which must continue to labour in antiquated plants. There was, to be sure, some notable investment growth in the early 1970s, but the sudden spurt in energy prices, coupled with a failure to allocate investment for new equipment, resulted in lower capital-output ratios being attained in the U.S. than in Japan and some other countries, which had not been so neglectful of investment.[22]

In addition, there has been a shift of the U.S. labour force out of certain sectors in which relative skills had been developed and into new, service-sector enterprises. This is held by some to have lessened productivity.[23] What should be remembered, however, is that this shift reflects a change in the comparative advantage of manufacturing of certain goods from the DMEs to the NICs. During the period bounded by the years 1960-73 and 1973-79, slower productivity growth rates were widespread throughout the DMEs: average annual growth rates, expressed in percentage terms, fell in the United States from 3.1 to 1.1, in Canada from 4.2 to 1, in France from 5.9 to 4.2, and even in Japan from 9.9 to 3.8.[24] Because it has been difficult for developed market economies to monopolise the technology they generate (a source of anxiety to many techno-nationalists), countries in the developing world, including the recent NICs, have been able to acquire technology and apply it in conjunction with their relatively abundant factor endowment in labour to compete with the DMEs. It should be stressed that it is not really the NICs (much less the LDCs) that have been of concern to techno-nationalists insofar as the high-technology security sectors are concerned; nevertheless, what we can state is that the recent technology erosion is a continuation of a pattern set some time ago. In low-technology markets, where one does notice the NIC/LDC challenge, DMEs have sometimes managed to regain competitiveness, usually through a combination of reducing wage costs per unit of output and downsizing.[25] This adjustment process can have high social costs, something that often prompts developed states to respond not by increasing productivity but rather by bestowing protection upon sectors deemed to be essential.

Among sectors considered to be of enormous essentiality have been those industries clustered near the apex of the triangle known as the defence industrial base, that is those sectors where the application of technology to materials is most pronounced. Significantly, the American comparative advantage in high-tech sectors has eroded in this decade; indeed, some say it has disappeared. As of 1986, the U.S. has been running a trade deficit in such sophisticated goods as computers, communications equipment, and scientific instruments — goods in which Americans had come to assume a certain continuation of industrial superiority. How much of the deficit can be associated with the formerly overvalued dollar, and how much with the general problem of declining productivity, we cannot at this point say. What can be observed is that the deficit has provided a dramatic impetus to techno-nationalist advocacy in the U.S.; for among other worries has been the fear that the country is becoming increasingly vulnerable to foreign suppliers (especially, the Japanese) who could inflict great potential harm on America "should they choose to hold back their high-tech gadgets."[26]

As we noted above, there is much that is familiar about the techno-nationalism question. In so many ways, the current unease felt by many in the U.S. about growing dependence testifies to the fear that America's trading partners might be either unwilling or unable (even if willing) to continue to supply critically needed components for the country's defence industries. In short, it reflects a long-standing apprehension about the security effects of trade. No one has more persuasively explicated those effects than Albert O. Hirschman, in his classic study of the political implications of trade.[27] According to Hirschman, trade possesses two unavoidably political implications: because the cessation of a trading relationship — or the mere threat of cessation — can endow one country with leverage over another, trade is said to possess an "influence" effect; conversely, because imports can contribute to a real increase in national power capability, trade is also said to possess a "supply" effect. In the case of high-technology production, we argue that Hirschman's thesis retains relevance for analysts of the security implications of interdependence. While it may be far-fetched, say, to imagine that Japan would choose to disrupt its high-technology trade with the United States, for whatever reason, it is less far-fetched to envision a situation in which forces beyond the control of either trading partner could have the effect of disrupting the flow of vitally needed defence equipment. Moreover, not only do techno-nationalists worry that America's own supply of this equipment might be disrupted; they also express apprehension that, through trade, the Soviet Union is enhancing its own military capability, thus demonstrating another "supply effect" of high-technology trade. For techno-nationalism, then, imports and exports represent but two sides of the same coin. In the following section, we focus on the import side.

IMPORTS AND TECHNO-NATIONALISM: THE CASE OF SEMICONDUCTORS

Evidence of an increasing U.S. dependence upon foreign suppliers of critical high-tech components and materials is not difficult to find. At present, for example, the United States is almost entirely dependent on foreign sources of supply for special silicon used in high-powered switching devices, for random access memories, liquid crystal and luminous displays for computers, and high-quality titanium sponge for aircraft.[28] Not only this, but the supply of sub-components in finished form is also increasingly acquired abroad. In particular, U.S. computer companies are now heavily dependent upon Japanese firms for their supply of semiconductors, a matter to which we shall shortly return. Within the general civilian economy this situation is regarded with some disquiet; within the defence industrial base, there exists something verging on paranoia over the consequences of growing dependence. Given that there are few if any "attrition fillers" in today's sophisticated arsenals, it is clear why ensuring the continued supply of complicated electronics and avionics components can prove worrisome to some planners.

There are two aspects of the technological-dependence question worth introducing here. The first relates to the phenomenal degree to which war-fighting and -deterring have both come to depend upon technological considerations. Newer and smarter conventional weapons (to say nothing of their nuclear brethren) have been injected into the arsenals of both NATO and (to a lesser degree) the Warsaw Pact, and this has had the dual effect of raising costs of defence and elevating, certainly for the U.S., the security consequences of import-dependence. Perhaps the most graphic illustration of the effect technology has been having on force postures comes when one studies the current U.S. defence budget. Although Washington now faces, and will continue to face, the likelihood of stagnating or even declining defence spending in real terms, there can be no question that the U.S. during the first half of the 1980s experienced the biggest peacetime buildup in its history. Even the Fiscal 1989 defence budget of $285 billion is equal, in dollars adjusted for inflation, to the level of defence spending at the peak of the Vietnam effort in 1969. Yet when one asks what the Pentagon is able to get with this money, one finds that, in large measure because the cost of high-technology weapons is so great, there are fewer troops, planes, and ships than there were 20 years ago. During the Vietnam era, the U.S. Army had a million and a half soldiers; today it has 772,000. (On the other hand, it has 50 percent more tanks today than in 1969.) The Air Force's personnel strength has been reduced from 862,000 to 576,000, and there are today fewer pilots (22,312 compared with 41,490) and aircraft (9,353 instead of 13,688) than in 1969. For its part, the Navy has shrunk from 890 to 580 ships, and its number of uniformed personnel has declined from 776,000 to 593,000.[29]

In and of themselves, figures such as these need not prove worrisome to U.S. and other NATO defence planners; after all, it is generally considered within NATO that the allies' superiority in technology can more than compensate for an imbalance in conventional weaponry and troop levels. However, as we shall show when we discuss the *export* side of the coin of techno-nationalism, there is a spreading conviction, at least among American military observers, that NATO's technological edge is eroding; some see the erosion to be progressing so quickly that unless arrested it is likely to pose a dire threat to Alliance security.[30] However, even if the U.S. did not see its comparative advantage in weapons technology *vis-à-vis* the Soviet Union slipping away, it would still have to face the uncomfortable knowledge that its technology advantage in respect of its *allies* has been whittled down drastically in this decade. And this, when it is coupled with a recognition of the essentiality of the imported goods in question, can and does pose an acute dilemma for security analysts when they ponder the implications of a continuation of recent trends. It often seems to be the case that Congressional figures who have been following the defence-industrial-base debate have evinced a greater willingness to support protectionist measures against imports than have Pentagon officials; for the latter, it seems that the restriction of *exports* looms as the principal if not sole security issue. Imports, it is argued by some in the Pentagon (including the current Secretary of Defense), can have the salubrious effect of forcing domestic producers to become more efficient, and therefore to become a less-costly source of procurement.

To those who do focus on imports as the chief security problem, it is the growing high-tech dependence upon Japan that tends to get most attention. Quipped one senior Pentagon official recently, if another war occurs, "we're going to subcontract [it] to Japan."[31] Others, both in Congress and the Pentagon, treat this possibility with anything but lightness of heart; they worry that this is exactly what would happen. Especially pronounced is their fear that Japanese dominance in the manufacture of semiconductors will make the U.S. military dependent to an intolerable degree on a foreign (even though friendly) supplier — one who could, in the event of war, be cut off from the consumers in America's defence industries. Semiconductors are attracting such attention from the defence community because these microchips are critical components for the operation of all advanced weapons systems in the American arsenal. Their importance inheres in the role they play in the electronics associated with missiles, aircraft, warships, computers, and radars. Noted one recent Pentagon study: "U.S. defense will soon depend on foreign sources for state-of-the-art technology in semiconductors ... an unacceptable situation."[32]

It is sometime argued that disquiet such as that expressed in the above quotation represents nothing so much as a kind of incipient, or disguised, "Japan-bashing" — an attitude whose roots, it is held, are to be found in the lack of competitiveness of the American economy of late, which has little or nothing to do with security. To those taking this approach, arguments in support of trade restrictions that are couched in the language of national security — as is so much of the defence-industrial-base advocacy — are, in the words of the *Economist*, "the last refuge of a protectionist scoundrel."[33] It is doubtless true that at least a portion of the current defence-industrial-base anxiety owes its existence to commercial and not security imperatives; and it is certainly apparent that there has been, over the past few years, a growth in the American propensity to blame Japan and other trading partners for the declining competitiveness of U.S. industry, and this in a variety of sectors, ranging from low- to high-tech.[34] Nevertheless, it strikes us as imprudent to dismiss the current techno-nationalistic mood as one that is entirely, or even chiefly, born of commercial considerations — save in the sense that the latter can be understood to be instrumental to the attainment of other objectives, such as those relating to security. For given America's historic position of relative independence from the international trading system, and in view of the degree to which the U.S. sees itself as the guarantor of security for the entire West, it is to be expected that the contemporary experience with interdependence would generate a set of security worries; it would be surprising were it otherwise.

It has long been understood by analysts of strategic issues that national security and the health of a country's industrial base were in some knowable and important manner correlated; one could not get or retain military capability, it was assumed, without at the same time developing industrial capability.[35] It has also been assumed that as a country's relative economic capability declined, it would perforce witness a reduction in its ability to safeguard either its own security interests or those of its allies. Indeed, many today speak of a declining American "hegemony," with all that this might entail for the security structure of the entire West.[36] Whether, as one currently popular thesis has it, the American empire is in eclipse, it is at minimum reasonable to suggest that the future of the Atlantic Alliance is going to witness a greater, not a lesser, tendency of economic forces and problems to generate security consequences.[37] So at the risk of sounding like economic troglodytes, we offer the modest suggestion that there is reason to take at face value the security anxiety expressed by many participants in the American debate over techno-nationalism. The debate, however much it may focus on commercial rivalries as instrumentalities, is really fundamentally about security and not commerce.

To be sure, it is not just in the high-technology sectors that one encounters proponents of a security-motivated protectionism. Notes one Pentagon production expert, John Mittino: "Many key industries, essential to expanded production in a national emergency, have encountered serious problems as a result of global competition." [38] It was the desire to address these widespread industrial-base problems that prompted IllinoisDemocratic Senator Alan Dixon to introduce legislation in November 1987, entitled the Defense Industrial Base Preservation Act, that could have the effect of limiting if not excluding foreign producers from bidding on U.S. defence contracts. At a time when the Pentagon is stressing the necessity of arms collaboration between the United States and its allies, the Dixon bill, which would exempt Canada, threatens the goal of greater arms interoperability and the cost-savings associated with common procurement; for this reason it has been criticised both by the Department of Defense and free-trade oriented journals. One such publication, the *Journal of Commerce*, wonders whether the net effect of the legislation would not be to render American industry even more inefficient, and therefore ultimately more untenable as sources of supply for the armed forces. According to this view, not only would the bill retard defence-industrial competitiveness, it would also drive a wedge between the U.S. and the very allies upon whom it must increasingly rely to carry a greater share of the burden of Western defence. [39]

As we noted above, the view from the Pentagon on the merits of protecting domestic industry from foreign competition is, at best, a mixed one. Some officials in the Department of Defense have shown themselves to be more disposed to import-restriction than have others. Significantly, a recent draft study done for the Undersecretary of Defense for Acquisition, Robert Costello (the so-called procurement "czar"), has called for a revitalisation of the U.S. defence industrial base with the active participation of America's allies. The report, entitled "Bolstering U.S. Industrial Competitiveness," reflects the current optimism among top-ranking Pentagon officials as to the utility and workability of common procurement efforts within the Alliance. [40] For those, especially in Europe, who have descried a greater willingness on the part of the U.S. to countenance restrictions on defence-related imports, the Pentagon report should come as a relief; for its drafters argue that it is fruitless for the U.S. to deny the existence of interdependence, especially in respect of the internationalisation-of manufacturing. "A keystone to the DOD industrial base strategy," states the report, "is cooperation with domestic industry, with allies and with friendly nations. The United States could not build fortress America even if this were a desirable objective." [41]

Whether the Pentagon's current official predisposition toward greater economic interdependence will prevail over the Congress's tendency to envision a defence-industrial-base approach that concedes more to import restrictiveness must remain a matter of conjecture. As we shall see in the next section, even the Pentagon must be considered a qualified supporter at best of greater trade liberalisation, at least in the realm of high-technology products with a real or potential military application; in this range of products, Pentagon personnel have until very recently been waging a bitter struggle to impose more, not fewer, restrictions on trade, albeit primarily on East/West trade. For the moment, however, it would be wrong to assume that it is only the Congress that has been showing itself disposed to import protection; for there have in the past few years been a series of trade-restricting initiatives in a variety of industrial sectors — initiatives that have caused some analysts to argue that a new protectionist tide is sweeping the U.S. Among those initiatives have been a few that are relevant to this chapter.

For example, in the spring of 1986 a seldom-used vehicle of U.S. trade law was employed to achieve the imposition of restrictions on machine-tool imports entering the U.S. from four foreign producers.[42] The legal vehicle was section 232 of the Trade Expansion Act of 1962 (as amended by section 127 of the Trade Act of 1974 and the Reorganization Plan of 1979), which allows the president to impose restrictions on imports that are held to impair the national security. This provision has been employed at various times to impose quotas and fees on imports of crude oil and products.[43] Should the Secretary of Commerce deem, after an investigation conducted by an office in the department's International Trade Administration, that imports of a given product are a danger to security, he must so advise the president, who has the discretion to take measures to "adjust" import levels. Given the well-known commitment of Ronald Reagan to free trade, it is significant that he chose in the machine-tools case to shelter the domestic industry from the full force of international competition. That he did so is testimony to the argument for protection that rested upon an assumption linking interdependence in this industry to a weakening of security.

During the spring of 1988, another security-driven import restriction was imposed. This time it was the American ball-bearing industry that was being protected from foreign competition, as the Pentagon announced that manufacturers of military systems would in future have to purchase their ball bearings at home. Given that Pentagon purchases account for nearly 20 percent of the entire American market for this product, it is clear that the imposition of a Buy American requirement would have a major impact on the fortunes of domestic firms. The ball-bearing industry can serve as a microcosm of the broader American dilemma associated with declining competitiveness: since 1980, the domestic industry has lost 15,000 jobs, which represents a 20-percent decrease in employment. While domestic production was down, imports were increasing, and by early 1988 were accounting for 65 percent of domestic consumption. Congressional proponents of import relief, highlighting the critical role of bearings in modern weapons systems, argued that a continuation of the trend would ultimately mean the country's defence industries would be unable, if required, to surge their production to meet wartime demand in a range of weapons systems.[44]

Other industries have also been receiving attention of late, both on the part of an executive branch and a Congress worried about the security implications of trade. The precision-gear industry, for instance, is now said to be in dire need of support, and for much the same reason as in machine tools or ball bearings: its inability to remain competitive and, therefore, capable of surging production in the event of a wartime situation.[45] Nor is the anxiety about an eroding defence industrial base restricted to manufacturing; for the growth of foreign engineers in the domestic talent pool has even been cited, by a panel of the National Academy of Engineering, as yet another challenge to national security stemming from interdependence. Some 55 percent of engineering graduate students in the U.S. — and a comparable proportion of the younger faculty at the nation's engineering schools — are foreigners living in the United States on either a temporary or permanent visa. Because these engineers are said to experience greater difficulty in getting security clearances than do U.S. citizens, the Academy fears that much of the country's engineering talent pool may simply be unavailable for work on critical areas of defence research, with obvious implications for security.[46]

In no area, however, has there been a greater tendency to stress the link between interdependence and adverse security implications than in semiconductors; it is in this sector that the import side of techno-nationalism is best illustrated. Moreover, this sector also serves as a logical bridge to our discussion below of the export dimension of techno-nationalism, for if one of the goals of American policymakers in combatting the planned takeover by Fujitsu of Fairchild was to safeguard the domestic supply base of critical electronic components, another goal was to arrest the decade-long seepage of American comparative advantage in semiconductor technology — even if, in this instance the seepage was to an ally and not, as in the Toshiba/Kongsberg affair, to the Soviet Union. Although the semiconductor case is complicated by its also being a trade dispute, it is with the security implications that our analysis is concerned, for we see these implications as having impelled the central organs of state in the U.S. to action.

Semiconductors are silicon chips that store and transfer electronic signals; in effect, they serve as the brain cells of a wide variety of high-technology products, including modern weapons systems. Until 1985, the United States had been the world's leading manufacturer of semiconductors; indeed, during the latter part of the 1970s, American producers had a stranglehold on world markets for chips. Throughout the 1980s the U.S. advantage continued to erode, however, so that in the space of a decade America's share of global production had declined from 100 percent to a mere, by 1987, 10 percent. Significantly, it was Japanese companies, initially working with licenced American technology, that replaced U.S. companies as dominators of world markets. One analyst has noted that "as recently as the early 1980s, American semiconductor makers were a symbol of America's technological might... [T]he Japanese assimilated everything the masters had to teach. Now the Japanese are the masters, and the Americans are scrambling to catch up."[47]

As the Japanese overcame America's early technological lead, many in Washington (and not just on Capitol Hill) arrived at the conclusion that the source of Japan's success could only lie in unfair trading practices. Subsidisation, to be sure, was cited as one such practice; but so, too, was the commercial practice of dumping (or the practice of selling a good, either at home or abroad, at a price greater than its price in a third country).[48] In September 1986, Washington and Tokyo concluded an agreement whereby the latter would seek to get Japan's chip manufacturers to raise their prices; by early 1987, the Reagan administration concluded that Japan was failing to live up to the agreement, and responded by imposing retaliatory tariffs against a range of Japanese electronic goods (but not semiconductors).[49] The tariffs, announced by President Reagan on 17 April 1987, constituted the first U.S. trade retaliation specifically directed against Japan since the Second

World War, and were targetted at desk-top and lap computers, colour television sets, and power hand tools. In explaining his decision, the president stated that "the health and vitality of the U.S. semiconductor industry are essential to America's future competitiveness. We cannot allow it to be jeopardized by unfair trade practices."[50]

While the administration was wrestling with its response to the dumping problem, a second front in the "chip war" opened up: the struggle to prevent Fairchild from selling 80 percent of its shares to Fujitsu. The Japanese purchase arrangement had been made public in October 1986, and it was assumed that Fujitsu would pay $200 million to the parent corporation, the French-controlled oilfield services concern, Schlumberger. Although some have interpreted the U.S. desire to halt the transaction as primarily a commercially motivated (if dog-in-the-manger) measure, comprehensible only in the larger context of Japanese-American trade friction, our view is that national-security considerations, interpreted both narrowly and broadly, underlay the administration's response.[51] In the narrow and immediate military context, there was genuine worry on the part of some that should Fairchild pass into Fujitsu's embrace, it would mean that yet another important supplier of electronics to the Department of Defense would become Japanese. For example, Fairchild was the only producer of a chip critical for the electronic guidance, sighting, and firing systems of the F-16. Not to have resisted the planned takeover, wrote one defence analyst employed by the U.S. Senate, "would have made our Air Force dependent on Japan for its most advanced aircraft. It doesn't take an expert to understand how that could pose a national security problem."[52]

More important, however, were the broader security implications of the proposed takeover. It wasn't simply that Washington felt the forces of international trade were having an unintended effect upon the security of the United States; something far more sinister was feared in certain precincts of the administration, particularly in the Pentagon. What worried American defence analysts was the prospect that Japan was deliberately, as a matter of national policy, seeking to dominate certain high-technology industries, among them semiconductors. Although this was not a consensus view within the administration, those who did tend to this interpretation were bolstered in their position by a secret analysis written by the Central Intelligence Agency, which made the case that Tokyo was indeed trying for domination in computer and semiconductor technology. The State Department did not share this perspective, but the Secretary of Commerce, Malcolm Baldrige, evidently did; for he told the Senate Finance Committee on 25 March, "I can only conclude that the common objective of the Japanese government and industry is to dominate the world electronics market."[53]

Among the American defence community there was even greater conviction that Japan might be launched on a predatory strategy of completing its conquest of U.S. electronics companies. In February 1987, a Defense Science Board task force reported that the country's reliance on foreign technology was posing unacceptable risks from the point of view of security. This warning was echoed by Charles Herz, general counsel of the National Science Foundation and a participant in a high-level group that was then engaged in a study of the national-security and economic consequences of Japan's challenge to the U.S. semiconductor producers. Although Herz was still uncertain whether Japan was consciously following a path that would lead to the continued erosion of the U.S. high-tech industrial base, he was clear on Tokyo's aspirations: "The Japanese have set out to be the world leaders in electronics and computers. Everybody knows that."[54]

At the same time that government interest in chips was peaking, the American semiconductor producers were devising a strategy of their own that would, they argued, enable them to mount an effective response to the threat implied by further interdependence. They would form a consortium, pool their research efforts, and seek to develop state-of-the-art semiconductor technology that could then be transferred to the private sector. Significantly, foreign enterprise was to be excluded from the venture. Equally significantly, federal subsidisation would be a necessary part of the enterprise. The consortium, to be called Sematech, was proposing to raise for research and development some $1.5 billion over six years in a clear effort to counter Japan's recent success in dismantling the U.S. industry. Because the Japanese industry was argued to be heavily subsidised, the new consortium would respond by fighting fire with fire. As one industry executive remarked at the consortium's launching forum in March 1987: "We can continue to sit back and watch the Japanese target and assault yet another critical U.S. industry, or we can get in gear and do what's necessary to repel this attack. Sematech is one of the strategies we're using."[55]

By late 1987 Congress would approve a grant of $100 million to get the new consortium set up; the remaining $150 million necessary for its first year would be raised from the contributions of member companies and from state and local funding.[56] As had been the case with machine tools, and ball bearings, and as was possibly going to be the case with precision gears, the U.S. government had again adopted a techno-nationalist response to the challenge of foreign competition. That it did so in this latest episode is primarily a function of the same security logic that had impelled the earlier efforts to combat import pressure. The method, to be sure, varied in this recent case, but the objective remained constant: to minimise the security risks associated with import penetration in a sector designated of critical importance to the defence industrial base. However, it was not lost upon some observers that efforts to limit foreign penetration of the American high-technology marketplace might potentially redound adversely for national security, if such efforts had the effect of keeping out superior technology. If it was easy to notice that an eroding defence industrial base might have negative implications for security, it was perhaps less easy for some to realise that protectionism — even if justified by considerations of national security — might also impose some major costs in a security context. The contradictions implied in this recognition would be well-demonstrated by the emotional debate over the Toshiba/Kongsberg affair, to which we now turn.

EXPORTS AND TECHNO-NATIONALISM: THE TOSHIBA/KONGSBERG AFFAIR

If the semiconductor dispute demonstrates the manner in which many in Washington relate import dependence to American security, the Toshiba/Kongsberg affair reveals in all its luminosity the potential security challenge posed by the *export* of sensitive technology. To be sure, the technology-export conundrum has long bedevilled relations between the U.S. and its allies, an observation to which the formation of COCOM (the Coordinating Committee for Multilateral Export Controls) as long ago as 1949 bears witness. There can be no question but that American anxiety over the security implications of East/West trade greatly predates the more recent concerns about the eroding defence industrial base.[57] That being said, we do maintain that some aspects of the Toshiba/-

Kongsberg affair do intermesh the older East/West-trade issue with the newer defence-industrial-base one.

In the first place, the recent decline of U.S. high-technology sectors, especially in electronics, has had the effect of intensifying the long-standing dispute within NATO over export controls, both because the U.S. is becoming more of a bystander — albeit an outraged one — in the technology-transfer domain and because of the costliness associated with correcting the damage done through leakage of technology in an era of modern, electronic warfare. Second, the Toshiba/Kongsberg case would have a direct bearing on the American defence industrial base in an industry-specific sense; for as we explain below, Tokyo's desire to placate the Reagan administration in the wake of the scandal contributed to the cancellation of Japanese plans to build their own modern fighter support aircraft (FSX) and instead enter into a co-production arrangement for an American plane, the F-16. Finally, it is becoming evident that one cannot isolate export controls from the broader question of the economic health of the defence industrial base, and it is also becoming clear that one of the costs absorbed by the U.S. as a result of its desire to inhibit the transfer of sensitive technology to its trading partners may well be a weaker domestic industrial base, for the good reason that stringent export restrictions can not only result in the loss of currently proposed sales, but can also deter future purchasers from shopping in the U.S. market — especially its high-tech market.

One of the consistent criticisms made by American allies over time has been that U.S. export-restriction policy can and does constitute an extraterritorial application of U.S. law. The effect of this, as seen by the allies, is that it causes them to lose business and deprives them of sovereignty. At times, such as during the controversy over the U.S. embargo on gas- and oil-related equipment to the Soviet bloc, unleashed in the wake of the Polish imposition of martial law in December 1981, intra-alliance differences can become so severe as to lead some to question the very long-term survivability of the Atlantic Alliance.[58] For their part, Europeans tend to be extremely skeptical of the utility of many of the economic restrictions advocated by Washington, and they particularly find puzzling what they see to be a U.S. obsession with embargoes and other forms of economic sanctions — actions that to the Europeans are feckless at best, counterproductive at worst.[59] In the United States, by contrast, there are many who see in the Europeans' laodicean approach to economic statecraft *vis-à-vis* the

Soviet Union an unwillingness to sacrifice the profits of trade for the longer-term goal of security. To many, especially those enamoured of "neo-conservatism," Europe's persistent pursuit during the 1980s of détente amounted to nothing less than a betrayal of core Western security interests.[60] This was held to be the case because regional détente and the trade it fostered was regarded by many in the U.S. as resulting in the transfer, in ways beyond enumeration, of the technological supremacy without which NATO could not hope to combat the Warsaw Pact. The most recent Pentagon assessment of Soviet military capability somberly notes — albeit with an absence of ally-bashing — that the USSR continues to eat into NATO's comparative advantage in high-tech war-fighting systems, so much so that "the technological advantages in military capabilities now enjoyed by the West have been threatened, if not eroded."[61]

Given the context, then, in which it developed, the Toshiba/Kongsberg incident could not help but become a major controversy in U.S.-allied relations. To the prevailing sense, on the Pentagon's part, that the Western countries were not taking seriously enough the matter of controlling technology transfer to the East was coupled the growing mood of anxiety in America about a disappearing defence industrial base. Thus it could be expected that certain quarters in Washington would explode with indignation at the news that two Western companies, the Norwegian (and state-owned) Kongsberg Vaapenfabrikk and the Toshiba Corporation's subsidiary, Toshiba Machine, had between them sold sensitive milling machinery and computers that were said to have enabled the Soviets to achieve a significant (and rapid) diminution in the noise emitted by the propellers of their SSNs. What perhaps was surprising, at least to Tokyo and Oslo, was not only the ferocity of the U.S. reaction, but the remarkable consensus in America concerning the gravity of the damage done by the technology transfer to security interests of not only the United States, but of NATO and Japan as well. It is our thesis that a large measure of this American anger can only be attributed to the sense felt by many in Washington that America's security interests were likely to continue to be compromised as a result of an inability to get allies to restrict their *own* technology to consumers in the West. This, in turn, is but another way of stating the predicament we discussed in the preceding section; for an unavoidable consequence of the loss of domestic industrial capability in high-technology sectors will be a continuation of the trend toward a loss of control in the area of technology security — a trend the Toshiba/Kongsberg affair, to repeat, illustrated so dramatically. To be sure, the episode did constitute a challenge to the West's anti-submarine warfare (ASW) capabilities, although how serious a challenge it was is open to some dispute.[62] More importantly, the affair symbolised to Washington something more portentous: the loss of autonomy, accompanied as it had to be by an increase in the country's vulnerability.

The details of the technology transfer need not concern us. Suffice it to note that the case had its origins in 1979 or 1980, when it is believed that the Soviets became aware, probably because of information passed to them by John A. Walker, Jr., that the position of their submarines was being given away by propeller noise. This knowledge triggered a Soviet quest for ways to reduce the cavitation noise and blade tonals associated with propeller action, and thereby make it more difficult for U.S. detection devices to locate their boats. By early 1981, a deal had been struck that would result in Toshiba Machine delivering to Soviet shipyards four multi-axis propeller-milling machines (forbidden under COCOM regulations to be sold to East bloc countries). At the same time, another contract was signed between the Soviets and Kongsberg, calling for the latter to supply numerical computers designed to guide the milling machines. Both Kongsberg and Toshiba would subsequently engage in a series of deceptions intended to obtain export licences from their respective national authorities. The first milling machine arrived in Leningrad in late 1982, but it was not until three years later that the transaction would begin to unravel publicly.

There are two differing versions concerning how Washington came to learn of the technology diversion. The Pentagon claims that, starting in 1986, it began to observe a marked quieting in Soviet submarines — a quieting that touched off deep suspicions about illegal technology transfer from Western companies. However, the Japanese insist that the story started to leak in late 1985, when a disgruntled Japanese executive with a Moscow-based middleman threatened to expose the illegal deal unless he was paid to keep silent. When this failed to occur, the executive, Kazuo Kumagai, sent a letter to COCOM officials at the organisation's Paris headquarters, who subse-quently forwarded the information to Washington, whence it eventually reached Tokyo. For much of 1986, investigations proceeded slowly in Japan, and not until early 1987 would the technology diversion become public knowledge.[63]

Both Oslo and Tokyo reacted with indignation to the news that their companies could be involved in such an illicit arrangement, and one so damaging equally to their own security interests and to their respective bilateral relations with the United States. Norway dismantled the offending division of the Kongsberg company, and tightened its export regulatory procedures, so that they have now become the most restrictive in NATO.[64] Japan also tightened its own export-licencing procedures, and brought criminal actions against executives of Toshiba Machine. As well, Japanese officials took pains to apologise to Washington for the incident.[65] To a degree, both the Norwegian and Japanese pacification efforts succeeded in limiting the political damage, but only insofar as mollifying the administration was concerned. Congress, where some conservative politicians were busily exploiting the issue, refused to let it drop. In particular, Congress was adamant that compensation be given by Norway and Japan to help defray the cost of repairing the damage. In addition, an amendment calling for a two- to five-year qualified ban on imports from Kongsberg and Toshiba Corporation (i.e. the parent company) was inserted into the Senate version of the omnibus trade bill, which the president vetoed in May 1988. The amendment calling for import sanctions remains a part of the revised trade bill passed in July 1988 by the House and the following month by the Senate, which is expected to be signed by the president and to become law later in the year. [66] Because of certain provisions for exemptions, and given the reorganisation of Kongsberg, it is expected that the brunt of the sanctions will be borne by Toshiba, which in any case seems to have been the centre of public outrage in the U.S., so much so that the incident has been almost always referred to as simply the "Toshiba affair."[67]

Without question, the American response to the technology diversion, which would have been vigorous in any event, was rendered more acute by the slippage of U.S. comparative advantage in high-technology trade. Symptomatic of this slippage, and one of the leading reasons for the Pentagon's (under Frank Carlucci) recent discovery of the virtues of arms collaboration, has been the dramatic turn-around the past few years of the U.S. trade balance in armaments. Historically, the U.S. in the post-World War II years has enjoyed a consistently "favourable" balance in arms trading with its allies, both in Europe and Japan. However, in the past two years America's trade surpluses in arms have shrunk to their lowest levels since the end of World War II. The rising levels of off-shore procurement being done by the Pentagon have not gone unnoticed in Congress, where there has been a resurgence of protectionist legislation introduced, such as the Dixon bill we discussed earlier.[68] The Toshiba/Kongsberg affair has witnessed the technology-diversion issue become linked with the broader arms-collaboration dynamic among the United States and its allies. It has done so because the U.S. has been able to offer the Japanese a carrot — namely, a reduction in administration anger with, and opposition to, the technology diversion. Thus, what was on the surface a matter concerning high-technology exports — and not American exports at that — quickly became transmuted into an issue of some moment for an important sector of the U.S. defence industrial base, the aerospace sector.

The quid pro quo, which was not particularly well-disguised, was that the Japanese would have to abandon their plans to build at home the replacement fleet for their aging F-1 fighters, expected to become obsolete during the latter half of the 1990s. As was the case in Israel, domestic production of such a high-technology weapons system as a modern fighter was seen to carry the promise of invigorating the domestic industrial base in the high-tech sectors and to contribute to national prestige. Moreover, the project was even going to enhance the country's security interests, although in the case of the Japanese plane it was perhaps more difficult to argue convincingly this last point than in respect of the Israeli Lavi.[69] However else the Japanese Fighter Support Experimental (FSX) program may have differed from the contemporary Israeli one, the two projects had one feature in common: they were both fiercely opposed by the Pentagon. In each case, the opposition was based on two objections. The first focused on opportunity costs, and held that the "build-to-print" option would be extremely expensive, and would necessarily mean that less security could ultimately be purchased for a given expenditure of defence dollars — an objection that in the case of the Lavi was made especially poignant because American aid was going to underwrite a large part of the development and production costs of the craft.[70]

The second objection, and the one of greatest relevance to our discussion of techno-nationalism and the U.S. defence industrial base, was the concern that the FSX and the Lavi would lead to a reduction in American fighter-aircraft production, both as a direct consequence of the failure of Japan and Israel to purchase an American aircraft in the first instance, *and* because of the likelihood that future U.S. sales to third parties would be lost as a result of competition for exports likely to be mounted by the Japanese or Israeli aircraft industry. To be sure, Japan's official policy has been to discourage arms exports, while Israel has been an active promoter of such exports; nevertheless, there was rising suspicion in Washington that should Japan become a producer of a sophisticated, domestically developed fighter aircraft, it would soon find itself in the export business. One trade analyst was only stating the widespread U.S. concern apropos of the FSX project in remarking that "the inescapable explanation is that Japan intends to develop a defense industry to export various types of military technology abroad."[71]

The Toshiba/Kongsberg scandal became a public controversy at the same time that the Japanese were arriving at the moment of decision for the FSX. Was it to be a domestic-development program, or would the Japanese Defence Agency opt instead for a foreign airplane, as it had done in the past, when it acquired F-4s and F-15s for the Air Self Defence Force?[72] Making it likely, throughout 1985 and into 1986, that the domestic-production option would be chosen were two important considerations: the FSX would, in supplanting the F-1, take the place of a symbolically important aircraft that, while based on American technology, had been the first supersonic fighter plane designed and built in Japan; and the FSX, at a cost of some $7 billion, would be an obviously lucrative proposition for the domestic aircraft industry and its political backers. Given the fact that the giant of the Japanese arms industry, Mitsubishi Heavy Industries, was leading a group seeking domestic production of the FSX, it seemed early in the decision process that the logic of events would lead to only one conclusion, namely that Japan should design and build the new fighter itself.[73]

However, the logic of events was to be derailed in part by the Toshiba/Kongsberg affair. It would probably be an overstatement to claim that in the absence of this affair Japan would definitely have opted for the domestic-production route. By early 1986, it was becoming clear to Tokyo that not only would Congressional ire be raised by a Japanese rejection of an American fighter aircraft, but so too would the reasonably well-disposed executive branch be opposed to such a course of action, for reasons we have already noted. As far as the Congress was concerned, it was primarily trade and balance-of-payments considerations that accounted for the displeasure with a domestically sourced FSX for Japan. Although by 1986 the dollar had started to fall against the yen, the U.S.

merchandise trade imbalance with Japan, which had skirted $50 billion in 1985, was showing no sign of reversing itself. For Japan to have chosen not to purchase one of the few commodities on the market in which it might be said the U.S. possessed a comparative advantage would have only fed the growing anti-Japanese sentiment on Capitol Hill.

What the Toshiba/Kongsberg scandal did do was to convince the Japanese of the danger that would be posed both to the trading and to the security relationship with America if a U.S. aircraft were not, in some important way, going to figure in the future FSX planning. In the wake of the public outcry in the U.S. over the technology diversion, it became the view among some Japanese business executives that the affair and its assumed damage to Western security were being magnified out of all proportion by the Pentagon, which was attempting to profit from the hysteria by forcing the Japanese to abandon the domestic production path. To those who shared this perspective, it was more than a coincidence that Secretary of Defense Weinberger had chosen to make a visit to Japan just as the American reaction to the Norwegian-Japanese technology diversion was at its sharpest. The implication to these analysts was clear: the Secretary had masterminded the timing of the release of the information about the transaction so that he could create a climate of fear among Japanese leaders.[74]

Although there is a surface plausibility to this argument, it appears to us to miss the point.[75] It is not that the Pentagon created the stir in the first place; it is rather that the Pentagon, and other executive branch agencies, would agree to limit the damage done by the technology diversion if the Japanese would renounce any plans to design and build the new aircraft themselves. In any event, that there is a linkage between the Toshiba/Kongsberg affair and the FSX decision seems obvious enough; indeed, an explicit connection between the two issues was made by no less a figure than Prime Minister Yasuhiro Nakasone himself, when he remarked in an August 1987 television interview: "We should place the highest priority on stabilized security ties with the United States when we think about the Toshiba case and the next fighters."[76] There can be little question but that, following the Weinberger visit to Japan (if not even before it) the domestic FSX was dead; what remained to be decided by Tokyo was which American plane would it choose, and upon what terms.[77]

It was not until mid October 1987 that Japan decided. Perhaps fittingly, given the parallels between the FSX and the Lavi, Tokyo would choose to enter into a co-production arrangement with General Dynamics to build a modified version of the F-16, something the Israelis would also do.[78] The Japanese decision came as something of a surprise to those who had been following the FSX, for once it became obvious that domestic production was not going to be pursued, it seemed that the operational requirements of the Air Self Defence Force, which was seeking a twin-engine fighter, would rule out choosing the single-engine F-16. Rumours circulating in the U.S. aircraft industry in September had the Japanese selecting the McDonnell Douglas F/A-18 as the FSX, for reasons related both to safety (the extra engine) and to the prospect of achieving more domestic value-added with this craft than with the F-16.[79] However, when the choice was made public in October, it seemed that the F-16 won out not over the F/A-18 but over another McDonnell Douglas craft, the F-15, and it did so on the basis of cost and versatility (the F-16 can serve in either an air-to-air, air-to-ground, or air-to-sea capacity, while the F-15 is primarily an air-to-air fighter).[80]

The third important consequence of the Toshiba/Kongsberg affair for the U.S. defence industrial base concerned the way in which the technology diversion focused attention on the simmering debate within the Washington policy community over the proper policy America should follow in the matter of export-restrictions on sensitive trade with both the East bloc *and* its own allies (as well as with neutrals that, like Switzerland or Sweden, were deemed to be trustworthy). At issue was the degree to which bureaucratic power should continue to be vested in the Pentagon's export-control office, which since the early 1980s had been rapidly accumulating influence in the area of trade, so much so it was becoming one of the capital's most feared bureaucracies. By early 1987, i.e. before the Toshiba/Kongsberg affair had become well-publicised, there was growing concern outside of the Pentagon over the costs of America's very restrictive export policy.

One widely circulated report released in February by the National Academy of Sciences conservatively assessed those costs at $9 billion in exports lost, at the ultimate price of nearly 200,000 jobs a year, as a result of what it held to be excessive regulation at the export-licencing stage.[81] With President Reagan's State of the Union address the preceding month calling for the government to do "everything possible to promote America's ability to compete," it appeared that the final stage had been set for a bureaucratic showdown in which the Pentagon would be vanquished by other

Departments, such as Commerce, that were mandated to liberalise not restrict American export possibilities. The situation seemed to be calling out for action because America's high-technology trade balance, which had been more than $25 billion in surplus in 1980 and 1981, had deteriorated after 1985. By early 1987, the 1986 high-technology trade-balance figures were in, and they showed a shocking *deficit* of more than $2 billion.[82] American business leaders, who for some time had been expressing dissatisfaction with the restrictive U.S. export policies, had a good idea what caused this recent turnaround. According to Oliver Smoot, president of the Washington-based lobbying group, Computer and Business Equipment Manufacturers Association, "international customers increasingly are buying non-U.S. high-tech products because our export controls are far more stringent than those of our allies."[83]

Techno-nationalists within the Pentagon, who generally would not agree with Smoot on much else, were in complete accord with his assessment of the relative stringency of export controls within the Alliance. To them, the real problem was that America's allies were not being brought up to U.S. standards of restrictiveness; for them, the principal danger in the talk of reforming the export-licencing system was that U.S. standards would be lowered to those of the allies,' that is, to the level of the least-common-denominator. This certainly was the view of former Assistant Secretary of Defense for International and Security Policy, Richard Perle, probably the most hard-line of the trade-restrictionists within the Washington policy community. Perle has been and remains extremely critical of provisions in the 1988 omnibus trade bill that would ease the restrictiveness of current export-licencing procedures, as well as de-emphasise the role played by the Pentagon's Defense Technology Security Administration, an office created in 1985 by Perle and now headed by his ally, Deputy Under Secretary of Defense for Trade Security Stephen D. Bryen. With the Toshiba/Kongsberg affair in mind, Perle has argued the amendments to the trade bill will "open the way to dozens of Toshibas.... It is undoubtedly frustration with our allies' approach to export controls that has led some Americans to argue that we should weaken or abandon our own controls, sinking to the level of our least vigilant allies rather than working to raise them up to ours."[84]

The export-restriction issue became greatly exacerbated by the Toshiba/Kongsberg case, which had the effect of temporarily slowing the momentum toward liberalisation that seemed to have been building in the past couple of years. It also exposed three major policy cleavages regarding export controls. The first concerned the question of U.S. interests versus those of the allies; the second of American business versus the U.S. government; and the third of bureaucratic combat being waged between the Commerce Department and the Pentagon. As we noted above, there has been, for some time, a struggle between Washington and its allies over the degree and kind of trade that should be carried on between the West and the East. At the most general level, the perspective adopted by the U.S. is one that holds the Alliance to constitute a contract of sorts between its members: on the one hand, the U.S. obliges itself to guarantee the security of the allies; on the other, those countries undertake not to assist the Soviet Union in building up its military capability, *inter alia* by the transfer of goods and technology that might be employed to enhance the Kremlin's ability to use or threaten force. It is clear that both aspects of this "contract" have become attenuated in recent decades; the U.S. security guarantee to Western Europe has for years been regarded with unspoken but nevertheless genuine skepticism, and the Europeans (as well as Japan) have been much more inclined than the U.S. to engage in trading relations with the Soviet Union and its allies. It is well beyond the scope of this essay to comment upon the contemporary dilemma of extended deterrence, but it is germane to our discussion of techno-nationalism to explore briefly the allies and the question of strategic trade.

We stated at the outset of this section that much of the U.S. anger over the Toshiba/Kongsberg affair stemmed from a sense of acute frustration over the declining centrality of U.S. manufacturers to global high-technology trade — a decline that is held, quite rightly, to have some serious security implications for the U.S., as it finds itself less able unilaterally to stanch the flow of sensitive technologies to the Soviet bloc. In many ways, Washington really never did imagine that it could totally restrict such technologies if the allies refused to cooperate; but in an earlier era, when the United States was a more dominant player in high-technology manufacturing, the amount of technology that could seep to the Eastern countries without its approval was much less than it is today. Indeed, if a liquid metaphor were to be applied to such trade today, "freshet" not seepage would come to mind. In that earlier era, to the extent allied cooperation was both necessary and desirable, it was sought through the Coordinating Committee on Multilateral Export Controls, which consists of Japan and all the NATO members with the exception of Iceland. Little is known of this international organisation that is headquartered in Paris, save that it is underfunded, has only infrequent high-level meetings (two since its inception, one in 1982 and one in 1988), and tries to avoid publicity.[85] We can state, however, that in its early years, COCOM was usually seen as having a useful role to play in the regulation of strategic trade with the Soviet bloc.

It is worth commenting upon the conditions that were in existence at the time of COCOM's greatest imputed effectiveness, for these conditions do not appear to be present today. Three underlying reasons for the organisation's relative success in its early years may be cited: 1) the other participating members were highly dependent, during the 1950s, on economic support from the U.S., which made the aid it disbursed conditional upon the allies' accepting embargoes on strategic trade with the Soviet Union, China, and North Korea; 2) there was at the time, and perhaps still is, a widely shared perception within the group that the Soviet Union constituted *the* major security threat to the COCOM members; and 3) the group compiled a reasonably manageable list of goods to be sanctioned — a list that in the immediate aftermath of the Korean War amounted to some 500 or so items, most of which in any case were of American origin.[86] By the mid 1960s, the first of these conditions had fundamentally altered; as a result of this, relations between the U.S. and its COCOM allies tended to become more fractious, as the latter found themselves increasingly unable or unwilling to balance tangible export losses against much less quantifiable and hypothetical gains in military security.

COCOM monitors high-technology sales to the Soviet Union, but it has no enforcement authority. This latter responsibility resides with the members' domestic legal systems — about which there has been much apprehension on the part of the United States. The Reagan administration, though not the Congress, has been taking the view that at least some good has come out of the Toshiba/Kongsberg affair, in that it has led both Japan and Norway to adopt tougher national legislative and monitoring provisions in respect of transfer of sensitive technology to the Soviet Union. [87]

To track the potential flow of technology from West to East, COCOM maintains three lists of "critical technologies." The *munitions list* contains items of unambiguous military significance. The *atomic-energy* list contains equipment and materials necessary for nuclear energy generation. For both these lists, there is an absolute prohibition on sales to the Soviet bloc. It is the third list, the one that regulates *industrial/chemical trade*, that poses the most difficulties for COCOM members; for it contains items that are of a "dual-use" nature. That is, items on this list may not be directly intended for military use, but may nonetheless have strategic applications. Sales of items on this list are examined on a case-by-case basis. In addition, each country has its own list of controlled goods and technologies, with that of the U.S. being the most ambitious, consisting as it does of some 700 pages containing 300,000 items upon which judgement must be passed before they are permitted to be exported — to anyone.[88]

It is this last list, the American one, that is at the heart of the other two controversies, those pitting the U.S. business community against the American government, and the Departments of Commerce and Defense against each other. It is these two controversies that demonstrate most graphically the manner in which export policy can ultimately lead back to such considerations affecting import policy as those we explored in the previous section, on semiconductors. For the dilemma exposed by the Toshiba/Kongsberg affair is this: how can the health of the American defence industrial base be preserved if government policy is so restrictive of exports that it ultimately poses as the single biggest factor inhibiting the competitiveness of the U.S. high-technology industries? It was precisely this question that the National Academy of Sciences addressed in its above-mentioned report of early 1987, *Balancing the National Interest: U.S. National Security Export Controls and Global Economic Competition*. The report concluded that export controls were not attaining the goals set out for them by the Arms Export Control Act of 1976 and the Export Administration Act of 1979; in fact, the controls were failing "to promote both national security and economic vitality."[89] That economic vitality was being retarded by export controls had for some time been an article of faith among American business executives, who like the European allies had been dubious about the utility of sanctions as a means of trying either to secure leverage over the Soviets or to prevent them from bolstering their military capability. Significantly, in the wake of the NAS report, it now appeared as if the Commerce Department had been won over to the anti-restrictionist side.

In March 1987, the Under Secretary of Commerce for Trade Administration, Paul Freedenberg, testifying before the House Subcommittee on International Economic Policy and Trade, sounded the tocsin for those in the U.S. policy community desirous of reforming the export-control system. With implicit (but none-theless clearly understood) reference to the Pentagon office headed by his nemesis Stephen Bryen, Freedenberg warned that America could not continue to handicap its high-technology manufacturers with over-regulation. "U.S. national security requires that American companies must be healthy," he said. "We must not, therefore, continue to bite the hand that feeds us..."[90] Coming when it did, this statement was interpreted (correctly) as a sign that the balance of bureaucratic power had decisively shifted against the techno-nationalist hard-liners at the Pentagon. For several years, dating back to 1981, Richard Perle and other Pentagon offi-cials seeking to clamp down on U.S. technology seepage had been relatively successful in encumbering with security-motivated reg-ulations more and more U.S. transactions (even, and especially, those with other COCOM members). Although the Export Administration Act empowered it to review exports to Communist countries only, the Pentagon, availing itself of a controversial 1984 presidential directive, had for a couple of years been inserting it-self into what Commerce saw to be its own jurisdiction, namely the licencing of exports to Western countries. According to Commerce Department figures, some 16,000 of a total 110,000 export licences (to all markets) involved Pentagon review in 1986.[91]

The Toshiba/Kongsberg affair had the effect, at least in the short term, of stemming the shift of bureaucratic power over export con-trol to the Commerce Department. What could be a more dramatic illustration of the follies of laxity, asked the hard-liners, than the recent case of two of America's allies allowing such critical tech-nology to flow so easily to the Soviet Union? In the long term, however, the affair buttressed the arguments of those working for export-control reforms. It did so because it shifted the focus away from Washington and toward Paris, where in early 1988 the U.S. began to work for a rationalisation of the COCOM regulations on sensitive trade. Mindful that one — perhaps the most important — lesson of the Toshiba-Kongsberg affair was that U.S. security could be breached as a result of technology diversions over which Washington had no control, and cognisant of the economic ration-ality implied by the growing trend toward intra-Alliance arms collaboration, American officials sought and seem to have got agreement from other COCOM members that henceforth restric-tions would be made much tighter, though on a narrower range of products in West-East trade. At the same time, the U.S. committed itself to liberalised *allied* access to U.S. technology.

The net effect of the two initiatives, Washington hopes, will be to lessen the ability of the Soviets to acquire useful military technology from allied countries, and to strengthen the American defence industrial base in high-technology sectors.[92] Whether the reforms will achieve their goals remains to be seen. At the very least, we can observe that the need to present a coherent position in Paris has at least (and at last) forced Washington to end the bureaucratic bickering between Commerce and the Pentagon.[93] It also has brought a respite to the intra-Alliance wrangling over export controls, for one consistent European complaint has been that in attempting to interfere with their trade with the Soviet Union, the U.S. has been trampling upon the sovereignty of its European allies, all in pursuit of an unattainable goal. The consensus as of this writing is that U.S. export-control has become more realistic as Washington has opted for a strategy, to use a commonly cited metaphor, of "building higher fences around fewer items."[94]

CONCLUSION

Two major generalisations can be derived from this study of U.S. techno-nationalism. The first is that import policies cannot be isolated from export policies (and vice versa). To be sure, sometimes the mechanics of protectionism differ in each trade category, and one can find, as with the U.S. semiconductor producers, that an industrial sector can advocate at one and the same time both an increase in restrictions on imports and a decrease in restrictions on exports. However, there is little that is surprising or new about such a mix of policy preferences; one of the hallmarks of mercantilism, after all, was its simultaneous quest for import-reduction and export-enhancement. In the contemporary context, such "benign" mercantilist forms as techno-nationalism display a logical consistency not only with the previous pattern of mercantilism, but also with the contemporary requirements of security. For it is beyond dispute that access to export markets can spell the difference between success or failure of a domestic entity — especially in the realm of high-technology weapons systems or their components. Thus one should not infer from the recent example of U.S. liberalisation of export controls a necessary conclusion that techno-nationalism is waning. Indeed, it may be easier to argue the opposite.[95]

The second, and related, generalisation concerns the proposition that all cannot liberalise their exports and secure gain therefrom if all do not liberalise their imports. Although this statement might seem so self-evident as hardly to require stating, it is worthwhile to recall that what we have been discussing is not the ordinary range of commodities that enter into international trade, but rather a particular set of items about which states have exercised a great deal of worry. It may well be that the current U.S. thrust, as expressed by the Pentagon, toward allied arms collaboration will continue to gather momentum, but we remain rather pessimistic on this point, and for two reasons. The first reason is that so long as America's trading partners, above all the Europeans, continue to see in high-technology weapons manufacturing the prospect of gains in wealth, employment, prestige, and security, then they will continue to aspire to techno-nationalist solutions of their own. As two of the chapters in this book have shown, European collaboration on modern aircraft production almost inevitably results in a felt need not only to *include* as many European participants as possible, but also to *exclude* a major non-European actor, the United States. Although we have chosen to concentrate in our own chapter on U.S. techno-nationalism, it has been far from our intention to argue that the U.S. is the only country in which techno-nationalism has contemporary policy appeal. Should the promise of 1992 in Europe be realised, it will likely lead to a more problematical arms-collaboration regime in the West, with all that this would imply for transatlantic political and security relations.

Moreover, in respect of the American defence industrial base, we would anticipate a continuation in the recent upsurge in security-generated protectionism. The American economy is hardly the most protectionist of current Western economies; but the American polity is still relatively uncomfortable in coming to grips with the security dilemmas associated with interdependence. For the United States, only over the past few years has trade begun to register as a major element in GNP. However, even if the U.S. had been as economically interdependent as its major trading partners — or as dependent as them upon trade for wealth-generation — it would still stand apart from them in one critical respect. It sees itself, and is seen by its allies, as by far the single most important guarantor of the security of the West. As a result of its position, and so long as it maintains the aspiration to play the role of guarantor, it will regard itself as having a dispensation toward   partial defence-industrial autarky to which the allies are not entitled. That the allies will continue to reject this claim to entitlement can also be anticipated. Thus we conclude by observing that, in the sector of high-technology weapons manufacturing, the future will likely be marked by heightened tension between allies, all of whom can be expected, aspirations of inter-operability and collaboration notwithstanding, to continue to vie among themselves for advantage at the crowded apex of the West's defence industrial base.

Notes

[1] Clay Chandler, "National to Buy Fairchild Semiconductor," *Washington Post*, 1 September 1987, p. C7.

[2] Clyde H. Farnsworth, "Toshiba, Norway Unit Assailed in Soviet Sale," *New York Times*, 1 May 1987, p. D2; Eduardo Lachica, "U.S. Is Investigating if Foreign Concerns Sold Gear to Enhance Soviet Submarines," *Wall Street Journal*, 30 April 1987, p. 36. Also see James M. Dorsey, "Pentagon Targets Companies in Japan, Norway," *Washington Times*, 20 March 1987, p. 1.

[3] *Congressional Record*, 19 June 1987, p. S8372.

[4] Fred Kaplan, "Administration Opposes Boycott against Toshiba," *Boston Globe*, 2 July 1987, p. 3.

[5] Stuart Auerbach, "Senate Approves 2-Year Ban on Toshiba's Sales in the U.S.," *Washington Post*, 1 July 1987, p. 1; Jerome Cahill, "Ban on Toshiba Asked in Senate," *New York Daily News*, 19 June 1987, p. C14. The $30 billion figure was demanded by California Congressman Duncan Hunter, who insisted that it would take the construction of at least an additional 30 *Los Angeles*-class SSNs to remedy the damage done to U.S. anti-submarine warfare capability. "Strong Defense, not Weak Trade," *Detroit News*, 7 July 1987, p. 6.

[6] For a seminal discussion of the phenomenon, see Robert B. Reich, "The Rise of Techno-Nationalism," *Atlantic Monthly*, May 1987, pp. 63-69.

[7] Good starting points for a discussion of mercantilism are two classic works: Eli Heckscher, *Mercantilism*, trans. Mendel Shapiro (London: George Allen & Unwin, 1935); and Jacob Viner, "Power versus Plenty as Objectives of Foreign Policy in the Seventeenth and Eighteenth Centuries," *World Politics* 1 (October 1948): 1-29. Although not addressed to the question of mercantilism, an invaluable analysis of economic instruments in foreign policy is David A. Baldwin, *Economic Statecraft* (Princeton: Princeton University Press, 1985).

[8] For U.S. raw-material policy, see Alfred E. Eckes, *The United States and the Global Struggle for Minerals* (Austin: University of Texas Press, 1979); and Stephen D. Krasner, *Defending the National Interest: Raw Materials Investments and U.S. Foreign Policy* (Princeton: Princeton University Press, 1978).

[9] George Leopold, "U.S. Chipmakers Fret over Export Restriction Proposal," *Defense News*, 8 June 1987, p. 15.

[10]For a discussion of interdependence that insists the term must imply the mutual dependence (or vulnerability) of states, see Kenneth N. Waltz, *Theory of International Politics* (Reading, Mass.: Addison-Wesley, 1979).

[11]For a summary of this perspective by one writer who does not necessarily embrace it, see Robert Gilpin, *War and Change in World Politics* (Cambridge: Cambridge University Press, 1981), p. 219.

[12]What some of these consequences might be is analysed in Klaus Knorr, "Economic Interdependence and National Security," in *Economic Issues and National Security*, ed. Klaus Knorr and Frank N. Trager (Lawrence: University Press of Kansas, 1977).

[13]Robert Gilpin, *The Political Economy of International Relations* (Princeton: Princeton University Press, 1987), p. 129.

[14]R. J. Barry Jones, *Conflict and Control in the World Economy: Contemporary Economic Realism and Neo-Mercantilism* (Sussex: Wheatsheaf Books, 1986), p. 151.

[15]Gilpin, *Political Economy*, pp. 31-32.

[16]Alexander Hamilton, "Report on the Subject of Manufactures," in *Industrial and Commercial Correspondence of Alexander Hamilton: Anticipating His Report on Manufactures*, ed. Arthur Harrison Cole (Chicago: A. W. Shaw, 1928), p. 284.

[17]David G. Haglund, "Strategic Minerals: A Conceptual Analysis," *Resources Policy* 10 (September 1984): 146-52; Idem, "The New Geopolitics of Minerals: An Inquiry into the Changing International Significance of Strategic Minerals," *Political Geography Quarterly* 5 (July 1986): 221-40.

[18]For excellent analyses of the problem, during the early postwar period, see Edward S. Mason, "American Security and Access to Raw Materials," *World Politics* 1 (January 1949):147-60; and Percy W. Bidwell, *Raw Materials: A Study of American Policy* (New York: Harper and Bros./Council on Foreign Relations, 1958).

[19]This disquiet was reflected in U.S. Congress, House Committee on Armed Services, *The Ailing Defense Industrial Base: Unready for Crisis*, 96th Cong., 2d sess. (Washington: U.S. Government Printing Office, 1980).

[20]Paul Seabury, "Industrial Policy and National Defense," *Journal of Contemporary Studies* 6 (Spring 1983): 6.

[21]Peter K. Clark, "Productivity and Profits in the 1980s: Are They Really Improving?," *Brookings Papers on Economic Activity* 1 (1984): 133.

[22]William J. Baumol and Kenneth McLennan, "U.S. Productivity Performance and Its Implications," in *Productivity Growth and U.S. Competitiveness*, ed. Baumol and McLennan (New York: Oxford University Press, 1985), pp. 9-11. Also see, for the lagging ability of the U.S. to use such productive equipment as new machine tools, Seymour Melman, "Limits of Military Power: Economic and Other," *International Security* 11 (Summer 1986): 78-79.

[23]Edward N. Wolf, "The Magnitude and Causes of the Recent Productivity Slowdown in the United States: A Survey of Recent Studies," in *Productivity Growth and U.S. Competitiveness*, p. 51.

[24]Baumol and McLennan, "U.S. Productivity Performance," pp. 13-14.

[25]David Greenaway, *International Trade Policy: From Tariffs to the New Protectionism* (London: Macmillan, 1983), p. 157.

[26]Reich, "Rise of Techno-Nationalism," p. 64.

[27]Albert O. Hirschman, *National Power and the Structure of Foreign Trade* (Berkeley: University of California Press, 1945).

[28]Jacques S. Gansler, "Needed: A U.S. Defense Industrial Strategy," *International Security* 12 (Fall 1987): 52.

[29]George C. Wilson, "Fewer Weapons and Troops to Fire Them," *Washington Post*, 25 April 1988, p. 4.

[30]Paul Bedard, "West Losing Its Edge in High-Tech Weapons," *Washington Times*, 27 April 1988, p. 1; Len Famiglietti, "NATO Leaves Technology in Laboratory," *Jane's Defence Weekly*, 28 November 1987, p. 1245.

[31]Tim Carrington, "Military's Dependence on Foreign Suppliers Causes Rising Concern," *Wall Street Journal*, 24 March 1988, p. 1.

[32]Quoted in Stas Margaronis, "Is Japan Outstripping U.S. in Defense Capability?," *Atlanta Constitution*, 10 November 1987, p. 29. By 1987, some 40 percent of the electronics in U.S. weapons systems was originating in Japan. Malcolm Gladwell, "A National Interest in Global Markets," *Insight*, 29 June 1987, p. 11.

[33]"Japan's Protected Telecoms," *Economist*, 3-9 January 1987, pp. 12-13.

[34]A good example of the tendency to view commercial rivalry with Japan as a security threat is Theodore H. White, "The Danger from Japan," *New York Times Magazine*, 28 July 1985, pp. 22ff.

[35]See Klaus Knorr, *Military Power and Potential* (Lexington, Mass.: D. C. Heath, 1970); and idem, *The War Potential of Nations* (Princeton: Princeton University Press, 1956).

[36]See especially David P. Calleo, *Beyond American Hegemony: The Future of the Western Alliance* (New York: Basic Books, 1987). Among theorists of international relations, it has become commonplace to speculate upon the consequences for an entire array of post-World War II international arrangements that are likely to attend a decline in U.S. relative economic capability. See, *inter alia*, Robert O. Keohane, *After Hegemony: Cooperation and Discord in the World Political Economy* (Princeton: Princeton University Press, 1984); Gilpin, *War and Change in World Politics*; and C. Fred Bergsten, "Economic Imbalances and World Politics," *Foreign Affairs* 65 (Spring 1987): 770-94.

[37]Paul Kennedy, *The Rise and Fall of Great Powers: Economic Change and Military Conflict from 1500 to 2000* (New York: Random House, 1987).

[38]Quoted in Jack Anderson and Dale Van Atta, "Can We Still Arm Ourselves?," *Washington Post*, 23 August 1987, p. B7.

[39]"The Business of Defense," *Journal of Commerce*, 16 March 1988, p. 8. For the exemption of Canada, which some sources argue could give Canadian defence producers a major advantage over European ones in the American market, see James Bagnall, "U.S. Bill Could Give Canadian Defence Firms Big Advantage," *Financial Post* (Toronto), 11 April 1988, p. 6. The logic and feasibility of a North American Defence Industrial Base (NADIB) being achieved is discussed in Beth L. Thomas, "The Environment for Expanding the North American Defence Industrial Base," in *Canada's Defence Industrial Base: The Political Economy of Preparedness and Procurement*, ed. David G. Haglund (Kingston, Ont.: Ronald P. Frye, 1988), pp. 220-37.

[40]For an analysis of current Pentagon thinking on the merits of weapons collaboration, see the chapter in this volume by Michael Moodie and Brenton Fischmann, "Alliance Arms Cooperation: Toward a NATO Industrial Base?"

[41]Quoted in Cheryl Pellerin, "Pentagon Eyes Major Steps to Bolster Industrial Base," *Defense News*, 16 May 1988, p. 1.

[42]"Reagan to Seek Cutbacks on Machine-Tool Imports," *Washington Post*, 21 May 1986, p. G1.

[43]U.S. Congress, House Committee on Ways and Means, Subcommittee on Trade, *Overview of Current Provisions of U.S. Trade Law*, 98th Cong., 2d sess. (Washington: U.S. Government Printing Office, 1984), p. 89.

[44]"Pentagon to Require American-Made Bearings," *Los Angeles Times*, 28 March 1988, p. 4:2.

[45]Erik L. Keller, "Defense Dept. Trying to Get Precision-Gear Industry Moving," *Manufacturer's Week*, 4 April 1988, p. 7.

[46]Robert Gillette, "Threat to Security Cited in Rise of Foreign Engineers," *Los Angeles Times*, 20 January 1988, p. 1.

[47]Steven Prokesch, "Stopping the High-Tech Giveaway," *New York Times*, 22 March 1987, p. F1. For a good analysis of 1970s trade rivalry in semiconductors, see Michael Borrus, James Millstein, and John Zysman, *U.S.-Japanese Competition in the Semiconductor Industry: A Study in International Trade and Technological Development*, Policy Papers in International Affairs, no. 17 (Berkeley: Institute of International Studies, University of California, 1982).

[48]For a thorough analysis of dumping, see Theodore W. Kassinger, "Antidumping Duty Investigations," Book 1, *Law & Practice of United States Regulation of International Trade*, comp. and ed. Charles R. Johnston, Jr. (New York: Oceana Publications, June 1987).

[49]For contrasting interpretations of the semiconductor-dumping case, see Japan Institute for Social and Economic Affairs, "The Semiconductor Trade Issue: Building an Open Global Market," KKC Brief no. 45 (Tokyo, February 1988); and Clayton K. Yeutter, "The Japanese Left Us with Little Choice," *New York Times*, 4 May 1987, p. 3:3.

[50]Quoted in Stuart Auerbach, "Sanctions Imposed on Japan," *Washington Post*, 18 April 1987, p. 1.

[51]Donald W. Brooks, Fairchild's president and chief executive officer, did not disguise his dismay at the administration's effort to halt the purchase, which he considered to have resulted from protectionist sentiment on Capitol Hill. Brenton R. Schlender, "U.S. Chip Maker Receives Offers to Fund Buyout," *Wall Street Journal*, 19 March 1987, p. 4. For another analysis that stresses commercial considerations to the exclusion of security interests, see John H. Makin, "The Problems Go Far Beyond Chips," *New York Times*, 4 May 1988, p. 3:2.

[52]This comment was made by Marco A. Caceres, Jr., in a letter to the editor of the *New York Times*, 14 April 1987, p. 30.

[53]Quoted in Stuart Auerbach and Peter Behr, "Japan to Seek Cancellation of Tariffs," *Washington Post*, 7 April 1987, p. E1.

[54]Ibid. Also see "Weinberger, Baldrige Fight Japanese Buyout," *Washington Times*, 13 March 1987, p. 11C.

[55]Irwin Federman, chairman of the Semiconductor Industry Association and vice-chairman of Advanced Micro Devices Inc., as quoted in Peter Waldman, "Chip Industry's Sematech Consortium Picks Austin, Texas, as Research Base," *Wall Street Journal*, 7 January 1988, p. 31. Also see Bill Sing, "Plan for New Chip Consortium Endorsed," *Los Angeles Times*, 14 May 1987, p. 4:1.

[56]"With Money to Spend," *San Jose Mercury News*, 29 December 1987, p. 12B. The members of Sematech are Advanced Micro Devices, American Telephone & Telegraph, Digital Equipment, Harris, Hewlett-Packard, Intel, International Business Machines, LSI Logic, Micron Technology, Motorola, National Semiconductor, Rockwell, and Texas Instruments. Waldman, "Chip Industry's Sematech."

[57]A good analysis of the ongoing debate over the merit and workability of export controls on sensitive goods and technology is Gary Bertsch and John R. McIntyre, "The Western Alliance and East-West Trade: In Pursuit of an Integrated Strategy," in *The Politics of East-West Trade*, ed. Gordon B. Smith (Boulder, Colo.: Westview Press, 1984), pp. 209-35.

[58]For an analysis of the effect of such tension on the Alliance, see Robert W. Tucker and Linda Wrigley, eds., *The Atlantic Alliance and Its Critics* (New York: Praeger, 1983). Also see, for a discussion of the gas-pipeline sanctions triggered by Polish developments, Thane Gustafson, "The Soviet Response to the American Embargo of 1981-82: The Case of Compressors for the Export Gas Pipeline," in *Politics of East-West Trade*, pp. 129-41.

[59]A skeptical assessment of sanctions against the Soviet Union, written by a British Sovietologist, is Philip Hanson, "Western Economic Sanctions against the USSR: Their Nature and Effectiveness," NATO Economics Directorate, *Colloquium* 1983, "External Economic Relations of CMEA Countries: Their Significance and Impact in a Global Perspective" (Brussels, April 1983).

[60]See, for a forthright statement of this perspective, Melvyn Krauss, *How NATO Weakens the West* (New York: Simon and Schuster, 1986).

[61]U.S. Department of Defense, *Soviet Military Power: An Assessment of the Threat 1988* (Washington: U.S. Government Printing Office, 1988), p. 140. For an elaboration of this argument, one focusing on the Toshiba-Kongsberg case, see William C. Triplett, II, "Crimes against the Alliance," *Policy Review*, Spring 1988, p. 8.

[62]The Assistant Secretary of Defense for International Security Affairs, Richard Armitage, remarked in a letter to Congressional leaders in March 1988 that original estimates of the damage caused by the technology diversion had been greatly exaggerated. See David E. Sanger, "U.S. Reverses Position on Damage by Toshiba," *New York Times*, 14 March 1988, p. D1. Also see David Silverberg, "Toshiba's Role in Quieting Soviet Subs Is Disputed," *Defense News*, 14 December 1987, p. 23. It now appears that Soviet Sierra- and Akula-class SSNs were incorporating quieter propellers as early as 1984, that is prior to the installation of the Toshiba milling machines in the autumn of that year. "Toshiba Bashing, Truth Bashing," *Oakland Tribune*, 16 March 1988, p. 8.

[63]This account is based on David E. Sanger, "A Bizarre Deal Diverts Vital Tools to Russians," *New York Times*, 12 June 1987, p. 1.

[64]Elaine Sciolino, "Norway Sanctions Opposed by U.S.," ibid., 15 December 1987, p. 7.

[65]Margaret Shapiro, "Japan Set to Tighten Law on Illegal Strategic Exports," *Washington Post*, 31 July 1987, p. 18.

[66]Clyde H. Farnsworth, "House, 376-45, Passes Revised Trade Bill," *New York Times*, 14 July 1988, p. 27; Idem, "Major Trade Bill Sent to President by Senate, 85-11," ibid., 4 August 1988, p. 1.

[67]Marcus W. Brauchli, "Board Approves Kongsberg Sale of Defense Unit," *Wall Street Journal*, 25 September 1987, p. 23. On the tendency for Toshiba but not Kongsberg to be targetted for vituperation, see Edward A. Olsen, "Picketing Electronics but not Sardines," *Christian Science Monitor*, 26 October 1987, p. 14.

[68]David Buchan, "Penetrating the Thicket," *Financial Times* (London), 13 July 1987, p. 14. By 1986, the ratio of U.S. defence-trade exports to imports, in respect of the NATO allies, had declined to 1.59:1. In the early years of the alliance, it had typically been about 10:1, sometimes more. David Silverberg, "Pentagon Targets Protectionism," *Defense News*, 5 October 1987, p. 1.

[69]For the underlying security rationale of the Lavi, see the chapter in this volume by Galen Perras, "Israel and the Lavi Fighter-Aircraft."

[70]A widely discussed estimate, one accepted by Israeli politicians, was that the United States was paying some 90 percent of the costs associated with the project. James Rupert, "U.S. Tells Israel Its Plans for Plane Are too Costly," *Washington Post*, 13 August 1987, p. 29.

[71]Margaronis, "Is Japan Outstripping U.S.?," p. 29. Japanese policy on arms exports is discussed in Andrew J. Pierre, *The Global Politics of Arms Sales* (Princeton: Princeton University Press, 1982), pp. 116-20. For the evolution of the contemporary Japanese arms industry, see Reinhard Drifte,

Arms Production in Japan: The Military Application of Civilian Technology (Boulder, Colo.: Westview Press, 1986).

[72]Part of what follows is based on the account given in Masaru Kono, "Japan's Decisionmaking and Japan-U.S. Interdependence: The Case of the FSX Selection, 1985-1987" (unpublished manuscript, University of British Columbia, Department of Political Science, 1988).

[73]Eduardo Lachica and Masayoshi Kanabayashi, "Japan's Arms Builders Openly Vie for Orders after Long Hesitancy," *Wall Street Journal*, 19 August 1987, p. 1.

[74]This thesis is argued by Yoichi Clark Shimatsu, "Was Toshiba Flap a U.S. Bid to Horn in on Fighter Deal?," *Los Angeles Times*, 25 August 1987, p. 2:5.

[75]At least it is more plausible than the Soviet version of the U.S. role in the Toshiba/Kongsberg affair, a version that holds America's ultimate aim to be nothing less than "drop[ping] an 'iron curtain' on the economic exchanges of the Soviet Union, and other socialist countries, with the West, to put a brake on our process of perestroika ..." Yuri Bandura, *Soviet News & Views*, no. 15 (August 1987), pp. 1-2.

[76]Quoted in Clyde Haberman, "Joint Project Is Seen on Japanese Fighter Jet," *New York Times*, 20 August 1987, p. 19.

[77]"Japanese Caving to U.S. Pressure on Using U.S. Airframe in FSX Program," *Inside the Pentagon*, 7 August 1987, p. 1. But for the view that Japan is actually getting the better of the F-16 arrangement, is in effect so modifying the aircraft as to make it virtually a domestically produced plane, see Sam Jameson, "Ex-U.S. Official: Japan Scheming to Get F-16 Technology Cheap," *Los Angeles Times*, 11 April 1988, p. 4:2.

[78]Richard Halloran, "Japan Likes F-16 as Its Next Fighter," *New York Times*, 20 October 1987, p. D5.

[79]John Koten, "McDonnell Emerges as Likely Supplier of Design for Japan's Next Fighter Jet," *Wall Street Journal*, 14 September 1987, p. 10.

[80]Halloran, "Japan Likes F-16."

[81]Calvin Sims, "Rift over High-Tech Exports," *New York Times*, 14 January 1987, p. D1; Stuart Auerbach, "High-Tech Export Panel Defended by Chairman," *Washington Post*, 15 January 1987, p. E1. In aggregate terms, the report put the cost for the U.S. GNP at $17.1 billion in 1985.

[82]Tim Carrington and Robert S. Greenberger, "Pentagon's Firm Control over Export Licenses May Lessen in Face of Politics, Big Trade Gaps," *Wall Street Journal*, 13 March 1987, p. 52.

[83]Quoted in Steven J. Dryden, "The Pentagon Won't Budge on High-Tech Trade," *Business Week*, 7 December 1987, p. 114.

[84]Quoted in Susan F. Rasky, "What Is Good for Security May Be Bad for Business," *New York Times*, 18 October 1987, p. E5. Also see Richard Perle, "Welcome to Moscow on the Ginza," *U.S. News and World Report*, 29 June 1987, p. 31.

[85]Stuart Auerbach, "Talks Set on Export Control, Verity Says," *Washington Post,* 11 November 1987, p. F3. For a recent study of alliance attempts to resolve the export-control problem, see Gary K. Bertsch, ed., *Controlling East-West Trade and Technology Transfer: Power, Politics, and Policies* (Durham, N.C.: Duke University Press, 1988).

[86]J. Fred Bucy, "Technology Transfer and East-West Trade: A Reappraisal," *International Security* 5 (Winter 1980/81): 147; Thomas C. Schelling, *International Economics* (Boston: Allyn and Bacon, 1958), p. 492; Gary K. Bertsch, "Technology Transfers and Technology Controls: A Synthesis of the Western-Soviet Relationship," in *Technical Progress and Soviet Economic Development,* ed. Ronald Amann and Julian Cooper (Oxford: Basil Blackwell, 1986), p. 131.

[87]Stephen E. Nordlinger, "U.S. Sees Progress in Controlling High-Tech Exports," *Baltimore Sun,* 2 January 1988, p. 1. Among the COCOM members the U.S. would like to see tighten export restrictions are Spain, Portugal, Greece, and Turkey. These countries, however, do not supply much high-technology goods to the Soviet Union, for obvious reasons.

[88]John Witherow, "US to Clamp Down on Techno-Bandits," *Sunday-Times* (London), 24 January 1988, p. 15.

[89]Quoted in Jonathan Dunn, "National Academy of Sciences Report Attacks Export Controls," *Multinational Monitor,* November/December 1987.

[90]Quoted in Steve Hirsch, "Export Control Policy," ibid., p. 29. The Freedenberg-Bryen feud had attained legendary proportions in Washington, especially in the wake of a bitter battle in September 1987 over who had authority to licence exports to Soviet-controlled firms in Western Europe. See Stephen Koepp, "Shoot-Out at Tech Gap," *Time,* 12 October 1987, p. 50; Eduardo Lachica and Tim Carrington, "Pentagon Faults Commerce for Licensing Shipments to Communist-Backed Firms," *Wall Street Journal,* 30 September 1987, p. 24; and Eduardo Lachica, "U.S. Reimposes Tight Review on Exports to Companies Controlled by Communists," ibid., 28 September 1987, p. 72.

[91]Richard C. Gross, "Technology Transfer," *Defence Science,* March 1988, p. 9.

[92]Eduardo Lachicha and E. S. Browning, "West Tightens Technology-Export Rules but Shortens List of Controlled Products," *Wall Street Journal* 29 January 1988, p. 16.

[93]David Silverberg, "Defence,Commerce Officials Mend Export Control Fences," *Defense News,* 29 February 1988, p. 3.

[94]Clyde H. Farnsworth, "West Is Easing Policy on Sales to Soviet Bloc," *New York Times,* 15 February 1988, p. 1.

[95]One analyst writes that the 1988 trade legislation, with its stress on stimulating U.S. exports in a wide range of sectors, civilian as well as military, has "finally brought the United States with full force into the mercantilist world." Clyde H. Farnsworth, "U.S. Push on Exports Sets Up a New Battle of the Barriers," ibid., 7 August 1988, p. 4:1.

Notes on Contributors

Marc L. Busch was a Research Assistant at the Queen's Centre for International Relations during the 1987/88 academic year. He is currently pursuing graduate studies in international relations at the University of Toronto.

Alistair Edgar, a Graduate Fellow of the Queen's Centre for International Relations, specialises in the politics of aircraft procurement.

Brenton C. Fischmann is a Research Assistant at the Center for Strategic and International Studies in Washington, D.C.

David G. Haglund is the Director of the Queen's Centre for International Relations, and an Associate Professor in the Queen's Department of Political Studies. He specialises in U.S. and Canadian foreign and security policies.

Michael K. Hawes, an Assistant Professor in the Department of Political Studies and Faculty Associate of the Centre for International Relations, Queen's University, has teaching and research interests in Canadian foreign policy and international political economy.

Bernd Huebner was a Visiting Defence Fellow at the Queen's Centre for International Relations in the 1986/87 academic year. He is a Lieutenant-Colonel in the Bundeswehr whose current posting is in Cologne, where he is working on the Heeresstruktur 2000 program, which examines the future structure of the West German army.

Andrew Latham is a Ph.D. candidate in international relations at York University in Toronto. Among his areas of interest are transatlantic political and security questions.

Michael L. Moodie, a Senior Fellow of the Center for Strategic and International Studies, has written widely in the field of armaments collaboration within NATO. He was Special Assistant to the U.S. Ambassador to NATO, David Abshire, from 1983 to 1987.

Galen Perras is a defence consultant based in Waterloo, Ontario. He has taught in the War Studies Program of the Royal Military College of Canada.

Index